Academic Gamesmanship

Alexander W. Astin

Published in Cooperation
with the Higher Education
Research Institute

The Praeger Special Studies program—
utilizing the most modern and efficient book
production techniques and a selective
worldwide distribution network—makes
available to the academic, government, and
business communities significant, timely
research in U.S. and international economic, social, and political development.

Academic Gamesmanship
Student-Oriented Change in Higher Education

PRAEGER SPECIAL STUDIES IN U.S. ECONOMIC, SOCIAL, AND POLITICAL ISSUES

Praeger Publishers   New York   Washington   London

Library of Congress Cataloging in Publication Data

Astin, Alexander W
    Academic gamesmanship.

    (Praeger special studies in U.S. economic, social,
and political issues)
    Includes bibliographical references and index.
    1. Universities and colleges—United States—
Administration.   2. College environment.
I. Title.
LB2341.A755   378.73   76-12520
ISBN 0-275-56720-6

PRAEGER PUBLISHERS
111 Fourth Avenue, New York, N.Y. 10003, U.S.A.

Published in the United States of America in 1976
by Praeger Publishers, Inc.

Printed in the United States of America

This book is based in part on an unusual kind of social experiment. The main purpose of the experiment was to see if a diverse group of 19 colleges and universities* could be stimulated to undertake changes in their policies and programs that would be designed primarily to improve the educational environment for students. The stimulus for change consisted of comprehensive data showing the effect each college was having on its students—data that previously had not been available to any of the institutions.

In conducting the experiment we discovered a great many things about the processes of gamesmanship in academe: how decisions do (and do not) get made, how committees operate, how data are interpreted (and misinterpreted), and how and why faculty members resist change. At the same time, we developed a number of very practical ideas about how to design future change strategies to maximize the chances that constructive change will occur.

The book comprises two main sections. The first (Chapters 1 through 5) describe the details of the experiment and the impact it had on the participating institutions. The second section (Chapters 6 through 10) includes our analyses of committee functioning, academic defense mechanisms, and effective change strategies.

---

*The following institutions participated in the study: Allegheny College; Franklin and Marshall College; Mills College; Northwestern University; Ohio Dominican College; St. Louis University; St. Norbert's College; State University of New York (SUNY) at Oswego; Tulane University; University of Massachusetts; U.S. Coast Guard Academy; University of Denver; University of Michigan; University of Redlands; Vanderbilt University; Vassar College; Western Illinois University; Washington State University; and Williams College.

ACKNOWLEDGMENTS

A project of this magnitude and complexity requires the coordinated efforts of a large number of talented people. Major credit should go to Linda D. Molm, who carried the main burden of administering the project during the first year. Her skillful handling of the many special requests and complaints from institutions, of the preparation and pilot testing of the data packets, and of the various consultant and institutional site visits during the first year of the project is gratefully acknowledged. Information from her summary of the first year of the project was used extensively in drafting sections of Chapters 2 and 3.

A number of current and former staff members of the American Council on Education also made significant contributions during that first year: David E. Drew, Barbara A. Blandford, Jeannie T. Royer, Melvina Kelly, Jeffrey Dutton, Charles Fletcher, Terry Mahn, and Charles Sell.

For the UCLA phase of the project, I am particularly indebted to Diane Elvenstar and Elizabeth Weinberger for their help in evaluating reports, making institutional site visits, and collecting and analyzing followup data.

During this followup phase, I have also relied heavily on Margo R. King for assistance in manuscript preparation, Gerald T. Richardson for help in data analysis, and Beverly T. Watkins for assistance in editing the manuscript.

The quality of the project was substantially enhanced by the participation of a number of consultants: David Bushnell, Craig Comstock, David Epperson, Harold Hodgkinson, Joseph Katz, Joseph Kauffman, and Michelle Patterson. I am particularly indebted to Dave Epperson and Joe Katz for their many perceptive analyses of institutional reports and their participation in the on-site followup visits during the evaluation year.

The success of the project was, of course, totally dependent on the active participation of the 19 institutions. I am indebted to the chief executive officers of these institutions and especially to the members of the task forces that devoted so much effort to the analyses of data and preparation of recommendations. In particular, the contributions of the following task force chairpersons are acknowledged: Richard A. Andrews (University of Redlands); David Booth (Williams College); Glen F. Clanton (Vanderbilt University); Dr. Charles C. Gilbert (Western Illinois University); Sister Thomas

Albert Corbett (Ohio Dominican); W. Patrick Dolan (St. Louis University); Walden Irish (University of Denver); Edward Rogge (Tulane University); G. S. Sachidanandan (State University of New York, Oswego); Richard W. Story (University of Massachusetts); Ronald Webb (St. Norbert College); Malcolm J. Williams (U.S. Coast Guard Academy); Jeremy Wilson (Northwestern University).

This study was supported in part by funds from the National Institute of Mental Health and the American Council on Education. The financial support and investigative freedom afforded me by both organizations is much appreciated.

Finally, I wish to acknowledge the contribution of the many thousands of students whose cooperation in the freshman and followup surveys produced the data that made this project possible. Hopefully, future generations of students will be able to benefit from the results.

CONTENTS

LIST OF TABLES AND FIGURE

1

AN EXPERIMENT
IN INSTITUTIONAL CHANGE

One legacy of the student movement of the 1960s is a widespread acceptance among academics of the need for "change" and "innovation." The near reverence for these terms that has developed among members of the academic community is apparently based on the assumption that many traditional practices of colleges and universities are no longer beneficial to students and therefore in need of replacement. One concrete manifestation of this belief is the new Fund for the Advancement of Postsecondary Education, whose principal mission is to encourage institutions to adopt "innovative" policies and programs.

The recent history of the student movement shows clearly that institutions did introduce many changes in direct response to student protests.[1] The circumstances under which these changes were introduced, however, suggest that they were frequently more strategic or tactical than educational. Students were sometimes given a greater voice in decision-making, for example, not because existing theory or data indicated that such a change would improve the learning environment, but simply because pressure had been brought to bear on the administration. In short, it appears that a decision to implement any given change is typically based more on power relationships than on educational knowledge.[2]

This relationship between knowledge and decision-making was the basic concern of "Data for Decisions in Higher Education" (the original name of the project, which was later abbreviated to "Data for Decisions"). This project was designed, first, to provide a sample of colleges and universities with comprehensive data on the effect each college was having on its students and, second, to determine if these data could be utilized in institutional planning for change. Thus, the objective was to determine if constructive change could be stimulated by providing a college or university with information about its effect on its students.

RATIONALE FOR THE PROJECT

The purposes of this project are perhaps best understood by stating some underlying assumptions that prompted us to develop the original project proposal:

1. Decisions about changes in U.S. higher education have traditionally given only minimal consideration to student development. Consequently, the education of the individual student is usually subordinated to resource acquisition, internal politics, and lobbying activities.

2. Institutions that strive to give the student a central place in their planning are handicapped by inadequate information on how their students are affected by current policies and practices and how institutional impact might be altered by changes in those policies and practices.

3. This lack of knowledge is a major obstacle to constructive change in institutions. Current practices (the status quo) are supported because they "seem to work" and because new or untried policies and practices represent a significant "risk." In a sense, then, ignorance is bliss to those who oppose change.

4. Improving an institution's awareness of the needs, aspirations, and backgrounds of its students, its effect on the cognitive and affective development of its students, and the manner in which potential changes in policy and practice might lead to a different impact will result in more effective institutional planning and decision making. "More effective" institutional functioning would presumably be manifest in such outcomes as:

- A stronger institutional commitment to critical self-study.
- A greater willingness to question or challenge existing policies and practices.
- An increased commitment to monitoring student progress and to an ongoing data collection effort oriented around student development.
- A greater receptivity to experimenting with untried or otherwise innovative practices and policies.
- The adoption of institutional policies and procedures that will result in an educational environment that more effectively meets student needs and aspirations.

THE PROJECT DESIGN

One practical reason for undertaking this study at the American Council on Education (ACE) was that we had already developed there a comprehensive base of longitudinal student data from a national sample of some 300 institutions. (These data are described in detail in Chapter 2.) Among other things, this data base included information on changes in student aspirations, plans, attitudes, values, and behavior during the undergraduate years. Thus, we could compare the development of students at any given institution with that of similar students attending other institutions.

Another important asset was our working relationships with many presidents and other individuals at the participating institutions. While we had routinely sent institutions reports based on data collected each fall from their entering freshmen, we had never attempted to feed back longitudinal data from our followups, nor had we made any concerted attempt to encourage institutions to consider the data in terms of policy implications.

The project comprised two major phases. The first, the "dissemination" phase, involved the analyses and preparation of the data for feedback, the design of feedback techniques, the selection of participating institutions, and the actual dissemination of the data to each participant. The second, the "evaluation" phase, involved a preliminary assessment of the project's impact on the institution and an evaluation of the feedback techniques.

Dissemination Plan

The early months of the project focused on two major tasks: preparing data "packets" to summarize the empirical evidence showing how the institution was affecting its students, and designing feedback procedures to maximize the chances that the institution could use the data effectively.

The data packets were designed primarily to show each institution how it was affecting its students' educational achievement and aspirations, career plans, attitudes, and behavior. Each data packet contained a number of tables together with explanatory text to aid interpretation. (See Annex A for a sample data packet sent to a participating institution.) The data analysis and preparation of packets are described in detail in Chapter 2.

A team of six consultants helped design the dissemination procedures. Twenty institutions were selected to participate in the project. Each institution created a task force to evaluate the data and prepare a report with recommendations for institutional action. Details of the design and implementation of these dissemination procedures are presented in Chapter 3.

Evaluation Plan

The project required two types of evaluation. The first task, of course, was to determine if and how each institution was affected by participation. The second task was a self-evaluation: How effective were our dissemination techniques? What changes would we recommend for future attempts at improving colleges for students?

Evaluating the impact of the project on the institution involved several types of assessment. One information source immediately available, of course, was the task force report. How effectively were the data utilized? What recommendations for change, if any, were included?

Another source of evaluative information was followup visits to each campus. How accurately did the report reflect the activities of the task force? Was any action taken by the institution to implement task force recommendations?

A final source of evaluative data was a survey of innovative institutional practices that was carried out prior to completion of the task forces' work, and a repeat survey carried out approximately one year later. These surveys were used to assess changes in institutional policies and programs which might be attributed to the project. Since the surveys were administered to a national sample of institutions, we could select a control group of 20 institutions that matched the 20 participating institutions on a variety of characteristics (including innovative practices revealed in the initial survey).

Evaluating our dissemination procedures required a continuous assessment of the project as it evolved, as well as a detailed examination of the evidence from the task force reports, followup visits, and surveys. Our immediate objective was to develop a revised dissemination plan that might be tried out in the immediate future. As our evaluation proceeded, however, it became clear that we were also in a position to examine some more general issues concerning the functioning of colleges and universities. How are different types of institutions likely to respond to overtures from outside agencies? How can outside agencies work most effectively with institutions to assist them in self-evaluation? How do committees and task forces operate? What can be done to make them function more effectively? What types of data are most likely to be utilized by decision makers? What defense mechanisms are employed by institutions to resist change?

The entire dissemination project, principally supported by a grant from the National Institute of Mental Health (NIMH), was scheduled for two years. This period had to be extended an additional seven months, however, because of delays associated with the move of the author (who was also the principal investigator) from ACE to the University of California, Los Angeles (UCLA). One benefit of the delay, of course, was to extend somewhat the time over which the impact of the project would be evaluated.

The principal stages in the project were:

Dissemination Phase

February - May 1972	Analysis of 1966-70 longitudinal student data; preparation of preliminary data packets for feedback to institutions. Initial survey of innovative practices.
June - August 1972	Design of feedback procedures; revision of data packet.
September - November 1972	Selection of participating institutions; formation of institutional task forces.
December 1972 - January 1973	Pilot testing; final revisions in data packets; transmittal of data to institutions.
February - May 1973	Monitoring of task force activities; consultation with task forces.
June - July 1973	Receipt of task force reports.
August - September 1973	Hiatus in activity caused by transfer of NIMH grant from ACE to UCLA.

Evaluation Phase

October 1973 - February 1974	Review and analysis of task force reports.
March - April 1974	Followup evaluation visits to institutions.

May - September 1974   Collection and analysis of additional follow-
                             up evaluation data; completion of final
                             report.

The remaining chapters comprise two main sections. The first
describes in detail the major phases of the project: preparing the
data (Chapter 2), disseminating the data (Chapter 3), evaluating the
reports (Chapter 4), and the impact of the project on the institutions
(Chapter 5). The second section includes a comprehensive assessment of the project, a how-to-do-it for future projects of this type,
and some speculations about the functioning of institutions,[3] committees, and change agents: designing an effective intervention
strategy (Chapter 6), academic games (Chapter 7—an inventory and
analysis of mechanisms used by institutions to resist change), making
committees work (Chapter 8), data and decisions (Chapter 9—making
data useful for policy), and speculations on the future (Chapter 10).

NOTES

1. Alexander W. Astin, Helen S. Astin, Alan E. Bayer, and Ann S.
Bisconti, The Power of Protest (San Francisco: Jossey-Bass, 1975);
Harold L. Hodgkinson, Institutions in Transition: A Profile of Change
in Higher Education (New York: McGraw-Hill, 1971).
    2. Carnegie Commission on Higher Education, Dissent and Dis-
ruption: Proposals for Consideration by the Campus (New York:
McGraw-Hill, 1971).
    3. It is interesting to note that virtually no attention is given to
student development in most modern treatises on college governance
and management. See, for example, E. C. Bolton and F. Genck, "Universities and Management," Journal of Higher Education 42, no. 4
(1971): 279-91; William E. Jellema, ed., Efficient College Management
(San Francisco: Jossey-Bass, 1972); Robert E. Lahti, Innovative
College Management (San Francisco: Jossey-Bass, 1975); James A.
Perkins, ed., The University as an Organization (New York: McGraw-
Hill, 1973).

2

Social scientists have had limited success, at best, in applying their data and findings to the everyday problems of the real world. Practitioners in education and other applied fields are unaccustomed to basing their policies and programs on empirical evidence and frequently view data from the social and behavioral sciences with skepticism and indifference. Social scientists, for their part, have tended to denigrate applied research, emphasizing instead abstract "theories" and data that often bear only a remote relationship to problems confronting the practitioner.[1] These tendencies are, of course, mutually reinforcing, so that indifference or hostility by practitioners discourages researchers from undertaking applied work, and excessive emphasis on abstract or esoteric concerns in research discourages practitioners from giving much attention to the results.

This gap between research and practice has been somewhat narrowed by the Cooperative Institutional Research Program* (CIRP). To begin with, this program was admittedly applied in nature, and in designing the various items a concerted attempt was made to reflect the practical concerns of both students and educators as well as the research interests of the staff of the American Council on Education. Furthermore, through the presidents and CIRP representatives at each participating institution, we had already established some preliminary channels of communication between researchers and practitioners.

---

*This program, initiated in fall 1966 in the Office of Research of the American Council on Education, is now conducted by UCLA's Higher Education Laboratory, under continuing support from ACE.

Below we describe the background of this longitudinal data base and the manner in which it was utilized to prepare the data packets for the 20 institutions participating in the "Data for Decisions" project.

THE COOPERATIVE INSTITUTIONAL RESEARCH PROGRAM

The principal objective of CIRP is to assess the impact of educational experiences on the college student using longitudinal data collected from individual students over time. With data from nearly 3 million students and more than 600 collegiate institutions, CIRP is one of the largest and most comprehensive research programs in the field of education. Student data cover a wide range of variables: socioeconomic background, ability, race, sex, educational aspirations, achievements, career goals, values, attitudes, and so forth. Also, in contrast to the typical study of students at a single institution, CIRP encompasses a national sample of students at many types of institutions. Institutions are sampled to represent the entire population of two-year colleges, four-year colleges, and universities.[2] The number of participating institutions has grown from 300 in 1966 to over 600 in 1974. Hence, three of CIRP's major advantages over earlier research efforts are its size, the comprehensiveness of the student data, and its use of a national sample designed so that research findings can be generalized to the entire population of institutions and students.

A fourth advantage of CIRP is its longitudinal nature. In addition to the fall survey of entering freshmen at participating institutions (begun in 1966 and repeated each year since), periodic followups of students are conducted. The followups have made it possible to study the central question of the research program: What impact do colleges have on their students? The first four-year followup was conducted in 1970, the year in which most of the first entering class (1966) would presumably have received the B.A. degree. (Subsequent four-year followups have been conducted on the entering classes of 1967, 1968, and 1969.) These followups include items repeated verbatim from the freshman questionnaire to measure change, and new items on the students' experiences and achievements in college, their ratings of the college environment, and their future goals and plans. Data on the college environment are derived from the followup surveys of students, from special surveys of institutions, and from secondary sources such as the U.S. Office of Education.[3]

With the 1966 freshman data and the 1970 followup data on these same students, we could estimate the impact of college over the entire four years of the typical undergraduate's career and compare changes in students attending different types of colleges. For the first time, we could provide individual institutions with information on their effects on their students compared with those of other institutions. Furthermore, by comparing the policies and practices of institutions with different impacts, we could provide some clues to ways in which any given institution might modify its impact to meet its students' needs. These considerations reinforced our belief late in 1971 that the time was ripe to learn if indeed policy could be influenced through the dissemination of research findings from this project.

Earlier Feedback Efforts

Although no project of this nature had been undertaken previously, some earlier attempts at routine informational feedback had been made by the ACE staff. One objective of CIRP has been to provide participating institutions with descriptive information on their own students and with national norms for comparison purposes and to share information about the research program with other educational researchers and interested persons. In the past, this feedback had taken several forms.

The primary feedback to individual participating institutions has been an 8- to 12-page annual report on entering freshmen, which gives a statistical summary of the responses of the institution's freshmen to the Student Information Form (SIF) as well as comparable normative information for all institutions of the same type (two-year college, four-year college, or university). Accompanying this institutional report has been the annual national normative report from the SIF, the freshman survey instrument, which includes statistical summaries by sex, type of institution, and geographic region for all new full-time freshmen enrolled in institutions that provided representative or relatively complete coverage of their freshman classes.

A more limited feedback effort has been conducted for the followup studies. For example, a one-year followup survey of the 1966 entering freshmen conducted in 1967 included a group of items known as the Inventory of College Activities (ICA) dimensions.[4] Each college was sent an institutional profile that described the college environment according to the ICA dimensions. In 1972 the institutions were sent a dropout report based on data from the 1966 survey of freshmen and the 1970 followup. Each institution also received a copy of "College Dropouts: A National Profile,"[5] a norms report showing the national figures on attrition.

Although these reports represent potentially useful information for decision making, this potential has not been fully realized. The data analyses, the packaging of results, and the feedback were not undertaken with any idea of influencing policy and planning directly, and no assessment of such effects has been made.

Data from the 1966 freshman survey and the 1970 followup were the core of the materials included in the data packet sent to each institution. Since institutions had received no followup information on a four-year period other than the dropout report, the feedback began with data from the 1970 followup, the first CIRP assessment of the effects of four years of college. In preparing the packets for feedback, we conducted a series of special data analyses. Other information planned for the project (for example, tabulations of descriptive data from the annual freshman surveys) required no special analysis.

The Research Model

To understand the rationale for CIRP data and the analyses for the data packets requires a familiarity with the three-component research model (Figure 2.1) that has shaped the program since its inception.

FIGURE 2.1

The CIRP Research Model

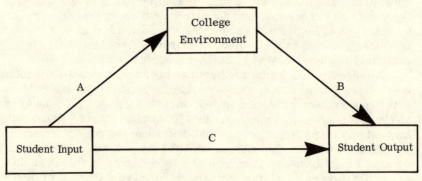

Source: Compiled by the author.

In Figure 2.1 student output refers to those aspects of the student's development that the college either attempts to or does influence. For research purposes, these must be fairly immediate outcomes that can be operationalized, such as completion of the baccalaureate, career choice, academic achievement, attitudes and values, and so forth: The 1970 followup survey measured a number of these outcomes.

Before one can accurately assess the role that the college plays to effect change in output, one must consider the attributes and potentials for growth and learning that students bring with them to college—the student input. These include family background, high school achievements and activities, attitudes, career plans, aspirations, and goals. These input variables, measured primarily through the 1966 entering freshman survey, include both static personal attributes (for example, race and sex) and certain items that might change with time (for example, attitude and career plans). The latter input measures can be regarded as "pretests" on certain output measures.

After considering the effects of student input on student output measures, one can evaluate the effects of the college. Thus, the final component, the college environment, enters the picture.

College environment refers to those features of a college or university that may have some potential effect on the student. The environment includes two broad classes of characteristics: between-institution variables that characterize an entire institution and presumably can influence all students (for example, type, control, size, administrative policies), and within-institution variables that are usually experienced by only some students at a given institution (for example, type of residence and major financial source).

In Figure 2.1 the principal research concern is to assess the relationship indicated by arrow B, the effects of the college environment on student output. A relatively unbiased assessment requires a control for the effects of student input on student output (the relationship indicated by arrow C). In other words, the student outputs of an institution (for example, the achievements of its graduates) can be taken as a measure of institutional impact only when they are viewed in relation to student inputs (for example, the achievement potential of entering students). Relationship A indicates that, for any individual student, the other college students make up part of the environmental factors that can influence that student's development. With a knowledge of the interrelationships and possible interactions among these three sets of variables, one can better estimate college impact.

DEFINING THE VARIABLES

The student input data used to analyze college impact were obtained from students who entered college as first-time freshmen in 1966, when they completed the 150-item SIF (see Annex A, Appendix A). We followed up a subsample of these students four years later (during late summer and fall 1970) when, presumably, many had received the baccalaureate. (See Annex A, Appendix A for the followup questionnaire.) To conserve costs, groups of 250 students for whom we had freshman data were selected randomly from the large institutions; at those institutions enrolling 300 or fewer students, we followed up all students who had completed the 1966 SIF. The final sample numbered 217 institutions. Data on the student's college grade point average, academic degrees completed, and scores on high school aptitude tests were obtained from a special survey of institutional registrars during fall 1970. Approximately 55 percent of the 51,721 students surveyed returned the followup questionnaires. Their followup responses were merged with their SIF responses on a single file.

Of these students, for whom both freshman and followup data were available, a one-fifth sample (N = 5,091) was selected for regression analyses.

Student Output Variables

The 1970 followup questionnaire included many items repeated verbatim from the SIF administered four years earlier, such as those on career choice and degree aspirations. In addition, the questionnaire contained new items asking about satisfaction with various aspects of the college. The followup data were used to construct measures of the following variables:

Career choice (15 dichotomous measures: artist, businessman, clergyman, and so on)
Major field (17 dichotomous measures: agriculture, biological sciences, business, and so on)
Degree aspirations (2 dichotomous measures: planning to obtain a bachelor's [or higher] degree, planning to obtain a doctoral [or equivalent] degree)
Religious preference (4 dichotomous measures: Protestant, Catholic, Jewish, none)
Life goals (17 measures: becoming accomplished in the performing arts, helping others in difficulty, being well-off financially, and

so on. Each scored on a four-point scale: essential = 4, very
important = 3, somewhat important = 2, of little or no importance
= 1)

Self-ratings (21 measures: academic ability, cheerfulness, political
conservatism, and so on. Each scored on a five-point scale. The
respondents were asked to rate themselves in comparison with
the average person of their own age: highest 10 percent = 5,
above average = 4, average = 3, below average = 2, lowest 10
percent = 1)

Daily activities (27 measures: listening to rock music, smoking
cigarettes, oversleeping and missing a class or appointment,
and so on. Each scored on a three-point scale: frequently = 3,
occasionally = 2, not at all = 1)

Overall satisfaction with the college (scored on a five-point scale:
very satisfied = 5, satisfied = 4, on the fence = 3, dissatisfied =
2, very dissatisfied = 1)

Satisfaction with specific aspects of the college environment (11
measures: overall quality of instruction, facilities for library
research, opportunities to discuss work outside the classroom
with professors in major field, etc. Each scored on a five-point
scale: excellent = 5, good = 4, satisfactory = 3, unsatisfactory =
2, very unsatisfactory = 1)

Ratings of the sufficiency of certain aspects of the college (10
measures: freedom in course selection, social life, personal
contacts with faculty, etc. Each scored on a three-point scale:
too much or too many = 3, just about the right amount = 2, not
enough = 1)

Except for the last three types of measures relating to satisfaction with the college, each student output or dependent variable listed
had been included on the freshman questionnaire. Thus, both pretest
and posttest scores were available for each student.

Student Input Variables

The freshman questionnaire covered much demographic and
background information, which was used to construct a series of
student input or predictor variables:

Sex (dichotomy)
Age (scored on a seven-point scale, ranging from 16 or younger to
older than 21)
Father's education (scored on a six-point scale: grammar school or
less to postgraduate degree)

Mother's education (scored on the same scale as father's education)
Parental income (scored on a nine-point scale: less than $4,000 to
     $30,000 or more)
Race (5 dichotomous measures: Caucasian, Negro, Oriental, American
     Indian, other)
Religious background (4 dichotomous measures: Protestant, Catholic,
     Jewish, none)
High school grades (scored on an eight-point scale: A or A+ to D)
Type of high school attended (4 dichotomous measures: public,
     private (denominational), private (nondenominational), other)
Extracurricular achievements in high school (12 dichotomous meas-
     ures: won a varsity letter in sports, edited the school paper,
     was a member of a scholastic honor society, and so on)
Pretests on 103 output measures (career choices, majors, degree
     aspirations, religious preference, life goals, self-ratings, and
     daily activities)

These input measures, together with scores on college admissions tests provided by the institutions, were used as predictor
variables in stepwise linear multiple regression analyses. The
aptitude test score and the basic pool of 31 demographic student
input variables (that is, all input variables listed above except the
103 pretests) were used in all analyses. Limitations in the capacity
of our computer program prevented our including pretests and post-
tests on all output measures in a single analysis. Consequently, four
separate analyses were run for the following groups of output measures: daily activities; life goals and self-ratings; majors, careers,
and degree aspirations; and religious preference and overall satisfaction with, as well as ratings of specific aspects of, the college
experience. Each analysis included as predictors only the pretest
measures for the particular outcomes in that analysis, plus the 31
demographic predictors.

Environmental Variables

The between-college measures included the following institutional
characteristics:

Level (3 dichotomous measures: two-year college, four-year
     college, university)
Curricular emphasis (3 dichotomous measures: teachers college,
     technological institution, liberal arts college)

Type of control (4 dichotomous measures: private nonsectarian,
    Protestant, Catholic, public)
Sex (3 dichotomous measures: men's college, women's college,
    coeducational college)
Race (predominantly black versus predominantly white)
Geographic region (4 dichotomous measures: Northeast, Southeast,
    Midwest, West and Southwest)
Selectivity (estimate of the average academic ability of entering
    freshman[6])
Enrollment size (scored on an eight-point scale: below 200, 200-499,
    to 20,000 or more)
Environmental factors from the ICA (33 measures of the peer environ-
    ment, classroom environment, administrative environment, and
    the college image)

The within-college measures—those applying only to subgroups
of students at a given university—were obtained from the followup
questionnaire:

Method of financing college (6 measures: support from parents,
    support from spouse, scholarship or fellowship, earnings from
    employment, loan, other sources. Parental aid was scored
    dichotomously: more than 40 percent, 40 percent or less. The
    other five measures were scored dichotomously: more than 20
    percent, 20 percent or less)
Residence during the freshman year (6 dichotomous measures:
    with parents; other private home, apartment, or room; dormi-
    tory; fraternity or sorority house; other student housing; other)
Married at the time of followup (dichotomy)
Had children at the time of followup (dichotomy)

ESTIMATING COLLEGE IMPACT

As indicated earlier, college impact can be defined as those
aspects of a student's development attributable to the effects of the
college rather than to the characteristics and potentialities of the
student at matriculation. Impact does not necessarily imply change;
in some instances a college may affect a student by inhibiting changes
that would have occurred if the student had gone to another college or
had not attended at all.
The college environment may affect student development in three
ways: by bringing about changes that ordinarily do not occur in college

students, by accentuating changes that do occur, or by diminishing or impeding changes. Our analyses were concerned with the comparative impact of different institutions rather than with the impact of attendance versus nonattendance.

Assessing comparative college impact requires certain statistical controls to compensate for the possibility that students in one institution may show changes that differ from those of students at another institution simply because the two groups themselves were different at college entry. Or, stated another way, we had to correct for the fact that colleges differ in the kinds of students they recruit. These corrections involved certain statistical controls that in effect "matched" students entering different colleges on their known characteristics at matriculation. Although it is impossible to know if all relevant input characteristics were considered, these statistical controls minimized the chances of error in estimating environmental effects.

A separate stepwise linear multiple regression analysis was carried out for each student output (dependent) variable above. In each analysis, student input (predictor) variables were permitted to enter in a stepwise fashion until no additional predictor could produce a reduction in the residual sum of squares exceeding $p = .05$. Thus, the residual scores on the dependent variable after the final step in each analysis were statistically independent of all input measures and could be used to assess the comparative impact of different environmental variables.

Next we computed, for each institution, an expected score on each output variable. The predictive equation for the output measure (obtained from these regression analyses) was applied to the freshman data for each student, yielding an expected or predicted response for that student. The expected responses for all students at a given institution were then averaged to yield a mean expected score for the institution on each output variable. This mean expected score was compared with the institution's mean actual score (obtained by averaging the actual followup responses of individuals). The actual score might be less than, greater than, or equal to the expected score.

Note that the expected score for any college was based on a formula derived from students at all types of colleges. Thus, if an institution's actual score was close to its expected score, one could conclude that the development of its students was similar to that of comparable students across the nation. This result would not mean that the college exerted no influence on the outcome in question, but rather that its influence was typical of that of most institutions. An estimated score that deviated from the actual score would indicate that influence on that measure was atypical for colleges admitting comparable students. In this sense, the data provided an assessment of the comparative impact of various institutions.

One must be careful to distinguish the impact of a college from the changes in students. Certain maturational changes occur in all persons of 18 to 22 regardless of where—or even whether—they go to college. Thus, even if students at a given college show substantial changes from their freshman to their senior years, one cannot be sure that these changes are attributable to that college's particular environment unless the expected mean response to the followup also deviated from the actual mean responses. These data enabled institutions to determine (a) the actual changes in their students between the freshman and senior years; and (b) whether the actual change (or lack of it) deviated from any change that could have been projected from the students' characteristics as entering freshmen.

Estimating Effects of Selected Environmental Factors

In these analyses the predictor variables included not only the student input measures, but also the measures of within-college environmental variables. Consequently, each respondent's expected score on a particular outcome was based not only on input characteristics but also on within-college experiences (financial support, residence, and so on). These measures were included in the pool of predictors to reduce the chances that a discrepancy between expected and actual scores for a college would arise not because of something inherent in the college environment, but because the proportion of students exposed to some within-college factor deviated from the norm. For example, living in a dormitory increased the student's chances of completing the bachelor's degree in four years. Unless we included this residence factor in the battery of predictors, the actual dropout rate for a community college could exceed its expected rate because most of its students lived at home, not because anything in the college contributed to the students' leaving. The expected degree completion rate of a commuter college would be lowered by including this variable in the analysis, and the expected rate for a residential college would be raised. After controlling for the effects of student input characteristics and within-college experiences, the partial correlations between various institutional characteristics and the student outcomes were examined. These analyses were conducted on the national sample of institutions.

Those within-college variables that entered the regression equation as predictors and those between-college variables that had statistically significant partial correlations with the student outcomes (after controlling for the effects of student input and within-college experiences) were listed in tabular form to help the institutions

understand the kinds of college characteristics or experiences that
may influence students. (See Annex A, Table A.9 in the data packet.)
Thus, an institution could gain additional insight into outcome variables on which it exerted a unique impact by examining the environmental characteristics that might be positively or negatively related
to that impact.

PREPARING THE DATA PACKETS

Selected results from these various analyses were utilized to
prepare tables for inclusion in the data packets for the 20 institutions.
Our principal objective was to assemble a packet containing those
empirical findings that might contribute to a better understanding of
institutional functioning and that eventually could be useful in planning
and decision-making. We wanted to provide enough detail to facilitate
interpretation of the data, but not so much as to discourage committee
members from working with those data. This need for balance applied
to the individual items provided as well as to the accompanying technical details of sampling, data collection, and statistical analysis.

The data packet was organized into ten sections as follows:

1. A covering letter explaining the project and the use of the packet.
2. A list of the 19 participating institutions together with the name
   and title of each committee chairperson.
3. A three-page summary of the design and purposes of the project.
4. A twelve-page guide to interpreting the data.
5. A four-page illustration of how the data might be applied to institutional policy.
6. Tables of data:
   a. College impact data. Actual and estimated changes (1966-70)
      in the following: career choice (Table A.1); major field (Table
      A.2); degree aspirations (Table A.3); religious preference
      (Table A.4); dissatisfaction with selected aspects of college
      (Table A.5); ratings of the sufficiency of selected aspects of the
      college (Table A.6); persistance rates (Table A.7).
   b. Trend data. Summaries of freshman class characteristics
      between 1966 and 1971 (Table A.8).
   c. Environmental data. Institutional and environmental factors
      associated with the various student outcomes (Table A.9).
7. Copies of the various questionnaires used in the longitudinal
   surveys (Annex A, Appendix A).
8. Coding scheme for majors and careers (Annex A, Appendix B).

9. Forms for requesting other analyses of data, including data from
    other participating institutions (Annex A, Appendix C).
10. Tables of data (if requested) from comparison institutions.

Annex A provides a copy of one institution's data packet. This
final form of the packet includes a number of modifications suggested
by the field testing and by our consultants (see Chapter 3).

NOTES

1. Arthur W. Chickering, "Research for Action," in The New
Colleges: Toward an Appraisal, ed. Paul Dressel (Iowa City: The
American College Testing Program, 1971), p. 26.
2. For a description of the sampling design, see Alexander W.
Astin, Margo R. King, John M. Light, and Gerald T. Richardson,
The American Freshman: National Norms for Fall 1974 (Los Angeles:
UCLA, 1974).
3. For further information on the objectives and activities of
CIRP, see Alexander W. Astin, "The National Study of Higher Education Moves to UCLA," UCLA Educator 16, no. 1 (Winter 1974): 28-31.
4. Alexander W. Astin, Manual for the Inventory of College
Activities (ICA) (Minneapolis: National Computer Systems, 1968).
5. Alexander W. Astin, College Dropouts: A National Profile
(Washington, D.C.: American Council on Education, 1972); vol. 7,
no. 1, ACE Research Reports.
6. From Alexander W. Astin, Predicting Academic Performance
in College (New York: Free Press, 1971).

3

DISSEMINATING THE DATA

The dissemination phase of the "Data for Decisions" project involved three major tasks: developing a preliminary design, pilot testing (with possible revision), and implementing the final plan. The initial design was to be completed during summer 1972, the pilot testing done in the fall, and the final plan initiated in November or December and completed by June 1973.

DEVELOPING A FEEDBACK PLAN

Before settling on a feedback strategy, we wanted to consider a wide range of possible approaches. For this purpose we selected a diverse group of six consultants to help the staff of the American Council on Education develop a feedback plan and to serve as an informal advisory committee for the project: David Bushnell, Human Resources Research Organization; Craig Comstock, Wright Institute; David Epperson, Northwestern University; Harold Hodgkinson, University of California, Berkeley; Joseph Kauffman, Rhode Island College (a member of the advisory panel for "Study of Campus Unrest and Change," supported earlier by the National Institute of Mental Health); and Michelle Patterson, University of California, Santa Barbara. A seventh consultant, Joseph Katz, Wright Institute and State University of New York at Stony Brook, joined the project during the second year. Each consultant had been involved with research in higher education, and several had had extensive experience consulting with other institutions.

The initial meeting of the consultants and staff was a two-day brainstorming conference in August 1972 to familiarize the consultants with the kinds of information that would be made available to institutions. A preliminary data packet, prepared and distributed before the meeting, included complete profiles on ten institutions. (Most of these were selected because one or more of the consultants had some personal knowledge of the campus.) After two days of intensive discussion, during which many possible strategies were considered, we were able to generate an overall project plan, specific feedback techniques, and a critical evaluation of the content and format of the data in the preliminary packets. With minor changes, the core elements of the feedback project are those designed at this conference.

A major concern of the participants was to avoid the weaknesses of traditional communication methods. For example, frequently used forms of presentation, such as written reports, are basically passive and require no active involvement by the recipients. Such reports are often read, filed, and disregarded. For this reason we chose not to send the institutions a research report containing a complete analysis, conclusions, and recommendations. Instead, by involving the institution actively in interpreting the data, we hoped to increase their interest in applying the results to campus concerns and, at the same time, to minimize any defensiveness associated with an outside data source. The institutions would be asked not only to report their analyses and interpretations to ACE, but also to translate these interpretations, where appropriate, into proposals for action.

Another problem with reporting results to a campus representative is that such a person typically has little power to effect change. Where possible, we wanted to direct the feedback to individuals or groups chosen for the power they wielded on campus rather than for the ascriptive categories they represented (for example, faculty, students, administration). We emphasized this intention to our initial contacts at each campus.

The Feedback Plan

Our first goal was to identify institutions in the Cooperative Institutional Research Program in which at least one key individual was known personally by an ACE staff member. Preliminary inquiries would be made to assess each institution's interest in participation. Selection of the 20 institutions for the experimental sample would be based on the responses and consideration of such criteria as institutional type and geographical location. All persons initially contacted at the campuses should be familiar with and favorably inclined toward the ACE research program. The intent of this selection procedure, of course, was to maximize institutional cooperation.

Each contact person at the 20 institutions would be asked to select five campus leaders interested in educational reform and regarded as influential campus figures to work with selected ACE student data. This committee would prepare a report—a local product—integrating ACE data with its own knowledge of the campus and students and suggesting proposals for change where appropriate. The committee would then be responsible for implementing these plans of action.

The ACE staff would provide individualized assistance to each institution. Colleges might need technical assistance to interpret the data, as well as guidance on strategies to implement proposed changes. Several of the original six consultants who had had experience working with colleges on self-renewal programs agreed to provide individual consultation upon request during the first year of this project. Each institution was informed that it could obtain on-campus assistance by requesting a visit from a team of one ACE member and one consultant. Even if all institutions did not request such visits, we would maintain close communication by telephone and letter.

To insure support at high levels, the cooperation and approval of the president would be sought at the start of the project. A personal letter to each chief executive from ACE president Roger Heyns would serve this purpose.

As an additional incentive to secure full institutional involvement, expenses up to $500 (for the report writer's honorarium, clerical work, and so on) would be reimbursed upon request. In turn, we proposed that each institution provide a matching contribution to indicate its own commitment.

The opportunity for participating institutions to exchange data was a key element in the plan. Each college would be encouraged to request copies of the data packets of other participating institutions as a "reference group" to compare the development of their students with that of students at similar institutions. To facilitate the exchange, the sample of 20 participants was designed to include several sub-groups of similar institutions. Consultants and staff members had observed that meetings involving small consortia of institutions with similar goals and problems often stimulate constructive change. By learning from other institutions' successes and mistakes, a given college could make more informed decisions. Thus, it appeared that the potential of the consortium would be enhanced by providing empirical data so institutions could make direct comparisons on identical measures of college impact.

Alternative Plans

To settle on a committee as the primary vehicle to implement the project seemed anticlimactic and perhaps even prosaic to some, given the nature of the brainstorming group and the freewheeling atmosphere in which the discussions took place. Formation of a committee was, in fact, one of the most unpopular ideas at the beginning. As alternatives developed, however, it became clear that the project would have little hope of getting off the ground if our recommended approach was initially seen as too far out. We were not part of the faculty, nor did we have any administrative power or authority. We assumed, of course, that the institution's prior relations with ACE and CIRP would facilitate cooperation, but we had no reason to expect that the people who would be given the responsibility to carry out the project would see us as having any special wisdom, power, or authority. In short, our consultants agreed that our only leverage would come through personal persuasion.

Like it or not, the internal governance of most higher educational institutions in the United States operates through committees. While committee work is frequently denigrated as unnecessarily time-consuming and often fruitless, a committee (or task force, as we called it) represents a widely accepted mechanism to give official recognition or sanction to an institutional activity. This is especially true for any new activity. Consequently, if the institution would appoint a committee responsible for the study, we would achieve two important first steps: We would have tangible evidence of the institution's formal involvement. And the energies of key members of the academic community would be formally committed (on paper, at least) to the project.

Although we did not realize it at the time, the project would eventually yield a great deal of potentially useful information about the functioning (and malfunctioning) of ad hoc committees (see Chapters 7 and 8). Although we gave extensive thought to the structure and selection of the committee, the project outcomes (see Chapter 5) suggest strongly that we might have devoted more attention to this aspect of the design.

A major point of controversy in the two-day brainstorming conference was the extent to which we should provide on-site consultation for participants. Extensive assistance was pushed especially hard by two consultants experienced at working intensively with individual colleges. They thought consultation was necessary to diagnose each campus's individual problems and needs. This initial diagnostic evaluation would presumably make it possible to focus the presentation of data more directly on the institution's most pressing problems. Furthermore, some argued that a series of initial consultative contacts would help to break down institutional resistance and develop a spirit of trust.

Despite these persuasive arguments, extensive on-site consultation was not included in the final study plan for a number of reasons. The most obvious was economic: The budget for the dissemination phase could not support extensive consultation without a major reduction in the number of participating institutions. (The number was already considered precariously small for any statistical evaluation of the project's impact which might be carried out during the second phase.) Another reason for rejecting consultation was a concern about further confounding the independent variable (that is, the student data). A major consultative effort could independently produce changes in the institutions that had no relationship to the data per se. (If resources had been available to examine a somewhat larger sample, it would have been informative to employ a factorial design in which both intensive consultation and student data were tried separately and in combination. Those consultants promoting intensive on-site consultation were, in effect, arguing for the existence of an interaction effect between consultation and data.) We were also concerned about keeping down the per-institution costs of this pilot dissemination so the approach could be applied economically on a larger scale if warranted by the results.

The generality of the findings and their applicability on a large scale are interrelated. Clearly, if the design of an experiment is such that a researcher has difficulty generalizing the findings beyond an experimental sample, policy makers may subsequently be reluctant to apply the approach on a larger scale, even if the results of the experiment are positive. Introducing a small number of select consultants as a major factor in the dissemination could impair the degree of generality of the findings, since these same consultants clearly could not carry the entire burden of a larger project. At the same time, positive results would stand a greater chance of widespread impact if they were obtained with relatively inexpensive dissemination procedures that could be replicated on a larger sample with reasonable confidence that results would be similar.

A final reason for rejecting intensive on-site consultation was a concern that it might be counterproductive. A critical difference between our project and the usual consultative visit to a campus was that the institutions had not requested our help. We were, in effect, asking their help. In return, we were providing them data they presumably did not have that might benefit their institution and students. Since such an effort might be seen as presumptuous on our part, some were concerned that on-campus visits by consultants early in the project might be regarded as heavyhanded and increase rather than decrease resistance. Indeed, one alternative considered but rejected was to present the study simply as a research effort, with no implied benefit to the institution. We discarded this idea primarily because we would be distorting the true purpose of the project.

The middle course eventually followed was as straightforward as possible. In brief, institutions were told this was a research project, but they might benefit from participation. Although we were open-minded about the possibility that the project might in fact turn out not to be of any benefit, we thought it would be beneficial to some.

We did not simply assume that being open about the project goals would allay all suspicions and break down all institutional defenses. No matter how elegant our rhetoric, we faced the possibility that a weak institutional ego would be threatened by the suggestion that some outside agency or individual possessed relevant and potentially important information that the institution itself did not have. The suggestion that a careful evaluation of such information can or should influence decision-making compounds the threat. That some persons on the campuses were indeed threatened by the project is documented in detail below and in Chapters 4 and 7.

Another suggestion given lengthy consideration was to provide each institution with an interpretive summary of its data. The major impetus for this suggestion was the large amount of raw data that would be reported back to each institution and the bewilderment that some consultants experienced on first encountering the data. While the limited personnel time influenced the final decision to reject this proposal, several other factors were also considered. By providing an interpretive summary of the meaning and implications of the data, we would, in effect, be doing a major part of the committee's work. This could discourage the committee from attempting to understand the data in light of their students' needs and encourage it instead to assume the role of critic of our interpretive summary. We wanted the summary to be the committee's, not ours. Furthermore, we were also concerned that errors of interpretation or fact resulting from our limited knowledge of the institution could provide a red herring to distract the committee from considering the major substance of the data.

Our negative decision was not based on any assumption that institutions would not need help with the data. Rather, we assumed that help would be more effective if it were provided in elaborate documentation and instructions accompanying the initial data packet, and by an offer of consultative assistance during the committee's deliberations. This latter, as it turned out, was probably not utilized to the extent that it should have been.

IMPLEMENTING THE PLAN

Work on the feedback phase was initiated immediately following the summer planning conference. Several tasks were to be completed by the end of the fall term: choosing the institutional sample, organizing the campus committees, revising the data packets, and mailing the revised packets. Completing these tasks by the end of the term would allow the institutions to spend the second half of the 1972-73 academic year analyzing the data, writing their reports, and initiating the changes based on their own recommendations.

Selecting the Sample

Selection of an initial sample of 50 institutions was based on several criteria: the institutions must be four-year colleges or universities (to make maximum use of the four-year followup data), they must have participated in CIRP since 1966 (so 1966-70 longitundinal data would be available), and they must have provided consistently representative data in the freshman survey. Once these requirements were met, we looked for institutions with an individual whom an ACE staff member knew personally and, ideally, who had supported our research program. Most often, this person was the institutional representative for CIRP; at several institutions it was the president. However, at a few campuses, our contact held neither position.

Personal invitations to participate were sent to these 50 people from the staff members with whom they were acquainted. (See Annex B for a copy of the letter.) Personal contact was emphasized from the beginning. The letters were followed within two weeks by telephone calls to obtain the response to several questions in the letter: First, was the institution interested in participating in a pilot feedback project? If so, what kinds of information would be most helpful in terms of present problems? Did the institution have the potential to implement policy recommendations implied by the research findings? Would the college or university be interested in exchanging data with other participating institutions?

The responses from the majority of colleges and universities were quite favorable. At only two institutions did the contact person refuse to let us consider the institution. The others, for the most part, were interested in receiving followup data on their students, were concerned with institutional self-study (several institutions were already involved in ongoing projects), and were willing to commit the necessary time and resources to complete the project.

Since the criterion "willingness to participate" did not appreciably decrease the sample size, we used several other criteria to select the final 20 institutions: our best guess about the probability of effecting real policy change, our ability to provide the college with the data it desired, geographical considerations, and the need to select a diverse group of institutions that also included several subgroups of comparable institutions to encourage data exchange.

The 20 participating institutions are listed in Table 3.1 by type and control, selectivity, region, enrollment, and sex. The slight bias toward private, eastern institutions primarily reflects oversampling of those institutions in the original CIRP sample. A third of the institutions had enrollments over 10,000, while nearly half had enrollments under 5,000. Only two were not coeducational, but three others— Williams College, Vassar College, and Franklin and Marshall College— had recently become coeducational. Only a few institutions were highly selective, but all were of at least average selectivity. The University of Redlands was the only four-year Protestant college, but the paucity of Western institutions in our sample warranted its inclusion.

The 20 institutions, informed by telephone of their selection for the feedback project, were given additional information and requested to organize a task force of approximately five influential, innovative persons interested in educational reform. Task force members could be faculty, administrators, or students, but one member should be a competent writer. The task forces at the 20 institutions would spend several months analyzing the data for their students, writing a report of their findings and recommendations for change if any, and implementing suggested policy or program reforms.

A letter with more detailed information followed the phone call. Letters were also sent to the remaining 30 institutions that were not included. (See Annex B for copies of both letters.)

The University of Michigan gave only a tentative acceptance: Its final decision was to be contingent upon its evaluation of the data packet. It chose a committee for this purpose.

Shortly after we had contacted all the institutions, we discovered that the records were in error on the inclusion of the City University of New York–City College in the 1970 followup. Consequently, we dropped City College from the sample but provided it with special analyses of the 1971 followup of the 1967 freshmen so that the time and effort the institution had expended would not be unrewarded. The final sample therefore included 19 institutions.

TABLE 3.1

Characteristics of the Original Sample of Institutions

Institution	Selectivity Code*	Region	Size	Sex
Public Universities				
University of Massachusetts at Amherst	5	East	20,732	Coed
University of Michigan	6	Midwest	36,967	Coed
Washington State University	5	West	14,667	Coed
Private Universities				
Northwestern University	6	Midwest	15,571	Coed
Saint Louis University	5	Midwest	9,383	Coed
Tulane University	6	South	8,453	Coed
University of Denver	4	West	9,350	Coed
Vanderbilt University	7	South	6,397	Coed
Four-Year Public Colleges				
SUNY at Oswego	4	East	8,283	Coed
U.S. Coast Guard Academy	6	East	969	Men
Western Illinois University	4	Midwest	14,307	Coed
Four-Year Private Nonsectarian Colleges				
Allegheny College	6	East	1,804	Coed
Franklin and Marshall College	6	East	2,787	Coed
Mills College	6	West	939	Women
Vassar College	7	East	1,900	Coed
Williams College	7	East	1,418	Coed
Four-Year Catholic Colleges				
Ohio Dominican College	4	Midwest	940	Coed
Saint Norbert College	4	Midwest	1,673	Coed
Four-Year Protestant College				
University of Redlands	5	West	1,970	Coed

*The selectivity codes are derived from the following table:

Selectivity Code	Median NMSQT Score of Entering Freshmen
1	Under 89
2	89-96
3	97-104
4	105-112
5	113-120
6	121-128
7	Over 128

Source: Alexander W. Astin, Predicting Academic Performance in College (New York: Free Press, 1971).

Preparing the Feedback

After the institutions were selected, letters were sent from ACE president Roger Heyns to the chief executive of each campus. Since several presidents had been our initial contacts, two forms were sent: a short letter to the presidents already familiar with the project, and a longer one to the majority with whom we had not been in touch. (See Annex B for copies of both letters.)

Shortly thereafter, a data release form and accompanying letter were sent to the presidents asking their permission to send their data to any project institution that requested them. (See Annex B for the form and letters.)

The 19 institutions are listed below by contact person: president, CIRP representative, or neither. Institutions at which someone other than the contact person was appointed to chair the task force are marked by an asterisk.

President	Institutional Representative
Franklin and Marshall College*	Allegheny College
Mills College*	Northwestern University
St. Louis University*	Ohio Dominican College
University of Michigan*	St. Norbert College
University of Redlands*	SUNY at Oswego
Vassar College*	Tulane University
	University of Denver
	University of Massachusetts at
Other Position	Amherst*
Vanderbilt University*	U.S. Coast Guard Academy
	Washington State University*
	Western Illinois University*
	Williams College

At six institutions, our contact was the president; all six presidents appointed another person as chairperson. Two appointees (at Mills College and Michigan) were institutional representatives. Our key person at all but one of the remaining institutions (Vanderbilt University) was also an institutional representative. Three contact persons who were institutional representatives appointed someone else to chair the task force. In summary, 11 task force chairpersons at the 19 institutions were institutional representatives for CIRP and therefore were quite familiar with our research program and data. Of the remaining eight chairpersons, five were administrators, two were faculty members, and one held a joint administrative/faculty position.

One key person at Vanderbilt was Nicholas Hobbs, provost and former chairperson of the Research Advisory Committee for ACE's Office of Research. Because of Hobbs' extensive involvement with our research program, we asked Vanderbilt to play a special additional role in the project. Vanderbilt agreed to be our pilot institution for both the data packets and the team visits. Preliminary versions of the data packet (revised after the two-day planning conference) were sent to the Vanderbilt committee on November 1 for pilot tests.

We asked the Vanderbilt committee to give us feedback on specific questions: How useful would the data be as an aid in policy-making? How clearly were they presented? Was there too little or too much methodological discussion? Was enough structure provided for the task force? Would the data exchange with other participating institutions provide a useful basis for comparison?

These questions were discussed at a meeting of the ACE staff and the Vanderbilt committee and during a telephone conference with some committee members. At the suggestion of those involved, we expanded the methodological section, adding some information on sampling. We did not increase the technical level of the presentation, however, for the sake of the less statistically sophisticated committee members. Vanderbilt suggested no other major changes, and the revised packets were sent to all 19 institutions on January 1, 1973. (See sample packet, Annex A.)

The mailing launched the actual data dissemination phase, which we now designated "Data for Decisions in Higher Education." As outlined in the packet introduction, we envisioned the work of the task forces as two-part: the data analysis and writeup of recommendations for change, and the implementation of these recommendations. The written report on the first part, originally due March 31, was to include several features: (1) an analysis based on the data and the task force's knowledge and experience of the effect the institution was having on its students; (2) a discussion of desired institutional effects on student development; (3) a discussion of any problem areas suggested by discrepancies between (1) and (2); and (4) specific plans for reform where needed.

Working with the Committee

The emphasis at ACE now shifted to offering assistance, guidance, additional data, and any other aid to facilitate the work of the committee (or task forces). We maintained close communication with the colleges through telephone, letters, and staff-consultant visits. This written and oral interchange between ACE and the task forces provided one of the primary methods of evaluating the project.

With the packets mailed, we prepared for visits by staff-consultant teams. Vanderbilt was once more employed as a test institution. A visit, scheduled for early January, had a dual purpose: (1) to provide a training session for consultants and staff before they were requested to go on additional visits, and (2) to answer Vanderbilt's questions on data interpretation and the scope of the project. In consideration of the primary purpose—training staff and consultants —all staff members then involved in the project (Alexander W. Astin, David E. Drew, and Linda D. Molm) and four consultants made the visit. In addition to the seven regular members of the Vanderbilt committee, three other persons (a dean, a resident psychiatrist, and a member of the mathematics faculty) were also present. In this meeting we encountered a number of problems. Several members of the Vanderbilt group expressed considerable irritation about what they saw as a lack of relevance to Vanderbilt's local problems. Others concentrated on technical deficiencies in the data and in the project design. The staff and consultants were immediately put on the defensive. Despite several attempts to refocus the discussion, the day-long meeting resembled a faculty colloquium (where a research project is presented and criticized) or perhaps an oral examination. Any lingering doubts about our decision not to provide each institution with intensive on-site consultation were removed by this Vanderbilt visit.

The experience with Vanderbilt prompted us to develop a set of guidelines for any future on-site visits requested by the other 18 institutions:

1. Staff-consultant teams should be small (no more than two or three persons) and meet with only two or three committee members. A small group should be more productive than the Vanderbilt-ACE group, where the meeting became an encounter with two sides gathering for battle.
2. All institutions requesting visits should submit a list of their questions and problems before the meeting. That way the institution would take the initiative for the discussion and the ACE team could prepare for the meeting. The college would be responsible for organizing the meeting and the agenda.
3. The ACE staff member should act primarily as a technical resource on matters of data collection, methodology, and so on, while the consultant should play the leading "change agent" role and handle questions of interpretation and application. This strategy should allow the staff member to maintain a neutral stance with regard to data interpretation and to keep his or her role from becoming defensive.
4. The discussion should be directed toward substantive, not methodological, issues. Methodological questions should be handled briefly so that they do not monopolize the meeting.

5. Institutions should be encouraged to begin the meeting with a discussion of their background and present concerns and then to
   move to the data for insights into the issues, rather than immediately turning to the data for problems.

These guidelines were applied with moderate success at Tulane
University and at a meeting held at ACE in Washington with the State
University of New York at Oswego committee. (Success here means
that the discussions seemed more productive than those held earlier
at Vanderbilt; the reports from the two institutions (see Chapter 4)
indicate, however, that the visits had little impact on the project
outcomes.)

Why did so few institutions request a visit? Perhaps we did not
emphasize this possibility enough in our correspondence with the
committees, or perhaps the analysis-interpretation phase is not the
time when visits are needed. The optimal time may be after the data
have been studied and applied to local needs, and the committee is
grappling with the problem of implementing its recommendations. A
visit at this point, solicited or not, might provide the catalyst necessary to translate recommendations into action. The task force report
would give the consultant or staff-consultant team the background
necessary to work more effectively with the local committee. (These
possibilities are discussed in Chapter 8.)

Our interactions with the institutions during this phase took
several forms. Table 3.2 illustrates the various types of communication that occurred between ACE and each institution. Telephone calls
or letters were sufficient to answer most questions. A few committee
members made informal visits to the council, usually when they were
in town for some other purpose. Most questions concerned methodological procedures used in the analyses. A few persons expressed
concern about organizing their committees, defining institutional
goals, writing the report, or developing strategies to implement
their recommendations. Only five institutions utilized the $500
honorarium.

Most colleges requested additional data. The most frequent
request was for comparative data from other participating institutions.
In fact, of the six institutions that did not request comparative data,
two (Michigan and Vassar) withdrew from the project and three (Mills
College, Washington State University, and Williams) failed to produce
reports (see Chapter 4). For the remaining institution, the Coast
Guard Academy, our sample probably offered no comparable institutions. Clearly, failure to take advantage of data exchange was a
symptom of committee failure.

We conducted special computer analyses for six institutions.
Because of technical problems, these were not completed until
February or March. With few exceptions, most institutions tolerated

TABLE 3.2

Forms of Communication with the Institutions

Institution	Telephone Calls[a]	Letters[b]	Data Requests	Requests for $500	Site Visit	Informal Visit[c]
Allegheny College	X	X	X			
Franklin and Marshall College			X			
Mills College						
Northwestern University	X	X	X			X
Ohio Dominican College	X		X	X		
St. Louis University	X	X	X	X		
St. Norbert College	X		X	X		
SUNY at Oswego	X	X	X		X[d]	X
Tulane University	X	X	X	X	X	
U.S. Coast Guard Academy	X					X
University of Denver		X	X	X		
University of Massachusetts at Amherst	X	X	X			
University of Michigan	X	X				
University of Redlands		X	X			
Vanderbilt University	X	X	X		X	X
Vassar College		X				
Washington State University	X	X				
Western Illinois University	X	X	X			
Williams College						

[a]Initiated by institution
[b]Letters from institution other than "form" correspondence (acceptance, committee names, etc.)
[c]Committee member visited ACE when in Washington
[d]Held at Council, not at Oswego
Source: Compiled by the author.

the delay well. One committee refused to discuss the impact data until they were tabulated separately for graduates, transfer students, and dropouts. Several mentioned that they did not have enough time to study the additional data once they arrived.

Unfortunately, we were not set up to perform special analyses at will. Vanderbilt requested over 100 cross-tabulations of variables in the freshman surveys for each year from 1966 to 1972. Because of the size of each file (300,000 students for each year), this request was impossible to fulfill. The task force report indicated that Vanderbilt was unhappy with our response, even though we did perform other special analyses for the institution.

During the first week of March, we telephoned all committee chairpersons to obtain progress reports. Since most data requests had been made rather late in the three-month period, we suspected that many committees were not far along in their work and would be unable to meet the March 31 deadline. We decided to grant an extension through the end of May if necessary. This additional time could be used both to complete the data analysis and to implement recommendations.

The time extension also enabled the research staff to complete the requested computer analyses. In addition to these supplements to the data packets, we supplied the institutions with a second major set of data, the 1971 followup survey of the 1967 freshmen. (These were the same data sent to CUNY-City College.) Late in March, a computer printout of the 1967 freshmen's responses to the 1971 followup questionnaire, tabulated by sex, was sent to each institution with a normative report of the national sample of students who were followed up.[1] These data provided the most recent available measure of student development. Only actual percentages for the 1971 followup were given in the printout, since time and resources did not permit us to carry out the regression analyses used to compute the "expected" scores with the 1966-70 data. However, by comparing these 1971 followup data with the 1967 freshman data from these same students, an institution could obtain a measure of change on a number of items. The data were also used to verify findings in the 1970 followup for similar items.

Withdrawals from the Project

Two institutions, Michigan and Vassar, formally withdrew from the project after several months. (Vassar had received the 1971 followup data before withdrawal; Michigan had not.) Michigan had

agreed to participate on a trial basis. After three months its verdict
was not to participate further. Its initial explanation included concerns about adequate data and a belief that no institution in the sample
was similar to Michigan. (Berkeley and Harvard, we were told, would
be regarded as comparable institutions.) In response to additional
inquiries, the Michigan chairperson reported that a major reason
for the withdrawal was strong resistance from one committee member who at the time was also conducting research on student development. Other committee members were reluctant to continue the
project in the face of his objections.

From such experiences, we became aware of some of the psychological reactions that can be expected and the barriers they may
present to a cooperative effort. The project was valuable for these
insights alone. In this particular case, however, we should not have
allowed Michigan to participate on a trial basis. The situation was
complicated when our contact person appointed another chairperson.
We originally spoke with the president, who agreed without reservation
to participate. It was his committee that subsequently made participation contingent upon review of the data packet. (The role of the initial
contact person is discussed in Chapters 5 and 6.)

At the time of the March 1 telephone call, the Vassar committee
was involved in another institutional project and had not yet met. At
that time, however, the committee said it still planned to meet its
commitments to the ACE project. In April Vassar notified us that it
was withdrawing because of insufficient time, because the data were
not well keyed to Vassar's problems, and because the sample did not
include a college that could be compared with Vassar. When we
initially contacted Vassar, the institution named several issues
directly related to our data. Vassar was, in fact, one of the most
enthusiastic potential participants. This example illustrates once
more the apparent lack of relationship between the degree of initial
enthusiasm for the project and actual participation.

We attempted to follow up Vassar's withdrawal with a site visit
to obtain more information on the reversed commitment and steps
we might take in the future to prevent similar occurrences. After
Vassar changed the meeting date several times, we decided that little
would be gained without its cooperation and abandoned the idea. One
consultant subsequently met briefly with the Vassar chairperson,
who again raised the issue of lack of time among committee members.

NOTE

1. Alan E. Bayer, Jeannie T. Royer, and Richard M. Webb, Four Years After College Entry (Washington, D.C.: American Council on Education, 1973); vol. 8, no. 1, ACE Research Reports.

4

EVALUATING THE REPORTS

By June 1973, 13 of the 19 participating institutions had written reports. Although the four remaining institutions presumably still participating in the project had promised to produce reports before the end of the summer, none was actually able to deliver.

The 13 reports were highly diverse. One ran to nearly 200 pages, while another was only six pages long. Some contained dozens of specific recommendations for change, while others contained none. (See Chapter 5 for specific recommendations.) Several reports were highly critical of the NIMH project, while others contained nothing but praise.

The review of these reports was designed to answer a number of questions: How had the institutions responded to the task? Are there distinct responses that characterize particular types of institutions? How cooperative were the institutions in following through on the assignment? Did they demonstrate an ability to make insightful data interpretations? What kinds of proposals for change were made? What is the likelihood that these proposals will be put into action? Are the proposed changes consistent with the data? Are the changes likely to improve the educational environment for students? Did the committee make useful suggestions for improvements in the project? What kinds of followups during the second year are most likely to provide meaningful data for the evaluation phase?

Seeking answers to such complex questions from a small sample of reports challenges the empirically oriented researcher. Perhaps the simplest approach would be for the principal investigator to develop his best answers based on careful reading and analysis. The problem with this approach, of course, is the idiosyncratic nature of any individual's interpretations of such material. How reliable are such judgments? Would an independent reader reach the same conclusions?

To minimize individual bias, we obtained independent assessments of the 13 reports by four different readers: two consultants and two staff assistants from the University of California, Los Angeles (Diane Elvenstar and Elizabeth Weinberger). One consultant (David Epperson) had been with the project since its inception; the other (Joseph Katz) joined the project during the second year.

Each reader was asked to evaluate each report according to detailed criteria. (See Annex C for a copy of the instructions.) The specifications asked the readers to include three sections in their written analyses: a taxonomy of institutional responses, generalizations about feedback procedures, and predictions and recommendations for the second year of the project.

Each reader reviewed the reports independently and prepared a written analysis that was forwarded to the principal investigator. After the reviews were completed, the principal investigator and the four readers met to discuss their respective analyses and to develop concrete plans for the followup phase of the project.

TAXONOMY OF INSTITUTIONAL RESPONSES

The readers were requested to develop a "taxonomic scheme into which the various forms of institutional response could be classified. Obviously, the scheme should have at least two major categories, but probably not more than six (considering the total number of participants)." Although each reader's evaluation was unique in certain respects, the four proposed taxonomies were similar in many ways.

One purpose of the meeting was to agree on the constructs used to rate or describe the reports. Rating scales for each construct could then be applied to each report to develop quantitative estimates of its contents. The five rating scales based on the independent readings of the 13 reports and the followup meeting are discussed below. Each construct was rated on a five-point scale.

Receptivity to Participation

The five-point scale for this construct had descriptions at three points: critical or rejecting (score 1), mixed or neutral (score 3), and highly receptive or favorable (score 5). This dimension closely resembles constructs suggested independently by three of the readers: "receptivity to feedback" (Epperson), "evasion" (Katz), and "receptivity to carrying out the goal of the project" (Elvenstar).

Depth of Understanding

This continuum also had labels for three of the five points: descriptive (score 1), interpretive (score 3), and insightful (score 5). In all likelihood this was the most complex dimension, in that it required some explanation beyond the scale labels for raters to utilize it. A descriptive approach to the data characterized those institutions that simply converted the numbers into prose form with little or no attempt to understand the implications of the data for students. A report was classified as interpretive if it included some attempt to understand the meaning of particular data. The highest point on the scale, insightful, applied to those institutions that utilized the data to enhance their understanding of institutional functioning as it related to student development. (These three levels of understanding are discussed in Chapter 9.)

Depth of understanding was suggested by the taxonomic dimensions of several readers. Consultant David Epperson proposed a dimension called "awareness of institutional functioning," which he defined as "the degree to which the institutional leaders revealed an increased awareness of critical aspects of institutional functioning." Staff member Elizabeth Weinberger suggested a dimension called "global versus specific," which she defined as the extent to which the committee "used the data in some overall context rather than responding to each finding as a discrete entity." Consultant Joseph Katz proposed two taxonomic dimensions that related to depth of understanding: "interpretive strength" ("identifying those features of the data that have particular relevance to one's institution, relating variables to each other, and forming basic conceptual and theoretical structures under which to use the data") and "general theoretical range" ("relating the data pertaining to several institutions to each other as a base for developing theories that help to understand institutional and educational processes").

Willingness to Change

Three points on this continuum were: "no change proposed" (score 1), "vague, overly generalized, or trivial changes only" (score 3), and "concrete, meaningful proposals for change" (score 5). This dimension was reflected in the taxonomies proposed by all readers: "receptivity to carrying out the goals of the project" (Elvenstar), "propensity for change" (Epperson), "action use" (Katz), and "likelihood of impact of data" (Weinberger). Since the instructions to the committee were quite explicit about formulating recommendations for change, it is not surprising that this dimension was reflected in all the taxonomies.

Data Relatedness

This dimension was defined as: "no changes based on data" (score 1), "some changes based on data" (score 3), and "most or all changes based on data" (score 5). While data relatedness was not suggested specifically by any one single reader, it was included to differentiate institutions whose changes were clearly data based from those whose changes had little or no relevance to the data. One university, for example, proposed 38 specific changes, but none could be traced to any particular data that we provided. Similar proposals for changes, although fewer in number, were scattered among several other reports, suggesting that some committees had used the project to promote certain proposals for change, rather than to generate proposals from enhanced institutional understanding. (Data use is described in Chapters 7 and 9.)

Constructive Suggestions for Changes in the NIMH Project

Since each committee was specifically asked for suggestions to improve the project design, we wanted to determine whether the reports actually contained any recommendations. The rating scale was: none (score 1), a few (score 3), many (score 5).

SCORING THE REPORTS

The five rating scales were included in a form used to quantify the content of each report. This form also asked the rater to count the number of separately identifiable proposals for change included in each report. (See Annex D for a copy of the rating form.) Each report was rated by three persons—the principal investigator and both UCLA staff assistants—independently to provide data to assess interrater reliability. Once these reliability estimates had been made, the three raters met to discuss discrepancies of greater than one point. After the discrepancies were resolved (in a "resolution" one or both raters agreed to change a rating so that the discrepancy was no more than one point), mean ratings were computed on each measure for the 13 institutions.

Reliability of the Ratings

The average intercorrelations of the three independent ratings[1] were high:

Scale	Reliability
Receptivity to participation	.94
Depth of understanding	.89
Willingness to change	.88
Data relatedness	.85
Constructive suggestions	.93

These data suggest that written reports can be evaluated with a high degree of precision, provided the qualities judged are reasonably well defined and the raters participate in the development of the scales.

Table 4.1 shows the means and intercorrelations of the various rating scales. Means of the first four scales reveal that the reports, on the whole, showed a moderate degree of receptivity to the project, depth of understanding, willingness to change, and data relatedness. With respect to constructive criticisms, the mean rating was about midway between "none" and "a few." The mean number of specific proposals for change was nearly 12, but this figure is inflated substantially by the inclusion of three reports with specific recommendations for 23, 31, and 38 changes, respectively. The highly skewed nature of this distribution resulted in a decision to rescale this measure before computing correlations with other variables (see note, Table 4.1).

All but one of the correlations in Table 4.1 are positive, and the majority are statistically significant despite the small sample size of 13 institutions. The ratings with the highest correlation are depth of understanding and willingness to change. Since the same individuals were judging both these characteristics, it is risky to postulate any causal connection between them, although one can speculate that an institution's willingness to change may depend on its ability (or willingness) to develop insightful interpretations of student data. The association could, of course, work the other way: Institutions that feel a strong need for some change may find some basis for change in the student data.

TABLE 4.1

Means and Intercorrelations of the Report Ratings
(N = 13 institutions)

Rating Scale	Mean	Intercorrelations				
		2	3	4	5	6
Receptivity to participating	3.4	.50	.59	.33	-.35	.58
Depth of understanding	3.0		.81	.62	.52	.56
Willingness to change	3.4			.61	.33	.75
Data relatedness	3.2				.43	.19
Constructive suggestions for project	2.2					.09
Number of specific proposals for change*	11.8					

*Median = 7. For computing correlations, variable was recoded:
1 (none), 2 (1-5), 3 (6-10), 4 (more than 10).

Note: $r_{.05}$ = .47.

Source: Compiled by the author.

The second highest correlation in Table 4.1 involves willingness to change and the number of specific proposals for change in the report: The raters' judgments of the institution's willingness to change were probably strongly influenced by the number of specific proposals for change. That these variables are not perfectly associated may be attributed in part to some changes that were judged "vague, overgeneralized, or trivial" by the raters.

The only negative correlation in Table 4.1 (r = -.35, .05 < p < .10) involved receptivity to participation and constructive suggestions for the project. Some of the most useful criticisms were made by institutions that were reluctant or even hostile about participation. However, constructive suggestions were positively associated with depth of understanding and willingness to change. Raters apparently tended to perceive institutions as relatively unreceptive if their reports contained substantial criticism of the project, even though these same institutions might be seen as willing to change.

WHO PRODUCES A REPORT?

Although all 19 participating institutions agreed to write reports summarizing the results of their participation, six institutions failed to do so in spite of frequent inquiries. Do these six institutions differ in any measurable way from the 13 that produced reports? Were their early participation patterns in any way symptomatic of an eventual failure to complete a report?

The small size of the sample precluded any highly sophisticated search for institutional or participation characteristics that would predict failure to produce a report. However, it was possible to compute some simple correlations between selected institutional characteristics and participation variables and the outcome of report versus no report (scored as a dichotomy). Significant correlations were obtained with the following preparticipation institutional variables:

Antecedent Variable	Correlation with Producing a Report
President original contact person	-.51
Selectivity level	-.49
Innovations in gate-keeping (pretest)	.44
Curricular and instructional innovations (pretest)	.44
Institutional representative original contact person	.42

As suggested in Chapter 3, the project was relatively unsuccessful in those institutions where the initial contact was the president. The president, the initial contact in four of the six institutions that failed to produce a report, was the first contact in only two of the 13 institutions that did produce reports. (In both these instances, the president appointed someone already familiar with the project to head it.) These findings strongly reinforce the notion that presidents should not be the original contact person unless someone already familiar with the project (or someone who can provide appropriate leadership) will be project director (see Chapter 6).

The most selective of the original 19 institutions were the least likely to produce a report. In fact, in two of the highly selective institutions that did produce reports, the project director was already strongly committed to the ACE research program and had to battle substantial odds to bring off the project successfully. The impressions of both consultants and staff who made followup visits were that selective institutions are characterized by at least two factors that interfere with participation: First, their faculty tend to be highly visible nationally and are reluctant to participate in such activities either because they have limited time or because their identification with institutional problems is minimal. Second, the faculty's perception that their institution is of high academic quality is inconsistent with the suggestion (implicit in this project) that the institution needs "change" or "improvement." Such a defensive posture is both paradoxical (faculty in the more elite institutions should, because of their more secure position in the academic hierarchy, be more receptive to self-criticism and self-study) and realistic (such institutions are presumably less in need of improvement in the sense that they enjoy most attributes traditionally associated with institutional quality: financial resources, highly trained faculty, the most able students).

It was both surprising and somewhat disappointing that producing a report was positively associated with the institution's pretest (1972) scores on two of the innovations measures. (The innovations questionnaire, administered before and after the project, was scored on the number of innovations in various categories; see Chapter 5.) Institutions with the fewest innovative programs should have the most to gain from participation in such a project. These institutions apparently are unlikely to carry through on their original commitment to produce a report. (This finding contrasts with the negative association between the quality of the report and the degree of institutional innovation.)

Is producing a report predictable from the style of the institution's early participation? To explore this question we correlated producing a report with numerous items about the institution's participation in the project prior to the report deadline. (Since most of these participation variables, as well as the dependent variables, are dichotomies, the correlations are actually phi coefficients.) Several participation variables correlated significantly ($p < .05$) with producing a report:

Participation Variable	Correlation with Producing a Report
Requested comparative data from other institutions	.76
Total number of data requests	.66
Requested additional impact data	.57
Requested assistance by telephone	.51
Requested special computer analyses	.46
Requested other ACE reports (i.e., Higher Education Panel)	.41
Requested all or part of $500 reimbursement	.41

Clearly, failure to take advantage of comparative data on students at other participating institutions is a poor prognostic sign for

producing a report. Only one of the six institutions that did not produce a report requested comparative data; all but one of the 13 institutions that did produce a report made such a request (as already
mentioned in Chapter 3, the one that did not was the Coast Guard
Academy). The next five items in the list reinforce the notion that
requests of almost any kind are favorable signs. The final item—
request for the $500 reimbursement—correlates modestly with pro-
ducing a report. No institution that failed to produce a report made
such a request; all five requests came from institutions that eventually produced a report. Apparently, the reimbursement is a sign,
although not a critical one, that the institution will eventually produce
a report.

In short, these findings suggest that in future projects of this
type, the activities of the institutional chairperson and committee
should be closely monitored. Although the monitor may regard
frequent requests for help and information as a drain on resources
or possibly even as a nuisance, they indicate a favorable outcome.
Their absence can indicate strongly that no product will be forthcoming
from the committee's activities.

CORRELATES OF REPORT RATINGS

Is the quality of the report related to these same antecedent
variables? To explore this question, we correlated institutional characteristics and participation variables with each mean report rating
(N = 13). Receptivity to participation correlated significantly with five
antecedent institutional characteristics:

Antecedent Variable	Correlation with Receptivity to Participation
Innovations in student life services (pretest)	-.76
University	-.56
Total innovations (pretest)	-.56
Curricular and instructional innovations (pretest)	-.53
Located in South	-.52

Institutions relatively innovative in student services tended to be
judged relatively unreceptive to project participation. Several interpretations of this finding are possible: Institutions already highly
innovative in their student service programs resent the implication
that some outside agency might be able to tell them something about
their students that they do not already know; or the relationship may
be attributable to the negative relationship with university status.

(While the correlations of receptivity with the three innovations measures above shrink to nonsignificance when the effect of university status is controlled, such partial correlations should be interpreted with caution because of the small sample.) It has already been suggested that research-oriented universities were the least cooperative of the participating institutions. Problems of committee malfunctioning and faculty defensiveness are likely to be exacerbated in the more research-oriented institutions (see Chapters 7 and 8). These institutions generally have more complex committee structures and much greater faculty autonomy.

One other correlate of receptivity not shown deserves mention: a site visit was negatively correlated (-.51) with receptivity to participation, a finding that again raises questions about the wisdom of on-site visits by institutional personnel. At a minimum it suggests that such visits should be carefully planned to avoid the problems mentioned in Chapter 3 (see Chapters 6 and 8, in particular, for recommendations on avoiding problems).

Depth of understanding has a negative correlation (-.53) with selectivity, again suggesting that the more selective or elite institutions were reluctant to make a critical, in-depth examination of their data.

Willingness to change was significantly (-.62) correlated with only one antecedent characteristic: the pretest score on innovations in student services. Again, the relationship between the quality of the report and the degree of innovation at the start of the project is negative.

Data relatedness of proposed changes was significantly correlated with several institutional characteristics:

Antecedent Variable	Correlation with Data Relatedness of Proposals for Change
Reliance on student evaluations of teaching (innovations pretest)	-.71
Total innovations (pretest)	-.60
Size	-.59
University	-.56
Curricular and instructional innovations (pretest)	-.53
Student life services innovations (pretest)	-.51

This correlation pattern is similar to that for receptivity to the project. Smaller institutions and those with relatively few innovative practices are most likely to develop recommendations for changes directly from the data.

Constructiveness of suggestions concerning the project was related to an eastern ($r = .51$) or midwestern ($r = .54$) location. Institutions that communicated via telephone during the project were unlikely ($r = -.54$) to offer constructive suggestions in their reports.

ACCURACY OF THE REPORTS

Followup visits to six institutions that produced reports (these visits are described more fully in Chapter 5) were designed in part to determine how accurately the reports reflected events during the course of the project.

Both consultants and staff who made these followup visits agreed that, for the most part, the reports were not accurate representations of many important happenings. In large part, these inaccuracies occurred when the report was the product of a single person, usually the committee chairperson. Most reports were not reviewed by committee members or others prior to submission to us.

At one university, for example, the brief (six-page) report was a carping criticism of the project, with neither interpretations nor any recommendations for change derived from the data. This report convinced the project staff that the committee had totally rejected the project and that the project had been an unqualified failure.

During the followup visit six months later, however, interviews with individual committee members yielded a somewhat different impression. Members' attitudes on the whole were far more positive than the critical and hostile report led us to believe. The chairperson, who could not be contacted for an interview, had apparently had the job pawned off on him. Other committee members saw him as an ineffectual leader, but they were too busy to carry out the committee activities on their own. Site visitors were convinced that the chairperson, apparently a lame duck waiting to assume a position at another institution, resented his appointment as chairperson and never became involved in the project.

The report of another institution contained more than three dozen suggestions for change. These suggestions, coupled with a generally enthusiastic tone, convinced the project staff initially that the project had been highly successful at this institution. However, during the followup visit, none of the five committee members could recall any recommendation until supplied with a list. When confronted with this fact, the chairperson indicated that the suggestions were merely "notions" that had resulted from committee brainstorming. Interestingly enough, this report had received a low rating on "data relatedness of proposed changes." Apparently, the committee chairperson had used the project as a vehicle to promote his favorite ideas about the future of the institution, but these ideas had little relevance to the project data.

At another institution, whose report appeared to be the work of the committee chairperson, the followup team was impressed with the remarkable degree of involvement of several other persons in the committee's deliberations. This involvement was simply not reflected in the report, which was subsequently described by the followup team as "the work of one man trying to get a job." However, this report was judged by the followup team as accurate in its portrayal of many institutional problems.

The followup visit an another institution raised still a different question about the veracity of written reports: Do they accurately reflect the institution as perceived by faculty, students, and administrators, or are they more reflections of just one constituency? The particular report in question was a reasonably accurate reflection of the consensus of the committee members, but it clearly did not reflect the interest or intent of the administration. The followup visit revealed that the president of this institution was seen by all committee members as much more conservative than they were. When questioned about the content of the report, the president replied, "It said just about what I thought it would say, given the composition of the committee." Clearly, this discrepancy between the committee and the administration does not present an optimistic picture of the fate of the recommendations.

At one private college, where the committee chairperson eventually became president (see Chapter 5), the problem of representativeness was again noted by the followup team. In this instance, the team concluded that the report accurately represented the intellectual feelings of the president but did not contain much input from other committee members and failed to reflect major aspects of the institutional climate.

In summary, these followup visits indicated strongly that reports obtained under the conditions of this study are not necessarily accurate indicators of events that transpired during the course of the project. The most important reason for this discrepancy is that the reports are usually the product of a single person often attempting to promote pet ideas or to grind a personal axe.

CONCLUSIONS AND RECOMMENDATIONS

The analysis of the 13 committee reports and of the followup visits to six institutions suggests several conclusions and recommendations:

1. An institution is unlikely to follow through on its commitment to produce a report if the initial agreement to participate in the project is secured from the president and the president passes along responsibility for the project to someone unfamiliar with it. If the initial contact must be the president, then measures should be taken to avoid repeating the same problems (see Chapter 6).

2. Poor project performance, including failure to produce a report as well as production of an unsatisfactory report, is more likely to occur in the large and more selective or elite institutions. In the future, special monitoring procedures should be introduced for such institutions to improve the chances of satisfactory performance.

3. Poor project performance (failing to produce a report) can be anticipated by the manner in which an institution participates in the early stages. Symptoms of eventual nonperformance include absence of any communication and failure to take advantage of special services. More intensive monitoring and followups of noncommunicative institutions are clearly indicated for future projects of this type.

4. Written reports summarizing committee activities and recommendations cannot be relied upon as accurate historical documents. Their accuracy and usefulness can probably be increased by following suggestions of the staff and consultants:

a. The report should include, perhaps as an introduction, a brief description of the administration and decision-making structure of the institution. If the report contains specific recommendations for change, they should be accompanied by a statement on the most appropriate strategy for implementation through this administrative structure.

b. Each recommendation for change should be accompanied by some rationale that refers to specific data or other information that constitutes the basis for the recommendation.

c. Reports should include dissenting views by committee members who disagree with particular interpretations of data or recommendations.

d. An early draft of the report should be reviewed by all committee members, with provisions made for addition of minority views in the event that suggestions for change are not adopted by the chairperson or writer of the report.

e. A draft of the report should be reviewed by a disinterested outside source, with special emphasis on accuracy of data interpretation and relevance of proposed changes.

f. Reports should also be reviewed by those members of the college administration and any key institutional committees that would be involved in implementation. Where possible, their reactions should be appended to the report.

NOTE

1. See J. P. Guilford, <u>Psychometric Methods</u> (New York: McGraw-Hill, 1954).

5

IMPACT OF THE PROJECT
ON THE INSTITUTIONS

The impact of participation in the "Data for Decisions" project was assessed by several followup procedures initiated during the first six months of 1974. This final data collection was designed to answer some specific questions: Had any recommendations from the committee reports actually been implemented? If so, to what extent could such changes be attributed to the project? Did participation bring about any additional changes not specifically mentioned in the formal report?

While on-site followups of all 19 original participating institutions would have been desirable, constraints on resources limited the followups to six. To maximize variability in the apparent success of the project, the six institutions were selected from the 13 that produced reports. These visits were expected to provide a basis for designing less expensive data collection instruments (mailed questionnaires and structured telephone interviews) to assess program impact at the other seven institutions that produced reports and at the six that produced no reports. The principal purposes of the followups were to determine each committee member's perception of committee activities, the current status of proposals for changes mentioned in the report, prospects for additional changes, and attitude about similar future projects. The followups also inquired about the decision-making apparatus of the institution and the likelihood that data like those in this project would be used regularly for student-oriented planning and decision making (see Annex E for a copy of the followup data collection instruments).

Teams of one staff member and one consultant took from one and a half to two days for each followup visit. They interviewed each member of the original campus committee, as well as several other key persons on campus: the chief executive officer, chief academic

51

officer, chief student personnel officer, and director of institutional research, if any. In some cases, one or more of these key individuals was also a committee member. On three campuses, interviews were also conducted with the committee as a group.

Followup data collection for the 13 campuses that were not included in the on-site visits occurred in two stages. First, the original chairperson (or another committee member, if the chairperson was no longer available) was contacted by telephone and informed that self-administering questionnaires would be sent to each committee member. Each contact person agreed to inform committee members that the questionnaires were being sent and that completion was important to success of the project. Next, questionnaires were mailed directly to each member, and nonresponding members were followed up by telephone. Although it was not possible to obtain data from all committee members, at least one member on all but two campuses provided the requested data (the two exceptions, of course, were the University of Michigan and Vassar College, which formally dropped out of the study before the followup).

Additional data to evaluate the impact of the project came from repeating the assessment of innovative practices originally carried out in 1972.[1] A slightly revised form of the innovations survey instrument (see Annex F) was sent to the institutional representatives (N = approximately 350) of all four-year institutions in the Cooperative Institutional Research Program that had responded to the first survey in spring 1972. This original group included 17 of the 19 project institutions. The followup survey was mailed in spring 1974, producing a two-year longitudinal interval to assess impact on institutional innovations.

IMPLEMENTATION OF PROPOSED CHANGES

The principal aim in conducting the on-site followups and the parallel telephone and questionnaire assessments was to determine the fate of recommendations from the committee reports and the extent to which implementation of these recommendations could be attributed to the project. Thus, followup interviews with committee members were used to obtain, where possible, some consensus about the status of each change proposed in the report and the degree to which the change could be attributed to the project. Implementation status was assessed on a three-point continuum:

Complete implementation: Committee members agree that the proposed change is fully implemented as described in the report.

Partial implementation: Procedures for implementing the proposed changes are under way, or committee members agree that the probability is high for implementation in the near future.

No action: Committee members agree that no evidence of implementation exists and no action is contemplated in the near future (or only a portion of committee members think such action likely).

Attribution of the change to participation in the project was also assessed on a three-point continuum:

Complete attribution: Committee members agree that the change would not have occurred without the project.

Partial attribution: The change may have occurred without participation, although committee members agree that the project provided impetus and/or speeded up the timetable for implementation.

No attribution: Implementation was not affected by project participation and/or only a minority of committee members think implementation was partially attributable to participation.

Table 5.1 summarizes the results of the followup analysis of changes proposed in the committee reports. Of the total 124 changes proposed, about one-third (42) were found in some stage of implementation one year later. Implementation of about one-fourth of the proposed changes was judged complete.

Committee members expressed substantially more doubt about the influence of the project in these changes. The project was seen as having significant influence in only about half (20) of the changes undertaken, and of these, only five were seen as completely attributable to the project.

What were these changes? Table 5.2 lists each change undertaken wholly or in part as a result of the dissemination project. These changes cover a wide range of institutional functions: hiring, appointment of committees, in-service training, student recruitment, job placement, extracurricular activities, faculty rewards and incentives, and institutional research. Perhaps most conspicuous by its absence is any change in the curriculum. Except for the Coast Guard Academy (where a minor revision in the timetable for student entry into the major field was partially attributed to the project), no change undertaken is directly related to curriculum or academic program. Although the 13 institutional reports contained several recommendations for curricular changes, few were actually implemented, and of those that were, none was attributed even partially to the project.

This absence of curricular change can be interpreted in several ways. One possibility is that the student data were not seen as relevant to curricular considerations, although they included changes in student major and career choice, and ratings of both the quality of teaching in different fields and flexibility in the curriculum. Another, perhaps

TABLE 5.1

Status of Changes Proposed by Participating Institutions, 1973, 1974

Institution	Number of Changes Proposed in Report (Spring 1973)	Implementation Status (Spring '74)			Attribution to Project		
		Complete	Partial	No Action	Complete	Partial	None
Allegheny	20	4	7	9	2	6	12
Coast Guard	12	2	2	8	0	3	9
University of Denver	5	0	0	5	0	0	5
Western Illinois	6	3	0	3	1	1	4
University of Massachusetts	2	0	0	2	0	0	2
Northwestern	38	5	2	31	0	0	38
Ohio Dominican	15	8	0	7	0	0	15
University of Redlands	8	1	0	7	1	0	7
St. Louis University	4	0	0	4	0	0	4
St. Norbert	8	7	1	0	1	5	2
Vanderbilt	6	0	0	6	0	0	6
Total	124	30	12	82	5	15	104

Note: Two of the 13 institutions submitted reports with no specific recommendations for change.
Source: Compiled by the author.

54

TABLE 5.2

Specific Changes Attributable to Project

Degree of Attribution/Change	Institution
Complete	
Hire additional black recruitment officer	Allegheny
Require faculty advisors to take advisees to lunch	Allegheny
Appoint second task force	Western Illinois
Undertake review of library	Redlands
Have two-day workshop to improve quality of teaching	St. Norbert
Partial	
Increase number of minority and older students	Allegheny
Increase contact between faculty advisors and counseling center	Allegheny
Develop occupational brochure	Allegheny
Provide undergraduates with more career information	Allegheny
Provide students with more opportunities for research	Allegheny
Collect more data on students	Allegheny
Permit earlier entry into major	Coast Guard
Provide additional outlets for creative activities	Coast Guard
Improve recruitment of minorities	Coast Guard
Increase out-of-class interaction between faculty and students	Western Illinois
Award certificate of academic merit to students	St. Norbert
Establish award ($1,000) for teaching excellence	St. Norbert
Establish Center for Student Development	St. Norbert
Conduct research on changes in student religious attitudes	St. Norbert
Appoint director of institutional research	St. Norbert

Source: Compiled by the author.

55

more tenable, explanation is that the committees avoided this area
because they were concerned that any recommendation might
generate resistance and hostility from the faculty. Most faculty view
curriculum and academic programs as their exclusive province; they
are likely to resist proposals originating outside traditional departmental structure (see Chapter 10). Thus, the committees may have
implicitly or explicitly avoided the curriculum, focusing instead on
institutional functioning where change was more probable.

Table 5.1 suggests that the project had little or no impact in the
research universities. All five institutions in Table 5.2 are primarily
undergraduate colleges; no university (Denver, Massachusetts,
Northwestern, St. Louis, Tulane, or Vanderbilt) was able to implement a single recommendation that could be attributed even partially
to the project. (See Annex G for a complete list of changes proposed
in each committee report.)

ADDITIONAL CHANGES NOT PROPOSED
IN THE COMMITTEE REPORTS

During the followup interviews some committee members mentioned spontaneously that the dissemination project had resulted in
some more or less serendipitous changes that had not been recommended or anticipated in the original report. For the most part, the
committees regarded that side effects as beneficial. Table 5.3 lists
the additional changes, together with the committee members'
judgments about the degree to which the changes could be attributed
to the project. Confidence in these judgments must be tempered with
caution since it was not possible to get each member's opinion about
the project's influence. If an additional change was mentioned by one
of the last persons interviewed, it was not always feasible to reinter-
view committee members to obtain judgments about attribution.

The additional changes in Table 5.3 contrast in certain ways
with those in Table 5.2. Several changes, for example, are concerned
with curriculum. Also, at least one additional change was reported
in all but one of the universities (Northwestern).

These contrasts prompt several conclusions: First, while changes
apparently can occur in universities, they are somewhat more difficult to anticipate (and, indeed, the impact of a dissemination project
such as this is more difficult to predict). Second, the contrast between
Tables 5.2 and 5.3 indicates that, while committees may be reluctant
to propose curricular change in a formal report, a student-oriented
project may have unforeseen impacts on curricular decisions.

TABLE 5.3

Additional Changes Not Proposed in Committee Reports
but Attributable to Project

Institution	Change	Degree of Attribution
Denver	Expand humanities program	Complete
Denver	Expand Early College Program	Partial
Franklin and Marshall*	Devote more attention to student needs outside class	Partial
Franklin and Marshall*	Increase emphasis on residential program	Partial
Massachusetts	Create "heightened awareness" among staff of usefulness of student data	Complete
Ohio Dominican	Modify academic calendar	Partial
Ohio Dominican	Reduce course requirements	Partial
Ohio Dominican	Establish new procedures for dealing with potential dropouts	Complete
Ohio Dominican	Show "greater concern" with college impact on students	Complete
SUNY at Oswego	Adopt open admissions	Partial
SUNY at Oswego	Adopt advanced placement program	Partial
SUNY at Oswego	"Greater use" of student data by administration	Complete
St. Louis	Creation of new position (Coordinator of Academic Development)	Partial
St. Louis	Undertake three-year planning effort	Partial
St. Louis	"Restructuring" academic administration	Partial
Tulane	Grant proposal based on CIRP data submitted to foundation	Partial
Tulane	"Increased concern" about need for more student-faculty contact	Complete
Vanderbilt	Changes in design of new student union building	Complete
Vanderbilt	Associate dean's proposal to reorganize university	Partial

*Did not complete report.
Source: Compiled by the author.

A proposal for curricular change, particularly in the universities, may constitute a red flag when it is presented as a formal recommendation in a written report. Stating recommendations in this direct manner may generate resistance or fear of resistance that reduces the likelihood of implementation. A possible strategy for dealing with this problem is to avoid specific recommendations and to focus the report instead on the interpretation of empirical data that highlight potential curricular problems. In this way, recommendations for change could be implied without being stated.

These speculations should be qualified: First, several changes in Table 5.3 are less concrete than those in Table 5.2 (such changes are flagged by quotation marks). Second, committee members in the research universities, confronted with the reality that none of their original recommendations had been carried out, may have felt obliged to provide the followup teams with other evidence that the project had had a significant impact.

IMPACT ON INSTITUTIONAL INNOVATIONS

The second assessment was carried out with the innovations survey instrument that had been administered first in spring 1972 and again in spring 1974. This phase of the evaluation was to determine if participation in the program was associated with changes in innovative practices at the institution. That part permitted the use of a control group of comparable institutions that did not participate in the project, but it was limited in the sense that the outcome measures (innovations) were somewhat remote from the immediate purposes of the project and the time interval (less than one year after completion) was perhaps too brief to provide an adequate assessment of impact. Nevertheless, this part of the evaluation proceeded on the assumption that any significant results would constitute strong evidence of the project's value.

Originally, the survey instrument was an omnibus list of innovative practices and procedures. Questionnaires were first completed in 1972 by CIRP representatives and returned to the American Council on Education. In 1974 a slightly revised instrument (see Annex F) was mailed from the University of California, Los Angeles, to the same representatives.

To provide a concise picture of the institution's responses to the entire instrument, four a priori scales were developed to measure different innovative practices.

Measure 1: Curriculum and Instruction (19 items)

Programs (for each program score 2 if tried, 1 if planned, otherwise 0): ethnic studies, women's studies, honors programs, career-related work/study, study abroad, off-campus study, individualized programs with distributional requirements only, individualized programs with no requirements, remedial programs, interdepartmental programs, independent undergraduate study programs, accelerated degree programs.

Instructional techniques and materials (do not have = 0, less than one-third of students exposed = 1, one-third to two-thirds of students exposed = 2, more than two-thirds of students exposed = 3): computer-assisted instruction, closed-circuit television, student-prepared multimedia, audio or video tape-recorded lectures, interdisciplinary seminars or discussions, open laboratories, modularized teaching materials.

Measure 2: Gate-Keeping Policies (21 items)

Criteria for awarding credit (score 1 for each criterion used): college level work completed in secondary school, education or training in industry or military service, work experience in industry or military service, successful completion of standardized achievement tests, correspondence courses given by this institution, correspondence courses given by other institutions, course credit by examination without taking the course, extensive travel and/or living experience.

Degree-granting policies (score 2 if tried, 1 if planned, otherwise 0): dual degree with other institutions, external degrees.

Grading methods (score 1 for each method used): pass-fail, pass-no record, descriptive reports by faculty, faculty evaluation of self-evaluative report by student, student self-grading.

Admissions (score 1 for each method used): special efforts to recruit students from specific ethnic groups, enrollment in some undergraduate courses by high school students, open admissions by lottery, open admissions on a first-come-first-served basis, open admissions to any high school graduate, open admissions (other).

Measure 3: Student Life Services (8 items)

Student-run judiciary (score 1), health service permitted to issue contraceptives (score 1), special policies for health-related guidance in sexual matters (score 1), coeducational dorms with sexes segregated by floor or wing (score 1), coeducational dorms with sexes segregated by rooms on same floor (score 1), students required to attend religious services (score -1), student publications subject to advice of faculty (score -1), student publications subject to consent of faculty (score -2).

Measure 4: Reliance on Student Evaluations of Teaching (3 items)

Student evaluations of teaching effectiveness are: used in all or nearly all departments (score 1), used in decisions about faculty promotions or salary increases (score 1), made generally available to campus community (score 1).

In addition to these four subscales, a "total innovations" score, the sum of the four subscales, was also computed.

Pretest and posttest questionnaires were obtained from 12 of the 13 institutions that completed reports during the first year, and also from 250 other institutions that completed both surveys. The control group was selected from the 250 institutions. For each experimental (project) institution, a matched control institution with an identical score on total innovations from the 1972 pretest was selected. Experimental and control institutions were also matched by type (four-year college or university), control (public, private nonsectarian, Protestant, Catholic), and geographic region (Northeast, South, Midwest, and West). If more than one control institution satisfying these matching criteria was found, the institution selected was the one whose 1972 pretest subscales were closest to those of the experimental college.

Changes from pretest to posttest for experimental and control institutions were compared on the five scales by t-tests for correlated means. None of the five comparisons approached statistical significance ($p < .05$). Although the size of the sample (N = 12 matched pairs) might handicap any attempt to identify statististically significant differences, note that the t-ratios on three of the five scales were actually negative, indicating that changes in the experimental group were actually greater than those in the control group.

While these findings indicate that participation in the dissemination project did not significantly influence the number of innovative programs at the participating institutions, several other factors may have contributed to the negative results. As already noted, the interval of time for evaluating impact was relatively brief. Since most institutional task force reports were not completed until late spring 1973, any significant impact on institutional innovation might not appear within the next 12 months. Another factor may be the relatively crude procedures for measuring institutional innovation. Basically, it was necessary to depend on one individual (the CIRP institutional representative) to complete both the pretest and posttest questionnaires. That this method of reporting may not be highly reliable is indicated by the relatively low correlations between some 1972 and 1974 innovations scores: Curriculum and Instruction (r = .33), Gate-Keeping Policies (r = .80), Student Life Services (r = .72), Reliance on Student Evaluations of Teaching (r = .31), and Total Innovations (r = .74). That these low correlations result in part from reporting errors is indicated by a comparison of the questionnaires from 1972 and 1974, which reveals numerous instances in which the 1972 and 1974 responses for the same institution were incompatible. Clearly, in future evaluation efforts of this type, factual reports of specific institutional practices should be verified by several independent observers.

CORRELATES OF INSTITUTIONAL IMPACT

The finding that some institutions were much more successful than others in implementing recommendations suggests that institutions may vary substantially in their responses to intervention projects. Do the more responsive institutions differ in any measurable respects from those unable to introduce changes based on the project? To explore this question, some analyses of institutional characteristics were repeated (see Chapter 4), except that the dependent variable in this case involved implementation versus nonimplementation of recommendations rather than producing versus not producing a report.

Two measures of implementation were used. In the first, institutions that implemented one or more of their recommendations (whether or not they were attributable to the project) were compared with institutions that implemented no recommendations (including those that produced no reports). Only one institutional characteristic proved significantly ($p < .05$) related to this measure: the pretest score on innovations in the Student Life Services (r = -.47). Possibly institutions that already have highly innovative programs of student services may feel less pressure to implement changes related to students than institutions that have few such innovative practices.

The second set of correlations compared institutions that implemented one or more changes attributable to the project with institutions
that implemented no attributable changes. Institutional selectivity was
negatively ($r = -.49$) associated with this measure, indicating that the
more selective or elite institutions tend to be less responsive to
projects of this type (see Chapter 4 for a similar finding on reports).
In addition, the pretest scores on two innovations subtests—those
concerned with curriculum and instruction and with gate-keeping
policies—were positively related (both r's = .44) to implementing
attributable changes. Apparently, institutions that already have innovative instructional and admissions programs are relatively responsive to projects of this sort.

While the small sample from which these correlations were
derived necessitates considerable caution in interpreting findings,
the significant correlations suggest that, for future studies, institutions most likely to be responsive could be identified. Less selective
institutions appear more responsive on two counts: implementing
changes as a result of project participation and producing a report
(see Chapter 4). The more selective institutions appear to offer most
resistance to such a project, particularly if they have relatively non-
innovative curricular programs and gate-keeping policies.

SUMMARY

This evaluation indicates that participation in the "Data for Decisions" project did have a significant impact on some institutions.
While the comparison of experimental and control institutions failed to
reveal any statistically significant effects on innovative practices,
followup interviews with task force members from the participating
institutions revealed that a number of recommendations were indeed
implemented and, in certain instances, these recommendations could
be attributed in part to the project. The likelihood of such positive
impact appears greatest in less selective institutions with relatively
innovative curricular programs and gate-keeping policies.

The followup evaluation also produced ideas for designing similar evaluation studies in the future (see Chapter 10).

NOTE

1. John A. Creager, <u>Selected Policies and Practices in Higher Education</u> (Washington, D.C.: American Council on Education, 1973); vol. 8, no. 4, ACE Research Reports.

6

DESIGNING AN EFFECTIVE
INTERVENTION STRATEGY

Perhaps the most important outcome of this study has been the insight gained into the design of an effective intervention strategy. While the original dissemination strategy was useful in many respects, changes and refinements would greatly increase the chances that any future intervention effort will have a significant impact on institutional policy and practice. Thus, a major objective is to outline an ideal intervention strategy for possible use in future attempts to encourage institutions to utilize student data in planning and decision making. These recommendations are based in part on the empirical data reported earlier and in part on speculations and impressions.

Although the project described in earlier chapters was initiated by an agency external to the institution (the Office of Research of the American Council on Education), most of the recommendations contained in this and subsequent chapters are applicable to projects that might originate within the institution. The reader can thus regard the ACE research staff as analogous to, say, the staff of an Office of Institutional Research, or to some similar unit within the institution that may be interested in using data to initiate student-oriented changes in policies or programs.

For convenience, consider that any data-based intervention comprises three major tasks: design and implementation of an overall strategy, development of an appropriate student data base for feedback, and selection and monitoring of an institutionally based committee or task force. Because both committee functioning and data base design are highly complex, these issues are treated separately (see Chapters 8 and 9, respectively). The focus here will be on designing an overall strategy, selecting the participating institutions, and approaching the institution to enlist its participation.

OVERALL STRATEGY

While many specific aspects of the intervention strategy should
be changed, the basic steps in the overall plan (pilot testing the data
base, forming a campus task force, monitoring task force activities,
and following up) were not seriously question by consultants or task
force members. However, the respective roles of the administration
and the faculty, the role of the committee, interaction among institutions, and the allocation of project resources should receive considerably more attention in future dissemination efforts.

Role of the Administration and the Faculty

Any effort at dissemination is unlikely to be successful unless
the top administration clearly supports the project. Strong administrative backing serves at least two critical functions: It provides
committee members with an incentive to move ahead with the project
and to find policy-relevant recommendations in the data; and it
maximizes the chances that recommendations will be put into action.
Administrative backing is important both in selecting and approaching
institutions.

Concerning the faculty, future dissemination efforts should be
designed with two principles in mind: Any change in the curriculum
or academic program must involve the faculty; and faculty, especially
those in the larger research institutions, are oriented primarily
toward their departments. Consequently, any recommendations for
significant changes in academic functions must gain departmental
support if there is to be any hope of implementation. If significant
changes in academic policy are recommended and key faculty members are not a party to their formulation, any such changes are
unlikely to be implemented.

Involving faculty in plans for institutional change does not, of
course, guarantee that changes will be accepted by faculty colleagues,
since faculty by nature are inclined to resist most changes (see
Chapters 7 and 10).[1] One strategy for avoiding heavy dependence on
faculty support is to concentrate on improving institutional functioning
in nonacademic areas, such as admissions, recruitment, orientation,
advisement and counseling, job placement, and residence life. Changes
in institutional policies and practices in these areas normally do not
require the support needed for changes in course requirements,
teaching techniques, grading, and other academic functions.

Role of the Committee

One major weakness in the original dissemination strategy was that little attention was devoted to how the committee should relate to the administration or how its recommendations might be converted into institutional action. Most committees assumed that the written report ended their work. The life of the committee should extend at least through some period of administrative and faculty review of its recommendations. Each committee member could be assigned some role in monitoring the fate of the recommendations. Extending the life of the committee would also help to clarify the types of administrative and faculty reviews necessary before final decisions on concrete action are made. The followup interviews revealed that most committee members were unclear about the review processes necessary before recommendations could be implemented. Clarifying these procedures at the beginning of the project would provide greater continuity and would enable each committee member to feel more involvement in the administrative and decision-making process of the institution.

A related consideration is the amount of committee time allocated to various phases. Some committees thought they were given too little time to consider the data and develop recommendations, whereas others thought the committee lost its momentum because of too much time. Less time is better than more time, if committee requests for additional data or for consultation can be handled rapidly. An academic year affords adequate time to contact the institutions, enlist their support for and participation in the project, form the committee, review the data, and produce a written report. Several institutions were clearly able to accomplish these tasks in substantially less than one academic year.

Interaction Among Institutions

Consultants, staff, and committee members were nearly unanimous in thinking that more interaction and interchange among participating institutions should have taken place. Clearly, active encouragement and support from the outside agency is critical. One way to initiate such communication is a workshop involving cooperating institutions early in the project. This workshop could enable task force members to become acquainted and to explore possibilities for exchanging data and ideas. It could also be a training device for those committee chairpersons not already familiar with the project.

Exchange of data will have little value if institutions believe that no other participating institution is "comparable," so each participant must see at least one and preferably more of the other institutions as similar to his or her institution.

Use of Project Resources

The design of any intervention strategy is constrained by available resources. If it had been possible to reallocate resources in this project, most consultants, staff, and task force members would have opted for more direct help and consultation from the staff. Such a reallocation would probably have necessitated a reduction in participating institutions and, possibly, a reduction in the data available for feedback. One problem with providing additional assistance is that the various recommendations cover virtually every phase of the project: selecting the committee chairperson and committee members, training the committee, interpreting the data, reanalyzing data, drafting and reviewing the report, and developing an implementation strategy for the recommendations. Taken together, these suggestions imply that institutions are incapable of carrying out any part of the project on their own and, in effect, require hand holding at every stage, Clearly, the resources needed for this much assistance would make the cost of most dissemination efforts prohibitive.

Some resources should probably be devoted to training institutional personnel (the task force chairperson, in particular) to carry out functions that outside consultants would otherwise perform. As it happened, two or three task force chairpersons actually did carry out many of these functions in a highly effective manner. These persons were familiar with the longitudinal student data and were strongly committed to the dissemination project from the beginning. For institutions without such a person, resources should be invested in selecting and training a task force chairperson early in the project (see Chapter 8).

Another aspect of resource allocation is the possible value of monetary incentives such as the "honorarium" offered to each committee. Among those institutions that produced a report, there was little association between use of the $500 honorarium and either the quality of the report or the success in implementing recommendations. During the followup interviews, one committee member suggested that the $500 would have been better used to support a long weekend retreat for committee members to discuss the implications of the data. The original intention, of course, was to offer the honorarium in recognition of the substantial labor involved in the

written report. Whether or not such an offer really has any value is,
at this point, moot. A more efficacious procedure might be to make
the money available to each committee to use as it sees fit, although
different uses (honorarium for the report writer, weekend retreat,
data processing, and so on) could be suggested. Another—albeit more
expensive—form of monetary incentive would be in the form of summer employment or released time.

SELECTING THE INSTITUTIONS

A remarkable feature of the project was the variation in institutional response, a variation by no means random (see Chapter 5).
Positive responses were limited almost exclusively to the four-year
colleges, whereas efforts with the research-oriented universities
(Massachusetts, Michigan, Northwestern, Tulane, Vanderbilt, and
Washington State) were almost totally unproductive. While one might
conclude that future attempts at dissemination in universities would
be futile, several mitigating circumstances should first be considered.
    With one exception (Northwestern), the person first approached
(usually the president) delegated the responsibility for running the
project to someone totally unfamiliar with the Cooperative Institutional
Research Program. Moreover, in the one university that produced a
meaningful report (Northwestern), the person initially approached was
already heavily involved with the program. Although the followup
visit during the second year revealed that prospects for meaningful
data-based change at Northwestern were not promising, this pessimism
was based not so much on a failure of the committee as on the particular problems Northwestern faced at that time.
    Another mitigating circumstance is that the universities were
generally among the most selective institutions. Since three of the
most selective colleges (Mills, Vassar, and Williams) failed to produce a report, difficulties with the universities may be attributable
as much to their relatively high selectivity as to their being universities.
    Chapter 5 suggests that the negative association between project
success and institutional selectivity may be attributed in part to the
faculty recruited by selective institutions and the manner in which
they are organized and rewarded. Faculty in selective institutions
are probably hired more for their research potential and interests
than faculty in less selective institutions. At the same time, they
are probably given smaller teaching loads and rewarded for research.
Research-oriented faculty are possessive of their time and likely to
resent participating in projects that require significant effort with
minimal scholarly rewards. Moreover, they tend to be critical of

projects by outsiders, particularly if the projects are regarded implicitly as evaluating their own institutions. Finally, the high degree of autonomy accorded professors in selective institutions makes them feel less obliged to cooperate in projects taken on by the administration.

Thus, several confounded factors may be responsible individually or collectively for the negative response: institutional selectivity, university status, delegation of responsibility from a top administrator to a person unfamiliar with the project, and the absence of a person on campus who is familiar with and committed to the project. While it is likely that several factors in combination produced the negative responses, a larger sample of institutions would be needed to assess the importance of each factor with any precision.

Regardless of the validity of these speculations, future intervention projects are not likely to have much impact on highly selective institutions unless the faculty or staff includes a person already familiar with the project and enthusiastic about participation. With that person, a different intervention strategy is called for. One possible alternative is to select a potential chairperson for the task force and to familiarize that person thoroughly with the project before forming the task force. (Selecting and training the chairperson are discussed in Chapter 8.)

In summary, the relatively passive intervention strategy utilized in this project is not likely to elicit much response from highly selective institutions or from research-oriented universities unless one person on campus is already committed to the project. In the absence of such a person, careful selection and training of a potential chairperson is clearly indicated before any actual committee work is undertaken.

Consultants Joseph Katz and David Epperson have proposed criteria for selecting participating institutions that would probably require an on-site visit before any final offer is extended. Katz proposes several questions to be considered in selecting an appropriate institution:

- Is the institution aware of its significant problems?
- Are institutional politics intractable? That is, are various departments so checkmated that change in any one is resisted to preserve the status quo?
- Is it possible to detect any institutional idealism? That is, are there key people who believe that the institution can and will improve and who can stimulate constructive thinking about policy changes?

Epperson focuses his criteria on institutional receptivity (see Chapter 4), suggesting that receptivity will be maximum under certain conditions: existing student data are either inadequate or out of date; new data complement rather than compete with old data; and the institution has previously used student data in policy deliberations.

Whether or not one chooses to invest in preliminary site visits, these criteria should be considered in developing any selection plan.

Consultants and staff who made followup visits to several institutions thought the most successful institutions were those experiencing serious pressures (budget deficits, low enrollments, high dropout rates, and so on), or severe internal morale problems. It was generally thought that such stresses lead a college to action and reform.

One institutional symptom that may militate against a successful dissemination effort is a rival project draining off institutional energies. A good example was the pending accreditation visit at one private college that, in the opinion of the followup team, substantially diluted the impact of what would otherwise have been a highly successful committee effort. All-absorbing institutional issues, such as widespread campus unrest, may prove an insurmountable rival for institutional attention. Unless the dissemination project can be incorporated into the competing activity, efforts at dissemination should perhaps be abandoned or at least put off until the issue is resolved.

Another potentially negative sign is the absence of an office or a director of institutional research or the equivalent. Some consultants thought this fact alone should be sufficient to disqualify an institution from consideration. While a director of institutional research does not guarantee success (several nonproductive institutions had directors), the followup visits suggested that the lack of a director was a major factor in the demise of the project at three institutions. While requiring a director of institutional research may be unreasonable, when such a person is unavailable some effort should be made to include on the committee a person who can play an equivalent role, for example, someone from the counseling center or the psychology department who conducts local research on students.

One final consideration in selecting participating institutions is the status of the chief executive. Lame ducks should be avoided. In at least one institution, the committee became discouraged about the project's prospects when it discovered that the president was resigning. In considering this handicap, however, one qualification is important: if the heir apparent is a local campus person who can be persuaded to participate in the project, the possibilities for significant impact may be even greater than when the incumbent is not a lame duck. At the one small college where the committee chairperson subsequently became president, the project had perhaps its greatest impact. At the time this institution was invited to participate, this person was both the institutional representative for CIRP and the academic vice president.

How does one weigh the various criteria for selecting participants? One could use all criteria to compute a receptivity score to
rate institutions on their potential response to a dissemination project.
Those institutions with the highest receptivity scores would be participants. In addition, a smaller sample of low-scoring institutions could
be added to the participants to test the validity of the measure as a
selection device and to examine possible interaction effects between
different intervention strategies and initial receptivity.

INITIATING THE PROJECT

Regardless of whether the project is initiated from within or
outside the institution, the initiating person or agency must decide
who is to be approached initially within the institution. In the pilot
project described in earlier chapters, that person was either the
chief executive or other top ranking administrative officer or the
institutional representative for CIRP. (The choice was dictated
largely by which person the principal investigator knew best.)

Approaching the institution through the chief executive officer
has the advantage of giving the project status and high-level administrative sponsorship, but it also entails certain risks. Indeed, some
findings indicate that making the chief executive the initial contact is
a poor idea, since it substantially increases the chances of project
failure (see Chapters 4 and 5). However, most presidents delegated
responsibility for chairing the committee to someone unfamiliar with
the project. By contrast, in those institutions where the initial contact person was the representative to CIRP, that person typically
chaired the committee. In all likelihood, the problem with presidents
as initial contacts is not the presidents themselves but the individuals
they appoint. In short, it appears that if the chief executive is the
initial contact, he or she should be given substantial guidance in
selecting a chairperson. To provide effective guidance would probably
require a consultant visit with the president, where the purposes of
the project and the ideal qualifications for the chairperson could be
discussed in detail.

Many persons thought the initial mode of approach—via letters
and telephone calls—was too passive. If such techniques were com-
bined with a personal interview, a number of potentially important
tasks could be performed before the project got under way:

1. Familiarize key administrative personnel (the president, in
particular) with the project objectives, securing some preliminary
commitment to consider seriously committee recommendations.

2. Discuss with top administrators various mechanisms to implement recommendations.

3. Discuss candidates for committee chairperson; interview potential candidates.

4. Discuss with top administrators (and possibly with the committee chairperson) committee composition, including the possible assignment of tasks and responsibilities to various members.

5. Discuss with the chairperson the likely modus operandi of the committee.

6. Gain some understanding of local institutional policies, practices, and problems to identify particular data that might be relevant (this analysis could also be performed during an earlier screening interview).

7. Determine the degree of administrative support for the committee and delineate commitments that are not possible.

8. Conduct a preliminary diagnostic evaluation of the functioning of the institution, with an eye toward problems that might arise during the committee's activities.

Another function of a preliminary interview would be to identify key individuals who should be involved in the project or who could be brought in later if the committee encountered major difficulties in its deliberations. Particularly important is an analysis of internal political functioning and identification of individuals whose opinions are highly regarded or who otherwise wield influence in decision making.

A controversy yet to be resolved is the extent to which the initiator of the project should assume the role of consultant. This role, somewhat like a client-counselor or doctor-patient relationship, involves two stages: a diagnostic phase with a review of symptoms ("tell me what your problems are"); and a treatment phase that attempts to devise possible solutions.

Proponents of the consultant approach argue that it is essential to initiate any data dissemination effort from the perspective of the institution and its particular problems, and that data introduced without any awareness of local problems will not be seriously considered and may even be regarded as intrusive or irrelevant. Critics of the consultant approach argue that institutions may not be aware of their own problems or, if they are, the "problems" may not be viewed as relating directly to student needs. Indeed, the major objective of the project was to encourage institutions to view their policies and practices more in terms of the consequences for students (see Chapter 1). Opponents also maintain that it is unrealistic and presumptuous to assume that student data will be useful in "solving" self-defined institutional problems and that, unlike the usual consultative relationship, a project of this sort is not a response to a request for assistance, but rather an effort directly aimed at improving institutions for students.

One possible compromise on consultation is to devote part of preliminary screening interviews to assessing salient institutional problems, with an eye to identifying those that relate to particular student data that might be available. Some effort should be devoted, however, to making sure that such a visit does not become identified as a gratuitous attempt to "help" with institutional "problems."

An important goal of the initial approach is to establish what consultant David Epperson calls relevance and credibility. In Epperson's view, minimal levels of credibility and relevance are first necessary "before the institution will invest enough energy to project its agenda onto the data displayed." While a preliminary institutional visit and diagnostic assessment may be useful in identifying institutional policies, practices, and problems relevant to the data, establishing credibility is not quite so simple. The institutional site visits during the pilot phase of the project proved that credibility is not just a matter of a substantial data base, a sophisticated analysis, talented and experienced researchers and consultants, and a prestigious organizational base (ACE). Indeed, these credentials and the sheer magnitude of the project may have threatened certain persons, particularly in some research-oriented universities, where a few faculty members apparently assumed a competitive stance toward the project. There is reason to believe that a highly competent and visible institutional research office on campus might well generate the same kinds of concerns.

It is important to design the initial approach to minimize institutional defensiveness. It is naive to expect, however, that good advance planning will always succeed in winning over all members of the academic community; some persons will probably resist projects of this type no matter what the initiating person or agency does. Likely hard-core opponents should be identified and, if possible, not put in a position where they can disrupt the project. It should be determined early if other persons on campus are already involved in student studies. These persons should be contacted to assess their interest in the project. If their approach is generally positive, they should be asked to participate actively and, if appropriate, to contribute their own local data to the deliberations. However, if their initial reactions appear hostile, competitive, or otherwise defensive, they should probably not be asked to participate, unless their involvement is essential.

Perhaps the surest way to obtain receptivity and credibility on campus is through respected or influential persons committed to the project; by displaying their enthusiasm, they can be invaluable in establishing support.

SUMMARY

The three major components of a general intervention strategy
are the overall design of the project, selection of the institutions,
and the approach to prospective participants.

Specific aspects of the dissemination process to be considered
in devising an effective strategy include academic games (those
devices employed by institutions to avoid dealing with the data [see
Chapter 7]), ways to make committees function effectively (see Chapter
8), and a design for a student data base that can be used effectively
in planning and decision making (see Chapter 9).

NOTE

1. Dwight R. Ladd, Change in Educational Policy: Self-Studies
in Selected Colleges and Universities (New York: McGraw-Hill, 1970).

7

ACADEMIC GAMES

One of the most frustrating and yet remarkable features of the reports produced by the 13 committees was the variety of defensive tactics the committees invoked to avoid coming to grips with the data. To paraphrase Eric Berne,[1] we have labeled these various defenses "games academics play" or simply "academic games."

The identification and description of some of these games, observed both in reports and in followup interviews with committee members, may seem somewhat tongue-in-cheek, but the reader should not regard them simply in terms of their entertainment value. Academics have become so expert at these games and so accustomed to playing them that the games pose a serious obstacle to any attempt to improve institutions for students. By identifying these games, readers should be better able to deal with academic gamesmanship when it occurs on their campuses.

While academic games bear some resemblance to the interpersonal games described by Berne, they are unique in certain ways. Academic games are less interactive than they are declarative: the typical academic game consists mainly of making a verbal statement. This statement may or may not be in direct response to a statement by another academic, and it may or may not require a response. Thus, many academic games may be played by one person because they are, in effect, ends in themselves. However, since the game also requires an audience of some sort, the player becomes, in effect, a performer.

Since academics place such a high value on intellectual competence, the immediate object of most academic games is to make the player look intelligent. A more subtle and sinister objective, however, is to relieve the player or the audience of any responsibility to act on a given task or problem. Psychologically, the function served here is tension reduction. The immediate source of these

75

tensions might be recognition that student needs are not being met or guilt about past failure to deal effectively with students. One immediate consequence of using academic games to reduce tensions is to preserve the status quo. By fending off action on new proposals, insights, or ideas, the player of academic games, perhaps unwittingly, becomes a party to a kind of institutional conservatism. Failure to act, in other words, is tantamount to endorsing current policies and procedures.

In the following catalog of major academic games, each type will be illustrated with actual examples from the reports and followup interviews. The list by no means covers all techniques used by academics to avoid coming to grips with problems requiring action. Also, some forms overlap, and a given quotation might well illustrate several forms simultaneously.

RATIONALIZATION

Rationalization, a familiar defense mechanism, is especially suited to the style of many academics, because it is highly verbal and depends heavily on abstract reasoning. Several reports tended to rationalize under two conditions: when data were perceived as unflattering or negative, and when the committee had not made concrete recommendations for change. In one institution where student ratings indicated considerable dissatisfaction with the inflexible curriculum, the report stated: "In a period when distributional and core requirements have been reduced significantly in most college and universities, this percentage may still seem low by comparison; but the special demands placed on (our) graduates require a strong basis in professional and technical competencies which are best taught in a core curriculum."

In a liberal arts college where student ratings of course offerings were negative: "Small colleges cannot afford to have a large variety of course offerings in any one semester because this leads to uneconomically small classes."

One institution, which compared its own data with those from several other institutions in the study, responded to a dropout rate much higher than expected: "Comparative data suggest that our institution looks worse than Williams College, Vanderbilt, and Northwestern University on student persistence, but better than the University of Miami [the University of Miami was not in the study; apparently, the institution got its data elsewhere] . . . in the last analysis, and maybe the best one, an absolute reference is needed."

Another similar example: "The proportion feeling insufficient contact with faculty is higher (slightly) than estimated—but when compared with the very high figures for Tulane and Northwestern, we aren't doing so badly."

Although participation in the project included a commitment by the institution to produce a report containing interpretations of data and recommendations for action, institutions that failed to carry through on this commitment were quick to rationalize their failure by reporting how busy committee members were with other responsibilities. One institution that produced a report with only criticism of the project and no substantive data interpretation included this statement: "Even though persons were selected who had higher education and its problems and issues well in mind, their priorities restricted the amount of time and energy they could give to the project."

The president of one liberal arts college that failed to produce a report wrote: "As I'm sure you appreciate, administrative officers of small liberal arts colleges have an enormous work load, and very little time to do anything over and above their normal routine."

At one small college that produced one of the better reports, the author apparently thought it necessary to rationalize what he perceived as only mediocre performance. His rationalization also contains a note of rejection: "Moreover, Council's May 31 deadline for the report gave us little time to digest the voluminous additional information which we received, which included a single computer printout of breakdowns of the responses of 1971 graduates and a separate book of national norms." (We had, at their request, provided a great deal of additional data.)

This rationalization of another committee's failure, obtained during a followup evaluation visit, is distinguished by its candor: "They were too busy for it, inexpert, and did not see anything in it for themselves."

A more bizarre form of rationalization is a game that, in Orwellian jargon, might be labeled Bad is Good. Here the academic manages to cope with a clearly negative finding by concluding that the finding is, in fact, positive. For example, in one college where students reported much dissatisfaction with their few contacts with faculty, this rationalization was utilized: "Furthermore, we hesitate to recommend or predict significant change in this area. For one thing, the system is completely institutionalized; and secondly, the discipline serves a positive purpose."

A variant on Bad is Good can be played by using the student rating data simultaneously in an absolute and relative sense. Evidence of negative impact (that is, actual student satisfaction substantially less than expected satisfaction) can be rationalized away by indicating that the absolute level of satisfaction is high. (Chapter 8 discusses this use of the data in detail.)

PASSING THE BUCK

A frequent method of sidetracking an issue in academe is to form a committee or a task force to study it—in short, passing the buck. Such ad hoc groups frequently try to deal with their own impotence by suggesting that "further study is needed" or that still other ad hoc groups be formed to carry on the task. Considering that each committee was explicitly charged with deriving concrete recommendations from the data, it was surprising that several institutions attempted to avoid this responsibility by suggesting that another similar group be established to carry on the work. At one institution, this game amounted to a paraphrase of the original charge: "In light of the data, it would seem appropriate to develop a task force to address itself to each of the seven problem areas. Starting with ACE data, the task force might well delve deeply into some of the reasons for the problem areas and develop plans to improve the situation."

At another institution, it seemed that the committee's inability to grapple with some parts of the data would be solved by some undefined "future study": "In terms of categories of data tabulated by the American Council on Education, then, we believe that a program giving optimum results should have positive impact . . . and that the data collected from future studies will clarify for us certain ambiguities which now exist in this area."

Or, more to the point, "We have left implementation of solutions in the report to the second task force." (Consultants and staff who made the followup visit to this institution expressed considerable pessimism about prospects for this second task force, the main problem being lack of continuity and leadership.)

OBFUSCATION

In some respects obfuscation was the most maddening of all the games played by the committees, since academics are masters at obfuscation, and this technique is often difficult to detect until it is too late. In reviewing one report, consultant Joseph Katz cited an extreme case of obfuscation: "Proposed changes are overly generalized and so multitudinous, with minimal attention to the 'how's,' that the best prediction is that any potential for action will be swallowed up in a sea of words." Katz offers an insight into the use of obfuscation: "The academic reflex is often to talk when faced with the need for action which requires some change of established habits. Academics often do not recognize this particular form of lassitude, because for academics words, after all, are action, perhaps the most favorite action."

One common form of obfuscation is to invoke platitudes or high-sounding generalizations that lead nowhere but that create the impression of genuine concern and interest. A few examples:

"The collection and use of data for the purpose of making rational change possible are of great value to higher education. Attempts at such methods of change are important and forward-looking, but must be geared to the presently limited institutional means for making change."

"Our students will always be the supreme judges of the worth of what we do. If we forget this fact in our day-to-day work, in the programs we devise, in the policies we establish, indeed even in the technicalities of running the institution, we violate their trust and we deserve nothing better than to disappear."

"Because of the long-range goal of graduating a professional motivated and prepared for a career, all aspects of the student's education and training must be seen in a relation to the overall objective of producing a well-educated (adult)."

Another form of obfuscation is the rhetorical question game. Here the academic poses what appears to be a serious and thoughtful question, but which in fact calls for no particular answer and either deflects the issue of shuts off further discussion and debate: "If students refuse to remain in such circumstances, are we to place the blame on them by hypothesizing some inherent deficiency within their skins, or could we admit that those who refuse and leave may sometimes be the best of the lot, not the worst?" (This statement concluded a discussion of findings that showed that the actual dropout rate of a college was substantially higher than the rate predicted from freshman characteristics.)

"Would students choose a large class with an excellent teacher, or a small one indifferently taught? Do student criticisms of advisement and counseling opportunities reflect the scale of values operative here in faculty assessment, that reward extra-university scholarly activity above concern for student needs?"

"Is this difference (in student dissatisfaction between 1970 and 1973) a manifestation of 'senioritis' or has there been a general increase in student dissatisfaction in that three-year period?"

CO-OPTATION

Co-optation, to borrow from the student New Left of the 1960s, is an especially effective defense against action because it incorporates an unqualified acceptance of the data. Briefly, co-optation involves the open acceptance of the existence of a problem, together with the suggestion that steps have already been taken to remedy the problem or, in its extreme form, that the problem has already been solved. The obvious danger of this technique is that it preempts any further action on the problem in the absence of evidence that the problem has, in fact, been solved. Data of the kind used in this study are especially susceptible to this game, since there is always some time lag between the collection of empirical data and the presentation of findings. Thus, the purpose of co-optation is to suggest that, in this interim, the problem has been solved. This is not to say, of course, that the problem has not been solved, but simply that co-optation in such circumstances may not be justified. Academics who fear that co-optation may be operating should ask themselves: How much faith do we have that the purported remedial action has alleviated (or will alleviate) the problem? If we had just now been alerted to the problem, would we have chosen the same solution?

One private university offers a good example of co-optation: "Though great unhappiness is also shown for library research facilities, the recent opening of the (new) library is assumed by the writer to have largely resolved this problem area."

At a state university where students complained about lack of curricular options, this example occurred: "At first the thought arose that this problem was due to the options available in terms of curriculum choice, but between 1970 and 1973 the options available have increased."

In response to the finding that students complained frequently about lack of social life, another report said: "Several recent changes may affect student evaluations in these areas, as well. For example, a large (student) recreation area and lodge was opened in the fall of 1972, which will provide the facilities for a wide range of outdoor activities."

Another example: "The proportion dissatisfied with advice from faculty is higher than estimated. We should note that we have already taken measures to upgrade and improve the advisory system."

The use of co-optation, like other defense mechanisms, does not necessarily justify the conclusion that the facts implied are untrue (it is entirely possible, for example, that the solution set forth has in fact ameliorated the difficulty). However, playing this game closes inquiry into the matter and precludes further discussions of solutions, even though direct evidence that the problem has been solved is lacking.

RECITATION

Some committees managed to avoid any serious attempt to relate the data to institutional policy by plodding methodically from one item to the next and simply converting the numbers into prose statements. (This game amounts to the excessive use of a "descriptive" approach to the data, discussed in Chapters 4 and 9.) Given a large amount of data, recitation tends to mesmerize the reader while at the same time creating the impression of serious concern and involvement. One report, by far the longest of the 13, consisted of literally hundreds of pages of recitation. Joseph Katz characterized the report as " . . . a veritable filubuster. Everything is laid out in the most tedious detail with little sense of the meaning of the data and their implications. . . . Here we have a use of the data quite like the use of royal comissions, white papers, self-studies, etc., a use not for action but as a substitute for or inhibitor of action." The ultimate futility of this exercise was perhaps best characterized by one statement following a recitation of many student dissatisfactions: "The past will play a much larger role in determining the future than the needs and pressures of students at any given time in the future."

DISPLACEMENT AND PROJECTION

The displacement and projection category covers a wide range of academic games that all shift attention away from the possible substantive implications of the data to some external source. Although in our project displacement and projection were frequently directed against ACE, in future projects they could just as well be directed against any unit within the institution such as the Office of Institutional Research or the president's office. The basic function of displacement and projection is to obviate the need for serious consideration of the data or for subsequent action by citing inadequacies in the data or in the services provided by the initiator of the project or supplier of the data.

The principla strategic advantage of these games is that there are deficiencies in any data, no matter how sophisticated nor how well analyzed and presented. Similarly, there will always be limitations on how much additional help the project initiator can provide. The critical distinction between legitimate criticism of the data or services, on the one hand, and the use of displacement or projection, on the other, is whether the criticisms are presented constructively (that is, to make appropriate qualifications in interpretations or to

clarify certain points about the data) or whether they are used to justify failure even to consider the significance of the data for students.
In some institutions, serious and legitimate questions about the data
were raised, but not the exclusion of any attempts at interpretation.
In others, defects in the data or services became the primary focus.

Some forms of displacement and projection address real deficiencies that indeed reduce the usefulness of data (see Chapter 9).
Pointing out such deficiencies becomes an academic game when it
is a means to avoid responsibility for interpreting the data or for
generating recommendations.

One form of displacement might be called caution. This game
involves a litany of technical limitiations in the data, followed by a
statement indicating that it would be hazardous to attempt to formulate
meaningful interpretations or generalizations concerning policy because of these imperfections. A striking example of this version is
illustrated in the report of one private university: "The data are assumed to be indicators of possible difficulties, or trends, or conditions rather than thought of as firm evidence. As indicators they point
more toward efforts to verify the indications or refute them than as
a basis for significant policy change. In fact, the report will not suggest any specific course of action for the faculty."

Another form of displacement is red herring. In this game the
academic identifies a real or imagined deficiency that could have
little or no bearing either on the validity of the data or on the committee's ability to interpret them. Attention is diverted from the task
at hand and, by implication, confidence in the project is undermined.
A striking example of red herring is provided by a public university:

"A final objection to the project felt by some committee members
was that the plan for the pilot utilization study originated in the minds
of those who provided the data, rather than with the immediate needs
of a particular university community." The report went on: "A number of committee members felt that there was a real gap between the
sort of shot gun provision of data and the particularly targetable needs
of the institution."

A close relative of red herring is innuendo. Here, the academic
gamesman attempts to discredit the data, the provider of the data, or
the entire project by suggesting that some minor deficiency might
indicate more far-reaching but undefined defects. The purpose of
innuendo is to discourage others from interpreting the data or making
recommendations by implying that the data cannot be trusted. For
example, one report cited what the committee considered a discrepancy in the data and then concluded: "The Committee wondered
whether other data that presented no obvious difficulties might not be
inaccurate, nevertheless." Playing innuendo allowed this particular
institution to avoid positive action by suggesting the need for additional

(presumably more valid) data: "Although the Committee is cautious about attaching great meaning on the data on hand, all members are anxious to see the results of subsequent materials. . . . The committee believes some way must be found either to verify the indications and take remedial steps, or to discount them."

A variation of innuendo is sarcasm. Once again, this game shifts attention away from the substance and, by implication, discredits the data. Institutions generally avoided playing sarcasm in their reports, with a few exceptions. For example: "Comparison with national norms show (our) students higher on academic, athletic, leadership, mathematical, mechanical, public speaking abilities, and on popularity with opposite sex and intellectual self-confidence, and lower on artistic ability. Again, all very nice, but so what?"

A common type of displacement and projection is "quantitative" games. Data can be rejected because there are either too little or too much of them. Several committees complained that they could not reach conclusions because certain data were lacking, although at least one committee reported that it could not function properly because there was too much: "The study committee was confronted with a superabundance of data which was impossible to fully analyze and utilize within the time period available for the prepation of this report." Or, at another institution: "The questionnaire was not definitive enough."

Still another projective device used to reject the data was that the time period during which they were collected was in some way atypical or aberrent. This type might be called "time" games:

"The fact that the data were several years old, that the years from 1966 to 1970 (the college years of student involvement) were years of very unusual student unrest . . . acted to retard enthusiasm for the possibility that the data could be relied upon to reflect important and presently relevant facts."

Another example combines the time game with co-optation: "A conditioning factor for these data, it should be noted, is the changing curriculum during 1969 and 1970. In this period the institution's curriculum was underoing comprehensive revision."

COUNTERMEASURES

The most important consideration in coping with academic games is to detect them in time to take appropriate countermeasures. Since committee deliberations ordinarily preceed the drafting of reports, one's best chance for early detection of gamesmanship is in the initial verbal interchanges among committee members.

The particular games preferred by any committee member are often related to the role that member plays in the committee meetings (see Chapter 8 for descriptions of these different roles). The "methodologist-critic," for example, is most likely to play displacement and projection games (caution, red herring, innuendo, and so forth). If someone demonstrates a predilection for particular roles and particular games early in the committee deliberations, that person will probably play similar games in writing the report. Neutralizing gamesman tendencies in the initial verbal exchanges among committee members, therefore, might help to discourage gamesmanship later in the writing of the report. In addition, the report should be reviewed first in draft form, so that there will be an opportunity to take appropriate remedial action before the final report is prepared.

Dealing with academic games involves two major components: identifying gamesmanship when it occurs, and taking appropriate remedial action. If one is familiar with the major varieties of games that can be played (see the previous section) and monitors early committee interactions carefully, detection should not be a major problem. A more difficult challenge is how to cope with academic games in a constructive manner.

Unless the task force members are a close knit group who know each other reasonably well and have established a mutual trust, a frontal attack on gamesmanship is probably inadvisable. By "frontal attack" is meant simply that the person countering the game simply points out the game when it appears and asks the player to adopt a more constructive approach. With persons who do not know and respect each other, the frontal attack is likely to provoke defensiveness, hostility, or other nonproductive responses.

A more effective approach for new committees is diversion. This technique is applicable to verbal interchanges where a particular task force member has disrupted committee functioning by playing displacement and projection games that focus the committee's attention on, say, methodological deficiencies. A potentially effective countermeasure is to divert such a discussion by suggesting that it is time to move to another topic, that other task force members cannot follow technical discussions, or that there will not be enough time remaining to consider what the data might mean.

Another approach is to isolate the gamesman. Persons who play displacement and projection games, for example, might be asked to prepare a written analysis of technical problems to be discussed at some future meeting. The request for the analysis in effect shuts off the discussion and provides a pivotal moment for shifting to more substantive issues. Isolation of games in a written report can be done by removing undesired portions (technical criticism, for example) from the main body of the report and locating them instead in an appendix.

Most academic games can be countered by suggesting that the player (and the audience) should consider also the implications of the data (this is particularly important with games such as recitation). For certain games, however, the player should probably be challenged more directly by suggesting that alternative explanations might be possible (this is particularly important for games such as rationalization and co-optation). Still another approach is to ask the gamesman to explain or elaborate on a particular statement (this approach is essential in a game like obfuscation).

Particularly difficult strategic problems are posed by games like passing the buck. Since academics are so used to playing such games, other task force members may be tempted to go along as a way to avoid the hard work of trying to interpret and understand data. Passing the buck also avoids the risk-taking that is usually associated with making recommendations for institutional change. Passing the buck should probably be confronted more or less directly, by pointing out that it represents an abdication of responsibility.

These suggested strategies represent only some of the many countermeasures that might be employed to cope with academic games. While their use by no means guarantees that the negative consequences of academic games will be eliminated entirely, task force members who are attuned to gamesmanship when it occurs will be in a much better position to reduce its impact on the project's progress if they have given some thought beforehand to possible countermeasures that might be used.

NOTE

1. Eric Berne, Games People Play (New York: Random House, 1964).

8

MAKING COMMITTEES WORK

Committees play a central role in the governance of most colleges and universities. In addition to standard committees covering major institutional functions, such as admissions, academic policy, and finance, institutions regularly utilize ad hoc committees to deal with such matters as hiring, planning, evaluation, and various crises. Even though committees normally advise rather than make decisions, administrators are usually reluctant to oppose the recommendations of any key committee.

In following the activities of our 13 institutional committees for more than a year, we found that they reflected not only our project, but also the general way committees work. Administrators tend to follow certain patterns in forming committees and in charging them with tasks. Committee members tend to view their roles in particular ways and to exhibit certain distinctive behavioral styles during committee deliberations. These observations convinced us that most institutional committees would function more effectively if somewhat more consideration were given in the planning stages to such matters as the role of the committee vis-a-vis the administration, the selection of a chairperson, the committee composition, and the probable fate of any reports or recommendations.

Our experiences with these committees are analyzed in terms of guidelines designed to enhance the effectiveness of any institutional committee. These guidelines should be useful not only to investigators who might undertake similar student-oriented projects in the future, but also to institutional administrators or faculty who are concerned about making their committes function more effectively.

These guidelines were designed to apply to a committee with a fairly well-defined assignment: to evaluate detailed data about the institution's student and to prepare a report containing recommendations for action where appropriate. While the data in this project primarily concerned students and their development, guidelines should also apply to committees assigned to evaluate other kinds of data (on institutional finances, for example). This project involved an outside agency (the American Council on Education) that initiated the undertaking and worked with each committee, which made the committee's role unusual. However, this initiating role could as well be played by persons or units within the insitution (see the section on working with the committee below).

This analysis of committee functioning will cover advance planning, committee selection, operating style, and the relationship between the committee and external agencies.

ADVANCE PLANNING

Most committees have two functions: a substantive function, which in this project involved evaluating data and preparing a report with recommendations for action, and a political function, which involves the way the academic community views the committee and the impact committee recommendations are likely to have. This analysis focuses on the former function: that is, how to establish a committee that will be maximally effective in evaluating evidence and preparing appropriate recommendations. We treat the political functions but primarily in terms of how political considerations influence committee effectiveness in carrying out substantive responsibilities. Overconcern with the immediate political impact of a new committee—its "image" or "legitimacy"—can produce a group that is unable to function.

The Committee and the Administration

Concern for the relationship between the committee and the top institutional administration was expressed often by members of each campus committee, as well as by the project staff and consultants. Committee members were nearly unanimous in feeling that a top administrator, preferably the president or chief executive, should view the committee's work as high priority and should make known from the outset that the committee's recommendations would be seriously examined as a basis for action.

These considerations strongly suggest that the committee should view itself as a creature of top administration. An important tactical question is, how much early publicity should be given to the administrator's backing? The committee will achieve visible status if the

chief executive personally announces its appointment and accompanies
the announcement with statements of high expectations and of willingness to act following completion of the committee's report. Such an
announcement would not only lend prestige to the committee's effort,
but would also provide members with moral encouragement and the
hope that their efforts would lead to something concrete.

Clearly the most difficult feature of this "up-front" approach is
the threat posed by implementation. Substantial changes in institutional
policy and practice will inevitably involve potential conflict or competition with standing committees and other governing bodies within the
institution. Any public announcement by the president of an intention
to make sweeping changes in institutional policy on the basis of a committee's efforts may well serve as a red flag to arouse strong resistance from entrenched institutional interests. Perhaps the most effective political solution to this dilemma would be to soft-pedal public
statements early in the game, and to reassure committee members
personally that their efforts will be seriously considered and that the
administration will push for any changes or reforms for which a con-
vincing case is made. As a matter of fact, perhaps the administration
should encourage the committee not only to make recommendations
for change, but also to suggest specific strategies for implementation.
Such strategies would probably involve the appropriate standing committees and governing bodies.

In retrospect it is remarkable that the establishment of the "Data
for Decisions" committee (or task force) on each campus did not generate more negative response from standing committees and governing
bodies. Among the dozens of followup interviews conducted during the
evaluation phase, only one committee member mentioned that the standing committees normally responsible for considering institutional
changes should have been consulted in the selection of committee members for the "Data for Decisions" project. (This person, incidently,
proved highly disruptive of the committee's activities and eventually
was asked to resign.)

There are probably several reasons for this apparent lack of defensive response by the standing committees. Such committees are
often involved mainly in routine activities; new activities or proposals
are usually assigned to ad hoc committees. Standing committees, of
course, are often asked to ratify proposals for change, but the responsibility for developing new ideas or proposals is typically not assigned
to such committees.

A related issue is who should be consulted in the selection of committee members? If this question is primarily substantive (how to get
the best members), the administrator should consult those sources
most able to identify people with appropriate personal qualifications
(see below). If the question is primarily political (how to pacify or

appease certain vested interests), then the administrator must weigh
the possible political gain from consulting these interested parties
against the possible political loss that would occur if their recomenda-
tions are not accepted or if certain other competing groups object because they are not consulted. As long as the function of the committee
is at least partly substantive, application of appropriate criteria for
membership should not be abandoned as the price for some expected
political advantage. Evaluating evidence and preparing a meaningful
report are too complex to justify such a trade-off.

Training and Orientation

Another question to be considered early in the planning stage is
whether potential members should be given training or orientation
prior to undertaking the committee task. Several consultants and institutional personnel suggested that it would have been useful to con-
vene new committee chairpersons from different campuses for an initial workshop to acquaint them with the data and give them a headstart
on the rest of the members. Such training would greatly strengthen
their hand in providing strong leadership for committee deliberations.
If the project initiator is unable to provide the training, the institution
could still consider bringing in one or more consultants to work with
the committee chairperson before the first meeting.

One consultant suggested that, in a large research university, the
entire committee should probably be given some formal training before
undertaking its task. This consultant felt that the structure and politics
of the typical research university are so complex that only a trained
team could possibly analyze data adequately and prepare recommendations that would have any hope of implementation. That our project
had the least impact in the research universities tends to strengthen
this view.

A related issue is the involvement of outside consultants in the
selection of committee members. Several consultants felt strongly
that consultation would greatly aid in selecting an effective committee.
If a consultant's active participation in screening candidates seemed
presumptuous, this screening could be just one part of a general consultation visit.

The Committee's Mission

The initial charge to the committee received little consideration
on any of the 19 campuses. Even though each committee chairperson
had detailed instructions and orientation materials (see Annex A),

the followups during the second year revealed that few, if any, committees were given much structure by the administration. Few committees, for example, had an agenda for their initial meeting. In future efforts of this type the committee chairperson, together with the responsible administrator, should work out a tentative plan that would become the preliminary agenda. During the initial meeting, the chairperson could assign specific responsibilities to each committee member, actively involving the entire committee from the beginning. Including each chairperson in an initial training session would facilitate such an agenda.

SELECTING THE COMMITTEE

Our experiences with various campus committees indicate that effective functioning depends on three major factors: qualifications of the chairperson, qualifications of members, and committee composition.

Qualifications of the Chairperson

Perhaps the most critical decision affecting the success of a committee is the selection of the chairperson. A poor chairperson can alienate an initially supportive administration and frustrate the efforts of even the most creative and dedicated committee members. By the same token, a strong and effective chairperson can lead a mediocre committee to substantial achievements and, where administrative leadership and support is lacking, can even seek out and corral wider institutional backing for well-conceived recommendations. The chairperson, in short, can make or break the entire project.

The proposition that strong, effective leadership is critical to the success of a committee is supported not only by the impressions of practically all persons connected with this project, but also by the evaluative data. We found no case where even a modestly successful committee did not have strong and determined leadership. On a few campuses relatively unproductive committees were chaired by highly qualified individuals, but in these instances the committee's efforts were frustrated by inadequate administrative sponsorship and support.

A strong committee chair is a necessary, but not the only, condition for an effectively functioning committee. In addition to leadership ability, a number of other qualities should be strongly considered in selecting potential chairpersons:

Status

The chairperson should command the attention and respect of the top institutional administration. If it is impossible to appoint a high-ranking administrative officer to chair the committee, the appointee should be in a position to communicate directly with top administrative officers. In other words, chairpersons should be influential by virtue either of the position they hold or of the respect they command. This requirement almost by definition excludes lame ducks—individuals who plan to leave the institution. Two committees that failed to produce reports had lame duck chairpersons; in both cases it appeared that these individuals had neither the motivation nor the support to follow through on their assigned responsibilities.

The need for a chairperson with clout presents special problems in the large research university. The natural tendency there is to appoint either a low-level administrator or a faculty member to head ad hoc committees. Faculty members in research universities, no matter how influential or widely respected, generally make poor chairpersons. One reason is that they are usually too far removed from day-to-day administrative and policy-setting functions. Another reason is the autonomy generally accorded faculty in the more research-oriented institutions. Such faculty—particularly the more prestigious or successful—are often jealous of their time and frequently regard committee appointments as an imposition or, at best, a necessary evil. And even if they are not too busy to devote a reasonable amount of time to the task, they are familiar enough with decision-making processes of the institution to regard such committees as relatively impotent. In short, research-oriented institutions should make every effort to find someone of influence within the administration to chair the committee.

Motivation

Our consultants and staff generally agreed that the committee chairperson should have an activist philosophy about the institution's mission. That is, the person should be strongly committed to the institution, but equally committed to its long-range development and improvement as an educational enviornment for students. The chairperson should not, in other words, be simply an apologist.

There was less agreement on the personal ambition of the committee chairperson. In at least two institutions, both consultants and staff thought that the personal ambition of the chairpersons (manifest, for example, in a desire to produce an impressive report) blinded them to some negative features of the data and made it difficult for them to face up to institutional problems or pathologies. Another consultant, however, felt it essential that the chairperson see a significant personal or professional payoff in the committee's success. It is difficult to argue, of course, that the chairperson should not be committed strongly to the eventual success of the committee, but it is probably unwise for the chairperson to see his or her status within the institution tied closely to the success of the project. Here again is a strong case for a chairperson whose status within the institution is secure.

Technical Qualifications

In a project such as this, knowledge of empirical data and of social science research is a desirable, but probably not essential, quality for the committee chairperson. At a minimum, the chairperson should be sympathetic toward systematic studies of institutions and students. Skill in creative writing is highly desirable, particularly since drafting or editing a report is likely to be a major responsibility of the chairperson.

Attitude Toward the Project

Ad hoc projects are almost doomed to failure unless the chairperson is committed to their general goals at the outset. In at least four of the six institutions that failed to produce reports, the chairperson was indifferent, or at best, neutral toward the project. (The same was true for at least three institutions that did produce reports, and the reports in general reflected this attitude.) The selection of indifferent or even hostile chairpersons is likely to occur in those institutions where the president passes along the responsibility for chairing the committee to some person who has no prior knowledge of the project and no prior commitment to this type of research or to student development. If the president insists on appointing such a chair person, then the person should be given an opportunity to discuss the background and design of the project with the administration and with one or more consultants before initiating any meetings with the committee. Consultative discussions should familiarize the chairperson sufficiently with the project to generate at least the beginning of interest and commitment to its aims.

Qualifications of Committee Members

Both consultants and staff have noted a number of personal qualifications that are characteristic of the most effective committee members:

- They have a substantive rather than a methodological orientation (they are not, as one consultant put it, "obsessed with methodological purity").
- They are secure and nondefensive.
- They are action-oriented people rather than simply contemplators and thinkers.
- The status of faculty members in the national community of their discipline is either high or irrelevant.
- Faculty members are regarded as either informal or formal faculty leaders.
- Administrators are either highly respected or at least not disliked or disrespected by the faculty.

Visits with committees during the dissemination phase and follow-up interviews on six campuses during the evaluation phase indicated that committee members can often be differentiated in terms of the roles they play. Below are capsule descriptions of seven of the most easily identifiable roles. While this list is stereotyped and incomplete, a careful review of each role should aid not only in identifying desirable qualities for potential committee members, but also in understanding the behavior of particular members once a committee gets under way.

The Methodologist-Critic

This role, perhaps the easiest to identify, is usually played by a social or behavioral scientist skilled in research design, statistics, and methodology. When there is only one social scientist on the committee, that person is likely to assume that he or she should play this role. Unfortunately, the methodologist-critic can be highly disruptive on an otherwise effectively functioning committee. Substantive discussions of the meaning of data can get sidetracked into highly technical critiques of alleged defects. The tendency to play this role is strongly reinforced if the social scientist is inclined to show off his or her methodological prowess or feels competititve with or possibly threatened by the project initiator or provider of the data. Although it is important to have technical expertise within the committee, methodologists will have limited value if they are expected primarily to be critics. When the committee is confronted with someone inclined to play this role, the chairperson needs strong control to prevent committee meetings from becoming hopelessly sidetracked.

The Substantive Critic

This role is usually played by persons who, for one reason or another, are unable to accept the idea that the data have any relevance either to the institution's problems or to student needs or concerns. The usual strategy of such critics is to put the provider of the data on the defensive by insisting that the relevance of each item to the institution's special problems somehow be proved. These critics may concentrate on minor or trivial items, or they may indict the entire data set for its failure to solve the institution's major problems: "This is all very interesting, but I fail to see how it is going to balance our budget."

Antidata Person

Like methodologist-critics, antidata persons are easy to spot. Their usual position is that "you can prove anything with statistics," and that the true essence of institutional impact on students cannot be captured in dry numerical data. Frequently, this role is played by persons whose disciplines are in the arts or humanities, although occasionally natural scientists will also play this part. Natural scientists tend to emphasize the primitiveness and artificiality of social science measurements compared with physical measures. Antidata persons tend to be among the most opinionated of all committee members.

The Prodata Person

This committee role is characterized by an enthusiastic acceptance of empirical data and a belief that meaningful institutional policy can be based on empirical information about students. Persons who play this role are frequently social scientists and very often in such a position as director of institutional reasearch. If their enthusiasm is tempered by methodological sophistication and by an ability to judge the quality of data, they can be most useful in helping the committee proceed with its task. The main danger with such persons is that their enthusiasm may blind them to ambiguities or other frailities in the data.

The Passive Resister

This role is characterized by a lack of involvement in committee activities and a general lack of enthusiasm for even the best ideas emanating from the committee's discussions. Often this role is played by disgruntled faculty members who resent their committee appointments or by busy administrators who view their committee responsibilities as an imposition. Committee chairpersons perceptive enough to spot a passive resister can sometimes reverse the role by assigning that person a meaningful task that contributes to the general thrust of the committee's work.

The Interpreter

This is a highly important role: committees that lack someone to play the interpreter may never get off the ground. Basically, the interpreter tries to draw inferences from the data that relate to institutional effectiveness and functioning. Analyses of the 13 committee reports revealed great differences in the extent to which the committee made meaningful interpretations of the data (see Chapters 4 and 9). There seems to be no disciplinary correlate to this role: social scientists often played it, but some of the most creative interpreters of data were from the arts and humanities (see below).

The Opportunist

This role is played by persons who see the committee as a vehicle to promote some favorite cause. Basically, the opportunist is interested in finding data that support preconceived notions about institutional policy or practice. The opportunist may be someone whose previous attempts to gain support for certain pet ideas or projects have been frustrated. In this project several committee chairpersons were opportunists. While the role can be effective in involving committee members and in pushing them toward substantive goals, the opportunist can mislead the committee into interpretations and conclusions unwarranted by the data. At the same time, the opportunist can cause the committee to overlook important items that do not happen to confirm the opportunist's particular pet ideas or theories. (See Chapter 9 for several instances where opportunistic chairpersons actually misinterpreted data to promote favorite causes.)

The Exhibitionist

Since this role relies heavily on verbal skills, it is a favorite of many academics. Basically, the exhibitionist likes to talk and to show off his or her knowledge, erudition, or verbal skills. Persons who play this role frequently combine it with other roles (for example, methodologist-critic, substantive critic, antidata person). Since they infrequently focus on substantive questions and often use up a lot of time, exhibitionists can be highly disruptive. Exhibitionists who have a good sense of humor or who are quite articulate are especially difficult to cope with, since they frequently entertain the other committee members.

Composition of the Committee

Although committees have two functions—substantive and political—
many administrators tend to view the appointment of committee members primarily in political terms, even when the primary function of
the committee is substantive. Typically, these administrators, in a
"United Nations approach," strive to placate various constituencies
within the institution by naming a representative from each to the
committee. The administrator is interested less in the individual's
personal qualifications than in the constituency that the individual
represents.

Several different political models can be utilized in appointing
committees. One is the curricular model, in which representatives
from each major curricular division are selected (for example, social
sciences, natural sciences, humanities, and so on). Curricular models
are common in institutions where faculty are perceived as having
power. In an alternative political model, characterized as administrative, an attempt is made to appoint representatives of the major administrative units or subdivisions within the institution: a dean, a
member of the faculty senate, the director of some staff office (research, planning, and so on), and possibly a student. Administrative
models seem more popular in smaller institutions.

The basic weakness of political approaches to appointments is
that those persons who end up on the committee may be incapable of
performing the committee's task. This problem will be exacerbated
if the appointees also perceive themselves as representing various
constituencies rather than as possessing appropriate skills to deal
with the assignment. If the committee members possess most of the
desirable attributes listed earlier, their representativeness will be
of secondary importance. This is not to say, of course, that one should
deliberately appoint a committee only of administrators or only of
faculty members from one department, but that considerations of
representativeness should always be subordinated to the candidate's
qualifications for the job.

The committee should include a strong, respected chairperson
and supporting members who possess appropriate skills and interests.
A respected and influential chairperson will not only provide the committee with clout, but will also help to enlist the cooperation of other
members. While one or two strong and influential members can help
a committee, to require that all members resemble the chairperson
in importance or status would be a mistake. Younger and less prestigious members will probably be more highly motivated to devote time
and energy to the committee's activities. A poor combination, of
course, would be a committee composed primarily of important people

led by a weak chairperson. (This occurred at one institution, with poor results.)

When weighing the disciplinary affiliations of committee members, several considerations must be borne in mind. Social scientists can provide valuable technical expertise and experience in dealing with empirical data, but they can also undermine the committee's activities if they choose to become methodologist-critics. (The beginning efforts of one committee were completely sabotaged by a social scientist who played this role.) Persons from the arts and humanities can be useful members, provided they can resist the temptation to play the role of antidata persons. In fact, some of the most creative and potentially useful interpretations of data were made by a committee that included only members from the humanities. Possibly, the technical knowledge of persons from the social sciences inhibits their ability to treat data creatively. To generalize from our experience about the effectiveness of persons from the natural sciences, business, or the professions is difficult. Although these members participated somewhat less in the committee's activities than persons from the social sciences and humanities, there were too few to draw any firm conclusions about their effectiveness.

Because so many academics deal with problems in abstract rather than concrete terms the committee should include among its members one or two persons with operational responsibility within the institution. A director of institutional research or a person of comparable position obviously should be included. Other likely candidates with operational responsibilities are the director of admissions, the registrar, the director of student personnel services, the chief financial aid officer, the director of the office of planning, and the chief budget officer. To have as much influence as possible, the committee should include at least one high-ranking academic administrator (president, academic vice president, provost, dean, and so on).

If the data to be considered by the committee are concerned with student development, student members can provide an important real world perspective. Unfortunately, they frequently lack any relevant technical, scientific, or literary experience or expertise. To counter this problem, the chairperson could go directly to the relevant departments (psychology, English, sociology, and so on) to obtain student nominees who possess appropriate skills, an approach preferable to the usual practice of appointing students who occupy particular offices within the student government. This latter practice, of course, is designed to fulfill political rather than substantive objectives.

Followup interviews with committee members revealed that students frequently were treated not as full-fledged working members of the committee but as spokesmen for the student body or as sources for student opinion. This approach not only relegates students to what

amounts to a token role, but it also invites unreliable estimates of
student opinion of only one source is consulted. More than one student
should be included on a committee. Students should be selected not
because they hold particular offices, but because they possess skills
appropriate to the committee's project.

At least one other category, the new faculty member or new administrator, should be considered for committee membership. Regardless of their status at time of employment, new members of the
academic community bring a fresh perspective and a lack of institutional bias that can greatly aid the committee in getting started. For
a while, at least, the new person can function almost like a full-time
consultant.

Some consultants and several institutional personnel felt that
committees assigned to evaluate data and to make recommendations
function more effectively if an outside observer or technical consultant meets regularly with the committee. Presumably, such a person
could provide detached and dispassionate input and could also assist
in answering technical questions about data or methodology. However,
outside observers or consultants may involve additional cost and certain other risks. For example, some consultants and staff felt that
the committee could become overly dependent on the outside observer
or, conversely, that it might view the outside observer as an interloper
or adversary.

STYLE OF COMMITTEE OPERATION

Once the committee has been established and the chairperson and
members selected, a number of decisions about the style of operation
must be made. Ideally, the initial agenda would be worked out between
the committee chairperson and someone high in the administration.
The first meeting of the group should include a discussion of the general background and objectives of the project, as well as possible revisions in the agenda.

The next important step is to move the committee from general
discussion to specific consideration of the data. To accomplish this,
one or two committee members could be assigned to examine the data
and generate a series of hypotheses to be discussed at the second meeting. The hypotheses could range from simple interpretations of particular items to possible changes in institutional policy based on data.
A list of hypotheses would help committee members as they begin to
study the data in terms of possible implications for the institution.

No matter how vigorously the chairperson tries to keep members
focused on substantive implications of the data, there will be a tendency in the early stages of the committee's work, particularly among

the social scientists, to play methodologist-critic or at least to raise legitimate technical and methodological questions. Such questions must be asked and at least partially answered. What should be avoided, as consultant David Epperson suggested in his review of the 13 committee reports, is the "use of the committee meetings as arenas to compete with one another to see who can be either the most 'tough-minded' or the most cynical about student motives." This area of committee functioning requires strong leadership from the chairperson.

The chairperson might assign a would-be methodologist-critic to monitor the interpretations and conclusions proposed by the committee as its deliberations proceed. The monitor could point out where data do not support recommendations or where extrapolations are questionable. This role of "keeping 'em honest," of course, does not have to be played by an expert methodologist. However, one member of the committee should be responsible for making sure that conclusions and interpretations are consistent with the facts. Committees are capable of reaching conclusions that have little to do with and may even be contradicted by the data.

How long should the committee allow itself to complete its task? Clearly, the committee must remain intact long enough to establish some connection between the data and the educational goals and aspirations of the institution. Several consultants and institutional personnel suggested that a committee retreat might bridge this gap between data and institutional goals. One committee member suggested that the $500 honorarium offered each participating institution might have been better spent to finance a retreat. In any case, the committee should set specific deadlines for completing various items on its agenda.

WORKING WITH THE COMMITTEE

Whenever an institution establishes an ad hoc committee to work with information provided by some other unit within the institution or by some outside agency, a number of issues must be considered. Since the initiative for undertaking the project does not originate within the committee, at first the committee is a passive body. Consequently, in the early stages, the initiating person or agency defines the nature of its working relationship with the committee.

Perhaps the most critical decision concerns the extent to which the project initiator or provider of data becomes directly involved in the workings of the committee. Although there was considerable disagreement among our staff and consultants, most persons connected with the project felt that involvement should have been greater. In particular, agreement was widespread that we should have provided the committees with more direction.

The need for greater direction and leadership was mentioned most frequently in connection with the initial orientation to the project. Since data-oriented persons or agencies are often regarded with a mixture of suspicion, resentment, and indifference, working closely with the committee during the early stages could serve to build trust and confidence. Whether orientation sessions by consultants and staff would have helped to break down resistance in our pilot project is not entirely clear, given the experiences at Vanderbilt and Tulane (see Chapter 2). Furthermore, even though the only other committee that received personal consultation showed no signs of active resistance or hostility, it ended up producing one of the poorest reports.

We probably tended to overgeneralize the unproductive session at Vanderbilt and to assign primary blame to the data and the project rather than to the particular situation there. In retrospect it seems likely that situational factors helped to create the negative atmosphere: the committee was too large and poorly selected, the outside consultant group was too large and intimidating, and the role the Vanderbilt group was asked to play (to help us "debug" our approach) was inappropriate.

Training and Orientation

To avoid similar problems, orientation sessions should involve only one or two persons outside the committee and should be presented to the committee as training or familiarization sessions rather than open-ended discussions about the merits of the project. Committee members should be provided with specific instructions about how to proceed and should be armed with a few key observations about the data to illustrate possible interpretive uses and to divert the discussion if it becomes unproductive. Ideally, the person doing the orientation should be prepared to point out how particular items of data highlight or otherwise illustrate a particular institutional problem. To use the data in this fashion, a certain amount of homework before the initial meeting is clearly indicated.

A precommittee training session could be put to several uses. At a minimum, the session should include instruction on how to read the data and how to write intelligible presentations based on them. This instruction would also help the committee establish its own level of aspirations with respect to its data. One apparent difficulty in our project was that most committees began to work intensively with the data before they developed any aspirations. What should the committee accomplish: Is it simply looking for evidence to support certain preconceived notions, or is it searching for something that might "shake up" the institution? Is it simply undertaking data interpretation as an intellectual exercise or is it seriously interested in evaluating institutional programs (for example, admissions, counseling, library, teaching practices) in terms of their implications for students? Establishing preliminary aspirations before they become immersed in the data should provide structure for the committee members and help them be more goal-oriented in their deliberations.

Early training sessions might also take some of the steam out of would-be methodologist-critics. Several institutional visits indicated that most legitimate objections to the data voiced by technical experts could have been resolved in a face-to-face discussion between these experts and one of our staff. Placing both persons in a larger group in effect puts both on the spot, which militates not only against productive committee work but also against any real appreciation of the underlying methodological problems. Encouraging methodologically inclined committee members to explore their legitimate concerns in a two- or three-person training session with project staff should contribute positively to effective committee functioning later.

Monitoring Committee Activities

Once the committee is formed and begins to meet, there are several options for monitoring progress and providing help. Monitoring can be done by the person or agency that either initiates the project or provides the data, or by some other persons within the administration. In the pilot project we attempted to provide several kinds of consultative assistance, although few committees took full advantage of this help. A staff research analyst was available to consult by telephone at almost any time during regular working hours. Additional special analyses of data were provided on request, although in some cases the requested analysis was too complex to perform with available staff and resources. Although each institution had the option to request a consultative visit to assist with the data, only one institution took advantage of this option. In addition to these offers, regular telephone checks were used to see how each committee's work was progressing.

It is difficult to know why the committees did not avail themselves of the consultative aid offered. Indeed, our followup visits revealed that many committee members felt strongly that more consultation and guidance should have been provided, even though these same committees seldom asked for clarification of questions or requested consultative visits.

Simply offering to make services available is evidently not enough. The project monitor would be better advised to be active and aggressive in following the committee's work. Several staff and consultants suggested that monitoring should be construed as a "formative evaluation" in which the committee regularly receives feedback concerning their progress. One way to formalize this feedback is to schedule two or three sessions with the project initiator or person providing the data during the course of the committee's meetings. If this is done, it is important that the committee not become too dependent on the monitor and simply mark time between visits.

If monitoring is only remote, periodic telephone calls should involve more than general inquiries—not just, how's it going? The caller should be armed with specific questions about committee progress and should be prepared to recommend alternative courses, depending on what the conversation reveals about the committee's activities. Individual committee members should also be encouraged to initiate communications directly with the monitor whenever they need advice or information.

Periodic monitoring would be useful in determining if the committee is having significant problems. If the monitoring indicates the need, a consultative visit should be offered but not imposed. Even if the monitor or consultant does not actually meet with the full committee, he or she could conduct informal discussions with individual members and offer specific suggestions to help the committee get back on the track.

Perhaps the most important function of active monitoring is not to provide the committee with assistance in interpreting its data (that is, to do the committee's work), but to provide evaluative feedback about the committee's progress. During the followup interviews many committee members reported that they would have benefited from feedback about the directions they had taken and the progress they had made. Such reassurance provides the committee with an additional incentive to continue its work.

A complaint commonly expressed by committee members during the followup visits concerned the slowness with which we responded to requests for additional data analyses. It goes without saying that quick response can be critical, and that committee enthusiasm can wane if delay in feeding back results is excessive. Most delays were connected with requests for new data analyses. Unfortunately, we were not well equipped to undertake such analyses on an ad hoc basis. (Indeed, to produce the original data packets strained our resources.) In future projects it would be prudent to develop software packages to enable the committee to have additional analyses done simply and on a quick turnaround. Some types of analyses that might be requested are discussed in more detail in Chapter 9.

Followup Evaluation

Staff and consultants who independently read the 13 committee
reports generally agreed that it would have been useful to provide
each committee with consultation and critical evaluation of a draft
report. For some institutions, particularly those where the report
was almost entirely the idiosyncratic effort of the chairperson, a
consultative discussion of the primary draft would have been useful.
(Some committee members reported that they saw neither a draft nor
a copy of the final report.)

Outside assistance might also be useful in implementing recommendations. A committee by itself is in no position to convert a written report into institutional action. As a matter of fact, most ad hoc
committees have a tendency to disband when the report is completed,
and the report either sits on a shelf or is filed. Under these conditions, there may be some advantage to keeping the committee intact
throughout the implementation stage. The committee could assume
a monitoring function of its own and follow the fate of its recommendations through the review and decision-making apparatuses in the institution. At a minimum, the committee wants to prevent its recommendations from simply being ignored; ideally, it would strive to
shepherd its recommendations through to some concrete action. Monitoring of this sort would probably be most productive if it were included in the original plan for the committee's activities and supported
by the administration.

The followup visit to six campuses convinced us of the desirability
of postproject evaluation sessions. While the principal purpose of the
followup visits was to obtain information on the fate of the recommendations, the visits sometimes provided an impetus for committee
members to take a renewed interest in the project and to consider the
possibility of additional work with the data. Moreover, in several instances, the visits seemed to rekindle the committee's interest in
seeing that its recommendations were acted upon. In short, it appears
that followup evaluation is useful not only to clarify the outcomes at
the institution but also to stimulate committee members to continue
to pursue the project's basic aims.

9

DATA AND DECISIONS

A number of questions arise about the use of empirical data in decision making: Is there any evidence that student data can really have a significant impact on institutional decision making? Are data on institutional impact useful in increasing institutional self-understanding? What are the circumstances under which data are likely to be misinterpreted? How relevant to institutional needs are the types of data used in our pilot project? What content areas are missing, inadequately covered, or irrelevant to decision making? How can empirical data be analyzed so results will be most useful? Are some forms of organization and presentation particularly effective? What sorts of additional analyses and related data processing services should be provided?

These issues will be discussed under several general headings: problems of interpretation, content, data analysis, timeliness, quantity, and organization and presentation.

PROBLEMS OF INTERPRETATION

A committee's treatment of any given empirical datum can show one of three different levels of sophistication: descriptive, interpretative, or insightful (see Chapter 4). Although these three levels are more a continuum than discrete classes, statements from the 13 institutional reports illustrate each level.

Description

Descriptive reporting of empirical data found in most reports is of extremely limited value, since it primarily converts numerical information into prose statements. This practice, quite common in published social science literature, is a substitute for thinking about what the data might mean. A few examples from the institutional reports:

> According to the 1970 survey, fine arts, health professions, and mathematics had fewer majors than projected, while education and English had more than projected. (No further discussion on this finding.)

> Numerically over 60 percent of withdrawals take place during the first two years students are at the university, and the overall tendency is for fewer students to leave the further they are along in their education.

> Present enrollment data indicate that minority groups have a lower representation, 2.1 percent as compared to 13.8 percent nationally, at . . . than at similar institutions.

Not infrequently, institutions try to dignify basically descriptive data reporting by stating that the data are "interesting" or "significant": "A particularly intriguing trend is the fact that the income level of the students' parents is on the increase."

A basically descriptive data presentation can also be given the appearance of something more through normative comparisons (which are, again, basically descriptive):

> A comparison of the father's occupation of . . . 's students with those of Northwestern, for example, suggests a great similarity except for the larger percentage of medical doctors in the . . . sample. . . . 's parents, according to these data, tend on the whole to be rather better educated than those of students at other private universities.

Descriptive analyses do not contribute to understanding the institution beyond a simple statement of observed facts. To make the data more relevant to decision making requires some attempts at interpretation.

Interpretation

Interpretative use of empirical data involves relating a given item or set of data to other information about the institution. By definition, interpretation involves speculation. This speculation is particularly important because it offers one means to understand the possible causal relations between decision alternatives and educational outcomes. The 13 institutional reports contain numerous instances where data are used interpretatively:

> 1970 levels of dissatisfaction were . . . substantially greater than would be expected . . . the results seemed to indicate a dissatisfaction with the faculty not in the technical performance in their jobs, but in terms of the atmosphere surrounding the academic community. The problem may be lack of "community"; the students seem to be looking for a more "personal" or open relationship with the faculty.

> Table A.5 reveals a comparatively high level of dissatisfaction with the degree to which undergraduate training has prepared the students for their future careers. This judgment was made by the graduates immediately before or very soon after graduation so it is not based so much on experience as on expectation or immediate results of the search for a first position. It may also reflect dissatisfaction with the college placement service.

> ACE data identified a substantial number of students at . . . from small towns or farms (31.1 percent compared to a national norm of 24.8 percent). Also, 32 percent of . . . 's graduates worked in a small town or farm compared to a national norm of 22 percent. This data is [sic] consistent with the role and scope statement which recognized . . . 's concern for . . . a rich agricultural area of small towns and cities. . . . "

> The committee noted with interest the discrepancy between the low level of dissatisfaction (2 percent) over the opportunities for discussion of work with professors in a major field and the high (29 percent) level of dissatisfaction with the advice and guidance from faculty and staff. Again, these figures are suggestive, but point toward several plausible interpretations. Most frighteningly, our students could be indicating that while our faculty is available for discussion, what the professors have to offer in the way of advice is either unwanted or irrelevant. Indeed, the question of the quality of academic advising has been frequently debated at . . . .

Insight

The distinction between interpretative and insightful uses of data is admittedly arbitrary. To the staff and consultants who read the 13 task force reports, insightful use of data included something beyond interpretation. This "something" usually involved relating an empirical finding to some aspect of institutional functioning which in turn implied something of significance for institutional policy and decision making. In other words, insight is an effort not only to understand or explain a particular empirical fact, but also to assess the significance of that fact or explanation in terms of institutional operations. Typically, such an assessment requires that the institution be seen in a new or unique light, hence the term insight. Although insightful use of data is rarer than descriptive or interpretative use, several reports contain impressive examples:

> The ACE predicted that 8 percent of the graduating seniors would respond that too much work would be required; the actual percentage was zero. Committee members were unanimous in their reaction that this result captured a truth about the academic program at . . .: that with a few notable exceptions it places a minimum of demands upon the student or serious involvement with the learning process. To merely increase the quantity of work would be folly, but more rigorous standards designed to encourage growth and mastery of meaningful skills seems a must. (The recommendations of the report included several changes designed to strengthen the academic environment.)

> Unless the character of those who withdraw is changing over grade levels, one can argue that the relatively comparable percentages for the first three years lead to the inference that possibly the same causes of unhappiness continue to persist during this period. Whatever the reasons, it is essential that these be explored in a crash research program. It is, of course, necessary to ask whether the University can tolerate an 11 or 12 percent per year withdrawal rate. To some this may appear low or to be expected considering the nature of the students; however, to the writers it is still more than adequate cause for self-scrutiny.

In response to evidence that the actual proportion of students seeking graduate degrees after four years is substantially below the expected proportion, another institutional report includes the following:

The committee feels strongly that one of the primary functions of a private, liberal arts college is to provide a rigor-
ous broadly based preparation for professional study; we view
with alarm the indication which the ACE data give us that the
process of earning a B.A. at . . . might discourage advanced
degree work. The conclusion of this report contains our specific recommendations in this area.

Misinterpretation

Although most committees were reasonably accurate in their
data interpretations, in a few instances potentially serious misinterpretations occur. In one report, misinterpretations justify certain actions to be taken by the administration, even though the data suggest
that no action or perhaps the opposite action is indicated.

Misinterpretation sometimes resulted from using the impact data
in a normative rather than an absolute sense. For example, on the
item about student satisfaction with research library facilities, more
than half the students at virtually every institution indicated that they
are either satisfied or very satisfied. So in an absolute sense, one
could be reassured since the majority of students express satisfaction. Thus, in one private college, data showing that 39 percent of
the students are dissatisfied with the library are cited as positive
evidence of good library facilities, although the expected rate of dissatisfaction was only 24 percent.

Some data are so complex and the interpretative process so time-
consuming that misinterpretations may not be detected. Decision
makers often do not have the time or the sophistication to verify interpretations by someone who may have a vested interest in the results. In any further dissemination effort, at least two persons should
examine all data and develop interpretations of implications for institutional policy. Any discrepancies in these independently derived
interpretations could be resolved by recourse to the original data.

In the report of one private college, the research staff detected
serious data misinterpretations only after the followup visit. These
misinterpretations came to light during the reliability studies of the
original report ratings, when major disagreement among the three
staff members occurred in rating the "data-relatedness" of the report. Returning to the original data to resolve the discrepancies revealed the interpretative errors.

Some difficulties in interpretation are due largely to the complexity of the data, a problem discussed below.

CONTENT

That the content of the student data is critical to a project such
as this was apparent because virtually everone concerned—committee members, consultants, and staff—had something to say about particular items, offering suggestions for modifications and for new data.
While these suggestions were sometimes contradictory, they were
sufficiently consistent to suggest that certain data were used more than
others and that additional data in other areas would have been useful.

Student Satisfaction

By far the most widely used data concerned student satisfaction
with the institution. Satisfaction with the undergraduate experience is
an objective probably shared by most institutions. At the same time,
student dissatisfaction is a potential cause for concern among faculty
and administrators.

Committees made most use of the items on satisfaction with particular aspects of the institution, such as outlets for creative activities,
instructional quality, and adequate advice and guidance from faculty,
noting frequently that these items were not specific enough. Members
of several committees wanted more detailed ratings on student academic and social life. They also wanted more information on student
services, including accessibility of counselors and advisors, quality
of counseling, and whether or not students thought they had been helped
by guidance. In the academic area, some members would have preferred student ratings of instruction in specific majors (for example,
chemistry, physics) rather than in broad curricular areas (for example, natural and social sciences).

Other areas where additional evidence of student satisfaction
would have been useful include the administration (too authoritarian?
too remote? too permissive?), faculty characteristics (too old? too
inexperienced? dull?), and the curriculum (not enough options? too
many requirements? too easy? too difficult?).

Another problem with most satisfaction questions was that the
level of satisfaction in any institution was usually too high to generate much concern among faculty or administrators; most students
in most colleges are more satisfied than dissatisfied with their undergraduate college experience. Most committees recognized this
problem and attempted to cope with it by focusing more on the discrepancies between expected and actual satisfaction levels rather
than on absolute levels of expressed satisfaction.

Attrition

For most committees, data on dropout rates were second in importance only to data on student satisfaction. Except in the most selective institutions, where attrition rates are extremely low, nearly every institution is concerned about its dropout problem.

Most of the 13 institutions that produced reports focused on the discrepancy between expected and actual dropout rates. Perhaps the greatest limitation of these data was the absence of reasons for dropping out. It is one thing to know that students are dropping out at a rate greater than expected from their entering characteristics, but quite another to know why. The data packets (see Annex A) contained some intepretative guides to help institutions understand these expected-actual discrepancies, but these guides were apparently much too generalized and difficult to translate into specific institutional action. A recent longitudinal study[1] indicates specific ways in which institutions can deal with high dropout rates. Any future efforts to disseminate information on attrition should include a detailed summary of these findings, as well as information on why students leave college.

More information on the current activities of dropouts would also have been useful. Several committee members expressed interest in how many dropouts had transferred to other institutions, how many were working, how many were married, and so forth. Such normative information, including expected-actual percentages for the college, would have been useful.

Careers and Major Fields

Although institutions used data on careers and majors, they were usually not able to grasp the major implication of such data: that expected-actual discrepancies in the proportions of students taking various majors or pursuing various careers say something about the relative appeal of different courses of study within the institution. Thus, if the actual proportion of students in a particular field is substantially below the expected proportion, it is possible that the field in question may be driving students away because of poor teaching, too many requirements, and so forth; or that competing fields may be drawing students away because of especially attractive programs or instructors. Some traffic among fields is the norm; the impact data on expected-actual discrepancies give the institution some basis to judge whether this traffic is typical or atypical.

The specific categories of these data were too gross. Because the number of students in any college was small (N = 100 - 200), detailed categories were not used. A striking example of the problem caused by the large categories occurred at the Coast Guard Academy, where the many students choosing "military officer" as a career were grouped together in the "other" category. Since academy officials were interested in the extent to which the undergraduate experience encouraged or discouraged students from pursuing such a career, confounding this choice with the mixed choices in the "other" category greatly reduced the value of these data for policy analysis.

This problem could be solved by generating the data for individual institutions by the finest possible categories permitting the institution to combine categories in whatever manner meets their policy needs. As long as the expected proportions of students in any given category are based on nationally derived formulas where the sample sizes for even the infrequent categories are adequate, any given institution with a few or no students choosing any particular category would not pose a serious problem in reporting data.

Educational Aspirations

A few committees used data on the impact of the institution on student plans for graduate and professional training. Such information is limited in that its relevance to institutional objectives is not always clear. Should the institution encourage the student interest in postgraduate training? Is such training appropriate for all students? Is it more important to stimulate interest in professional than in graduate training? Although few committees dealt with such issues, some reports implicitly place a high value on stimulating student interest in graduate or professional education. In these instances, the committee apparently considered student interest in postgraduate education a reflection of their attitudes toward their undergraduate education.

Religious Orientation

Committee interest in data on student religious orientation was minimal, with a few notable exceptions. This general lack of interest no doubt reflects the avowed secularism of most higher educational institutions.

Most religiously affiliated institutions were, of course, interested in the extent to which attendance there affected student religious orientations. This concern was not, however, limited entirely to institutions with a formal religious orientation. The committee at one nonsectarian institution, for example, made the following interpretative use of the data on religion:

> After four years, the number of students expressing a
> religious preference declined to 42 percent Protestant,
> 33 percent Catholic, with 19 percent expressing no re-
> ligious preference. Measured against the general na-
> tional decline in religious commitment during the college
> years, the impact of . . . appears to be positive, with
> actual minus estimated percentages computing at 15
> percentage points higher than projected. Since attend-
> ance at chapel has been mandatory, this figure is per-
> haps not surprising; it may also be that the relative
> socioeconomic homogeneity of the student population
> is an additional factor here. In any event, these impact
> data appear generally supportive to institutional goals.

This particular use of impact data provides another example of the value of expected-actual discrepancies. In spite of a decline between freshman and senior years in the absolute proportion of students electing a formal religious preference, the institution was able to identify a positive impact on religious preference by reference to the normative data on expected-actual discrepancies. In other words, even though the decline in the proportion of students choosing a formal religion was absolute, this decline proved substantially less than the decline among comparable students elsewhere.

Trends in Entering Freshman Characteristics

Although information on successive classes of entering freshmen was included in the data packet primarily because it was available (and therefore regarded by some as "filler" not really germane to institutional impact), several institutions used these data extensively. In one private college, for example, the committee made the following observation when it found that the entering freshmen were substantially younger than freshmen in general:

> When our committee looked at these figures, some mem-
> bers wondered whether liberal arts institutions like ours

might not be overlooking an opportunity to improve the
age mix within the student body. Nationally we find a
somewhat broader range.

Similarly, the report of a private university contains the following observation:

It is also apparent that our freshmen have been more
career-oriented than is the norm. Yet, a number of
policies and practices in the university do not seem
to acknowledge this factor. For example, students
are, at present, oriented more toward an academic
major than toward developing a career. . . . Unless
the university can adequately respond to the expressed
and implied needs of these students, it is likely that
many may choose to go elsewhere.

Private institutions tend to show more interest than public institutions in data on entering freshmen. In particular, the private
institutions, which at the time of the study were beginning to confront
declining enrollments, are concerned about preserving their attrac-
tion to potential students and, in some cases, appealing to new student
constituencies. Some committee members remarked that future surveys of entering freshmen would be more useful if they provided information on why students choose the institution they attend. Presumably, such information would provide a better understanding of
how to attract particular students.

National Results on Environmental Impact

The data packets also contained a summary of the major findings
on institutional characteristics that affect different student outcomes.
This section was included to provide committee members with some
basis to interpret their own institution's special impact on students.
These national data showed, for example, that large institutions tend
to generate more student complaints about faculty contact than do
small institutions; that is, actual student dissatisfaction tends to exceed expected dissatisfaction in the larger institutions. Institutions
were expected to use these data to interpret their own results (for
example, if a large institution had more student dissatisfaction with
faculty contacts than expected, this deviation could be regarded as
consistent with the norms for large institutions; however, if such a
deviation occurred in a small institution, the committee could conclude that their institution was atypical).

Both the institutional reports and the on-site followups indicated that committees made little use of these data, in spite of our expectation that they could help to interpret data for any given institution. In all likelihood, many committees were simply unaware of the relevance of this section, despite recommendations that they use it. Conceivably, the magnitude and complexity of the interpretative task was too great to incorporate this additional information.

Whatever the explanation, it would be premature to conclude that national data of this sort have no value. The results suggest that committees need more direct assistance in using normative findings. Clearly, utilization of national normative data on institutional impact should be a principal agenda item for any training sessions involving committee chairpersons or members (see Chapter 8).

Suggestions for Additional Data

Committee members made a number of suggestions about important areas of student development or institutional functioning not covered in the data packets. The most suggestions concerned academic life: student study habits, number of study hours, preferred instructional styles and techniques and, as one committee member stated during the followup visit, "data pertinent to the student's academic life that are easily interpreted into action by administrators."

Other specific concerns included sexual attitudes and behavior, drug use, interpersonal relationships between men and women and between different racial groups, fairness and adequacy of financial aid policies, reasons for staying in or changing major fields, and attitudes about controversial issues.

DATA ANALYSIS

Other than simple marginal tabulations based on the freshman data, the bulk of the data consisted of expected and actual scores for each institution on the various student outcome measures. Despite a lengthy explanation of the regression techniques used to compute these measures, many committee members had difficulty understanding these data. In some cases, telephone conversations or correspondence could clarify the data. However, in some colleges, continuing confusion within the committee was apparently exploited by methodologist-critics (see Chapters 7 and 8), who seized upon this uncertainty to undermine confidence in the data.

In spite of these problems, most committees, including some
that were methodologically unsophisticated, understood the basic
analyses underlying the impact data. One reasonably good grasp of
the analysis is shown in this excerpt from the report of a public
college:

> The presentation of both actual and "projected" responses
> is a very useful analysis device. It aids the institution in
> identifying abnormalities, or at least deviation from the
> expected. It gives the institution a reference to make
> judgments. It also allows the school to identify possible
> problem areas which would not normally be identified.
> For example, if 12 percent were dissatisfied with the
> social life on the campus, this might not be regarded as
> significant unless one knows that a "normal" level is
> 18 percent. This would allow a much different analysis
> picture than if the figures were reversed or if only the
> actual figure was provided.

Some institutions complained that the satisfaction scales were
dichotomized between the "on the fence" and "dissatisfied" points.
Before the pilot testing, the plan was to use the mean satisfaction
scores rather than the dichotomized measures. However, the pilot
testing showed that mean scores actually provided less information
than the percentage dissatisfied. While it is possible to provide dis-
tributions of actual responses to each satisfaction scale, it would
probably not be feasible to calculate separate expected scores for
each scale point, and it would be particularly difficult for the middle
points. One could, of course, use multiple group discriminant analysis
techniques to calculate such scores, although these techniques would
not capitalize on the ordinal character of the satisfaction scales.
Perhaps the best compromise would be to calculate the expected percentage only for the satisfied-dissatisfied dichotomy and to provide
the entire distribution of responses to the actual satisfaction scale.
Most committees had difficulty understanding that the formulas
for calculating the expected scores were obtained from the national
sample of students attending all institutions and that the expected
scores for their institution were obtained by applying these general
formulas to the data for their students. Another point sometimes
missed was that the general formulas were derived using the student
as the unit of analysis, whereas the data provided each institution
were aggregated across all students at that institution.
Some committee members would have preferred that statistically
significant differences for expected-actual discrepancies be flagged,
a refinement with both advantages and disadvantages. Should

institutions be encouraged to ignore discrepancies that fail to reach statistical significance? What levels of significance should be used? Should institutions be encouraged to emphasize differences that happen to be statistically significant, even if the magnitude of the differences is of little pratical consequence? While the balance of opinion from committee members, consultants, and staff appeared to favor the addition of significance tests to the data packets, others thought such refinements would clutter up the reports and discourage attempts by statistically naive persons to interpret the substantive findings. As a compromise, general guidelines for persons concerned about statistical significance could be provided to indicate, given the college sample size, the approximate size of an expected-actual discrepancy that would be required to reach statistical significance for different expected score values.

As a major refinement for future dissemination efforts, one could calculate results separately for certain potentially important student subgroups. Such subgroups would include men and women, blacks and whites, and—for the complex univiersities—schools or other broad curricular groupings (engineering, business, and so forth). A recent national study of dropouts,[2] for example, suggests that an undifferentiated analysis of the type used in this study can mask important interactions with variables such as race and sex. Separate subgroup regressions would enable staff members to consider such interactions and to provide the institutions with impact data on each subgroup. The principal requirement for such an analysis, of course, is sufficient students within any given category to provide reliable discrepancies between expected and actual scores.

One final refinement for future multivariate analyses involving expected and actual scores is corrections for measurement errors in the predictor battery. Such errors, which cause one to underestimate the relationship between predicted and actual scores, can produce biased results, particularly if the institution's entering students differ greatly from entering students nationally. Statistical corrections for such errors are possible.[3]

TIMELINESS OF DATA

Practically everyone agreed that the potential impact of student data is reduced if the data are no longer regarded as current. The fact that the longitudinal data for this project were two years old made it possible to obstruct committee activities by playing the "time game" (see Chapter 7). One must recognize, of course, that any data will necessarily be historical.

In future studies, every effort should be made to complete data analyses quickly so the delay between collection and feedback to institutions is minimal. Problems of timeliness, however, are not solved merely by having the most current data. No matter how recent, data on any single class of students may have limited value if that class is regarded as atypical or otherwise unique. Whether or not any institution was justified in rejecting data on this basis, the more skeptical committee members tended to dismiss certain findings for that reason. The best solution here is to have available data on several different classes. While such data are expensive and time-consuming to collect, they provide a way to replicate findings from any single class and negate claims that data on a single class are atypical. Of course, if data on several classes produce inconsistent results, the institution is justified in questioning the generalizability of data from any single class.

The more enterprising institutions in the participant sample (St. Norbert, Ohio Dominican, and Western Illinois) independently undertook studies of more recent student classes to verify trends in the data provided through this project. For the most part, these surveys produced results strikingly similar to those provided in the project, although the surveys of more recent classes usually followed different methodologies. Dropouts, for example, were not included, and surveys were administered at different times. While excluding dropouts should increase student satisfaction, expressed student dissatisfaction increased slightly in these additional surveys at all three institutions. These higher rates may be attributable in part to the particular time and conditions under which the additional surveys were conducted. Student criticism of an institution probably peaks during late spring of the senior year (when the extra surveys were conducted), declining somewhat during the summer and fall following graduation (when the ACE followup was conducted).

In short, institutions that want to replicate data from any given class of students should make sure that their survey techniques utilize comparable sampling procedures (all students from a given class, rather than just the graduating seniors), as well as comparable methodologies (surveys mailed at similar times).

QUANTITY OF DATA

This project provides no simple answer to the question of how much student data institutions really need and can utilize. The project was frequently criticized by committee members for providing too much data. At the same time, numerous suggestions for additional items indicated that more data were desired by many institutions.

That many institutions were not prepared to handle the amount of material they received is suggested by several reports that ignored major parts of the data. However, other institutions showed an almost insatiable appetite, innundating us with special requests for data from other samples of students and for additional tabulations.

The amount of data is a function of the number of questions in the student surveys and the number and complexity of the tabulations. The followup visits indicated that it is difficult to have too many different items of data, as long as the institutions are able to relate each item to some institutional issue. Providing excessively detailed data tabulations makes coherent presentations of results difficult. Future projects should provide only the simplest and most straightforward tabulations in the main data packet, reserving detailed breakdowns and analyses for supplementary reports or appendices.

Probably more significant than the sheer volume of data is the mode of organization and presentation. If data are organized in a meaningful way and presented coherently, institutions are probably capable of digesting a large amount.

ORGANIZATION AND PRESENTATION

Concern about content and analysis can cause one to forget that the organization of the data and their presentation to the institution are critical. Researchers who collect and analyze student data are prone to ignore a self-evident truth: The recipient will probably follow the data organization used by the provider. In this study, the data were not ordered by any particular plan, other than putting the most important first. Thus, an opportunity for a significant impact on the way data were used was lost.

The major reason to organize student data is to help the institution see their relevance to its program and policies. In most higher educational institutions today, much energy is devoted to two general problem areas: institutional survival and internal politics. If data can be related to either issue, institutions are likely to see them as relevant. For private institutions, admissions, student recruitment, fund raising, and dropouts are relevant to survival. Dropout rates and institutional accountability relate to survival for public institutions, where the problem is not so much a matter of remaining in operation as it is of receiving reasonable public funding. For both public and private institutions, evaluations of faculty and of student services are probably relevant to internal politics.

Organizing the data around major institutional functions, such as admissions, curriculum and academic program, and student services, would enable institutions to identify local policy concerns for which the data are relevant. Many items in the current study could have been organized in this way. Nearly all satisfaction items, for example, were concerned either with the academic program or with student services. Data on degree aspirations and careers are relevant to the academic program, while descriptive data on entering freshman classes are relevant to admissions. Impact data on attrition, however, are probably related to all areas of institutional functioning, although these data could have been related to more specific institutional functions if the reasons for leaving the college had been obtained during the followup.

The most frequent complaint about organization concerned failure to present results separately for student subgroups. This was a particular problem in the large universities, where schools and colleges within the institution are virtually autonomous units with different administrative policies and academic programs. Organizing the results around major curricular groups (such as natural sciences and humanities) would have been helpful to smaller colleges. Several institutions could have used data presented separately for students in experimental colleges or other special institutional subunits.

Organizing data by student subgroup, of course, requires knowledge of each subgroup. Sorting students into major curricular groupings or into traditional university schools and colleges, such as education or engineering, can probably be done with reasonable accuracy by using the student's initial choice of a major field, readily available from the freshman questionnaire. Sorting into experimental colleges or other special subunits, however, requires specific knowledge not usually available in a national survey instrument.

Although special tabulations by curricular units were provided to the few institutions requesting them, their value was limited because of the few student respondents at any given institution. In future studies, the minimum of students needed within each major subgroup should be determined before followup data are collected.

Some institutions could have made greater use of the data if they had been presented separately for persisters, transfers, and dropouts. Such breakdowns would have been particularly useful in evaluating the data on career changes, degree aspirations, and satisfaction. Again, a larger student sample would have been required, particularly for those institutions with relatively low dropout rates.

Most committees experienced difficulty in translating data into recommendations for action. For example, if the actual dropout rate is higher than expected from entering freshman characteristics, what remedial actions are possible? Or, conversely, if the actual rate is lower than expected, what practices should be continued to ensure that the institution will maintain its superior holding power?

This problem could be solved by presenting results on institutional impact together with summaries of potential remedies involving manipulatable variables. While this solution may seem unrealistic, a recent national study of dropouts[4] provides potential remedies directly controllable by the institution. Conceivably, other student outcomes could be similarly analyzed before any future data dissemination effort was undertaken.

The difficulty experienced by the committees in interpreting the expected-actual data on institutional impact might be lessened if the impact results were accompanied by more explanation of how they were obtained and what they might mean. For example, data on actual versus expected dropout rates might include:

1. The actual dropout rate for the institution.

2. The actual dropout rate for the population of institutions.

3. The expected dropout rate based on entering student characteristics.

4. An explanation for any deviation between 2 and 3 (above), for example, "Your expected rate is relatively high because your entering freshmen include a relatively high proportion of married students, veterans, and students with mediocre grades in high school; students with these characteristics drop out relatively frequently."

5. The difference between expected and actual dropout rates (1 and 3, above).

6. The explanation for 5 (above), for example, "Your actual dropout rate is less than your expected rate in part because a relatively high proportion of students have jobs on campus and a relatively high proportion also participate in extracurricular activities; both of these factors reduce dropout rates."

Another way to facilitate data use is to provide each institution with examples that show how other institutions have used various items. After seeing how items can be translated into recommendations for action, the recipient institution may be encouraged to attempt similar interpretations of its own data.

A number of committee members thought that the theoretical rationale for various items should have been provided in the data packets. While the underlying significance of student career choices and degree aspirations may seem self-evident, many committee members did not understand why such data were included. With career data, for example, one must understand how the institution affects student career choice, particularly if preparing students for particular types of careers is an institutional goal. Moreover, career changes during the undergraduate years also reveal something about the relative attractiveness or strength of different curricular programs. If students defect from a particular field more often than expected, this may be symptomatic of a potential weakness in that program or of excessive curricular demands.

In short, the usefulness of data can be enhanced by providing the underlying rationale and potential importance of each item together with the actual results.

Committee members and consultants made additional suggestions for enhancing the impact of the data by modifying presentation. These suggestions ranged from audio-visual aids to flagging or otherwise highlighting large deviations from expectation. One consultant suggested a computerized press release describing the major findings, with the actual values plugged into the individual institution's release. A similar release was used with the 1972 CIRP survey of entering freshmen. Although such releases are difficult to design, many institutions have spoken highly of their usefulness. If nothing else, such a release would draw attention to the data and their possible significance.

NOTES

1. Alexander W. Astin, <u>Preventing Students from Dropping Out</u> (San Francisco: Jossey-Bass, 1975).

2. Ibid.

3. Alexander W. Astin, "The Methodology of Research on College Impact: Part One," <u>Sociology of Education</u> 43 (Summer 1970).

4. Astin, <u>Preventing Students from Dropping Out</u>.

10

POSSIBILITIES
FOR THE FUTURE

This pilot project has demonstrated that many different types of colleges and universities are capable of investing a significant effort in reviewing a comprehensive set of data concerning their own students. Many institutions are able to make meaningful interpretations of relatively complex longitudinal data and, in certain instances, to develop recommendations for changes in policy based on these interpretations. Under certain conditions, they are also able to implement these changes within a relatively brief period. And finally, in spite of many limitations in the data and method of dissemination, most institutions expressed strong interest in participating in future dissemination efforts of this type.

While these findings suggest that further efforts to improve colleges for students on a larger scale may prove useful, the impact of these efforts can be increased substantially by certain modifications and refinements in the procedures. The previous chapters include specific recommendations for changes in several areas: the design of a student data base for use in decision making (Chapter 9), the overall strategy for dissemination (Chapter 6), identifying and coping with institutional defenses (Chapter 7), making committees work effectively (Chapter 8), and preparing and reviewing committee reports (Chapter 4).

Future attempts to utilize student data should consider at least three additional issues: institutional conservatism, dissemination resources, and evaluation of impact. These issues are examined here.

A THEORY OF INSTITUTIONAL CONSERVATISM

During the peak years of campus unrest in the late 1960s, U.S. higher educational institutions were frequently accused of conserv-

atism. While these allegations came largely from the political
left, the early 1970s have witnessed similar criticism from persons
all along the political spectrum.

Regardless of the validity of these charges, the U.S. system of
higher education is subject to internal and external forces that render
its institutions highly resistant to significant change. In retrospect,
it seems that most instances of failure in this pilot project are trace-
able, at least in part, to these conservative tendencies. If this impression is valid, future dissemination efforts will be more likely to succeed if they consider these forces and how they interact.

Institutional conservatism derives from the interplay of at least
three factors: the structure and function of institutions, the traditional
role and personal dispositions of administrators and faculty, and external societal demands. Of these, faculty are by far the most important single influence.

Institutional Structure and Functioning

The operation of colleges and universities has become highly
ritualized. Much of this ritual is keyed to the calendar, so fundamental
functions are repeated on an annual or seasonal basis almost like
clockwork: application deadlines, letters of acceptance, orientation,
registration, class schedules, midterms, finals, vacations, commence-
ment, and so forth. These regularly programmed activities create
an annual operation cycle that is repetitive, predictable, and thus
highly resistant to change.

The governance of most institutions has become highly bureau-
cratized. Not only has the formal administrative structure become
heavily laden with assistant and associate deans and vice presidents,
but also the faculty advisory and governance system has become a
maze of councils, standing committees, ad hoc committees and task
forces. Change under these circumstances becomes exceedingly difficult since decision-making power is highly diffused and proposals
for change must run the gamut of review committees, departments,
councils, and administrators.

Faculty and Administrators

The faculty role typically contains much personal and professional
autonomy. Faculty members usually have considerable freedom in
deciding what to teach, how to teach it, what to study, how to study

it, and how to allocate their time. This autonomy increases with
seniority and tenure. Naturally, faculty value their autonomy highly
and guard vigilantly against attempts to take it away.

Faculty often view administrators with a curious mixture of fear,
suspicion, and contempt. Fear arises from the potential threat to
faculty autonomy posed by the administrator's real or imagined power
Suspicion results from the faculty's traditional dislike for authoritaria
or hierarchical systems and their concern that administrators may
actually use their decision-making power. Contempt stems from the
belief that faculty become administrators either because they are in-
competent teachers and scholars or because they value power and
authority more than teaching or scholarship. Consequently, many
faculty, almost by instinct, oppose administrative proposals for
change. With the current trend toward faculty unionism,[1] this opposi-
tion is likely to increase.

At the same time, administrators (most of whom were once faculty members) have generally accepted the theory that faculty autonom
must be protected at all costs and that authoritarian or otherwise
nondemocratic practices must be avoided. Indeed, many administrators will argue that they have "no real power" and that they merely
carry out the will of the faculty. As a result, administrators usually
refuse to act on any proposal without first running it through cumbersome faculty review and advisory mechanism. Cohen and March[2]
have described this situation as "organized anarchy."

Even if a proposal for change originates within the faculty, the
background and training of most academics militate against acceptance. One major objective of graduate training in almost all disciplines is to develop skill in "critical thinking." Graduate students
are continuously rewarded by faculty for demonstrating their critical
abilities. What this often comes down to, however, is the detection
of flaws in the views or work of others. Typical arenas where these
critical abilities are exhibited by both faculty and students are departmental colloquia, faculty meetings, and doctoral oral examina-
tions. In short, this tradition of displaying one's critical skill naturally leads faculty to view any proposal for change initially in terms
of its defects.

Institutional conservatism does not go unnoticed by faculty members. Indeed, most faculty will readily admit that "it's hard to get
anything changed around here." Ironically, this partial recognition
of the difficulty exacerbates the problem by creating an atmosphere
of institutional pessimism, a belief that significant change is either
impossible or, at best, very difficult to achieve. This pessimism,
in turn, discourages many faculty from active support of attractive
proposals because they think their efforts will be futile.

When pushed to account for institutional inertia, faculty often cite the cumbersome administrative structure or even the conservatism or obstreperousness of their own colleagues. What many faculty are unable or unwilling to face, however, is how they personally contribute to the process: mistrust of and even contempt toward administrators and outside coordinating agencies, blind protection of faculty autonomy, a tendency to be critical of any new idea and to display these critical skills before colleagues, passivity in the face of obstructionist colleagues, pessimism about the prospects for significant change, and reluctance to volunteer time and effort to support promising proposals for change.

External Demands

Boards of trustees, alumni groups, and the local, state, and federal governments, on which most institutions now rely heavily for financial support, exert control over institutions. While these external agencies may on occasion provide the impetus for institutional change (for example, eliminating sex bias in hiring faculty), the fact that these agencies rely heavily on institutions to perform certain services in certain traditional ways makes them a potentially strong force supporting institutional conservatism.[3]

The trend toward more centralized planning and budgeting for public systems of higher education and the increasing pressures from outside agencies, such as legislatures, state budget offices, and coordinating boards, for greater accountability have been particularly effective in reinforcing faculty and institutional conservatism. No matter how it is presented, such central "coordination" is interpreted as a potential threat to autonomy. Thus, faculty and administrators are inclined to rush to the defense of the status quo and to stifle innovation. Traditional practices and procedures that might otherwise be subjected to regular review are accepted as gospel, so that attempts by individual faculty to apply their highly developed critical skills to established institutional practices and procedures are discouraged.

The net result of these forces—the interplay among faculty, administrators, and external agencies, coupled with the academic tradition of criticism—is that any proposal for change has a dubious future in most institutions. Even if a new idea is attractive enough to appeal to a majority of the faculty, their support is generally so fragile that a sufficiently determined and articulate faculty critic can usually succeed in scuttling the proposal. In this sense, then, individual faculty members in most institutions are capable of wielding a great deal of negative power.

MAXIMIZING RESOURCE USE

The pilot project was not designed to take advantage of the internal resources that many institutions have to enhance the overall impact of an effort to improve the educational environment for students. The greatest potential institutional resource, of course, is the time of students and staff. Could more students and staff be involved in the dissemination effort? Because of the complexities of interpreting data and making appropriate policy recommendations (see Chapters 8 and 9), it is probably a poor idea simply to hand over raw data to large numbers of persons around the campus. However, drafts of the committee's final report based on these data could be given much wider circulation. Obvious channels for communication and evaluation of the reports would be the student newspaper, alumni bulletins, and other periodicals circulated within the institution. Open forums involving all segments of the academic community could also discuss the report's conclusions and implications.

The entire dissemination effort could also be institutionalized. The committee or task force, for example, could be a standing institutional committee with responsibility to continue evaluation of new student data. At the same time, the office of institutional research or some comparable office could be given continuing responsibility to collect and analyze longitudinal student data on a regular basis. Close working relationships between the task force and this office would ensure that adequate data would be forthcoming regularly, that future surveys could be designed to fill gaps in the current data, and that data of limited usefulness could be eliminated. An initial dissemination effort could be used to train the office of institutional research to collect and analyze data for future projects.

The higher education community also has substantial resources to enhance the impact of a student data dissemination project at the interinstitutional level. If a future effort utilized data from the Cooperative Institutional Research Program, the effort could, in theory, involve the more than 600 institutions currently participating in that program. If resources to support longitudinal followups at each institution were unavailable, the most interested institutions might be willing to support the cost of their own followups.

In addition, multiinstitutional agencies, such as the National Center for Higher Education Management Systems, city and state-wide coordinating agencies, professional associations (for example, the Association for Institutional Research), and existing institutional consortia (for example, the College Research Center or the Associated Colleges of the Midwest) could contribute to a major dissemination effort. Many of these agencies and associations already have substantial student data bases that might be utilized in a coordinated effort to improve institutional programs.

EVALUATION

Evaluation of the pilot project (Chapter 5) was limited because of the small number of participating institutions and the relatively brief time available to assess the impact of the project. For any future dissemination effort, two aspects of the evaluation should be given major attention: criteria for assessing project impact and design of the evaluation research.

Outcome Criteria

In some respects it was unrealistic to assess such a short-term pilot project primarily in terms of implementation or nonimplementation of actions proposed in the committee reports. Indeed, the follow-up visits suggested that the project had had significant impacts unanticipated in the reports. These apparent effects were often defined in vague terms, such as "increased awareness" of students' problems and needs. Some suggested initially that the main impact of the project might be a placebo effect rather than changes derived directly from data. It was reassuring, when these side effects did occur, that they concerned student development, which was after all the main focus of the study.

For future studies, these indirect effects of project participation could be assessed in several ways. The values and attitudes of faculty and administrators could be surveyed to determine if student development, in contrast to scholarly productivity, fund raising, and other competing goals, has increased its position in the hierarchy of priorities. Unstructured interviews could determine of faculty and administrators make spontaneous statements about students and their development more frequently than they did before they were involved in the project. A longer term evaluation could assess parallel changes in the students' perceptions of institutional concern for their development.

Another apparent side effect of the pilot project was to increase institutional interest in student data and, for some institutions, to strengthen their capability for collecting and analyzing such data. While these impacts were difficult to demonstrate empirically because pretests of these capabilities were inadequate, anecdotal evidence from the followups convinced the visiting teams that such changes had occurred.

A related measure of behavioral change that could be incorporated into future evaluations is the frequency with which top administrators ask for and read reports derived from student data. It would be important to know, for example, whether administrators of institutions participating in CIRP are more likely to study and use reports from the annual freshman survey after they participate in such a dissemination project.

Ultimate criteria for evaluating future dissemination projects would, of course, involve assessments of changes in student development. One would hope the project would reduce dropout rates and increase student satisfaction with the undergraduate experience. Other areas of possible influence are student aspirations, interests, and attitudes.

An examination of data on consecutive entering classes led some institutions to recommend that larger proportions of students be recruited from certain subgroups (such as minorities, older students, and low-income students). These recommendations suggest that future evaluations should include data on changes in the characteristics of entering students as additional outcome measures.

Methodology and Design

Two basic elements in the evaluation design for the pilot study should probably be used again in evaluations of future dissemination efforts: longitudinal data and a matched control group of institutions that are not participating in the dissemination effort. These two design features are, of course, mutually reinforcing: The value of an experimental and matched control group is enhanced if pretest and posttest data are available from both groups. In the pilot effort, the value of the control group was diminished substantially because data on recently proposed and implemented changes were not available for comparison with the experimental institutions.

Because the initial impression of institutional enthusiasm for the research project frequently proved misleading, the fact that the control institutions were not a strictly random sample from the project population was probably not a major handicap. Nevertheless, for future dissemination efforts it would be preferable to select, on paper, twice as many experimental institutions as needed and then select the actual participants randomly. Those not selected would become control institutions. In this way, causal inferences about program impact could be made with more confidence.

The sample for the pilot effort was too small for any sophisticated empirical analysis of program impact. Resources permitting, a minimum sample of 50 experimental and 50 control institutions should be selected for future dissemination projects. In addition, the longitudinal time to assess project impact should be extended to at least two and preferably three years beyond completion of the one-year dissemination phase. An interim assessment of early impact could be carried out after the first followup year.

Interpreting evaluative data from the pilot project presented some inferential problems, particularly in determining whether participation in the project caused changes (see Chapter 5). If a report contains a recommendation for change and followup assessments indicate that the change has been implemented, it is difficult to conclude that the change cannot be attributed at least in part to the project. But, in fact, most such changes could not be attributed to the project. Apparently, the report was often used to promote pet ideas for change already conceived before the project got under way.

A comprehensive assessment of changes that are ongoing or proposed should be made before any project is launched. These pretest data could provide the basis for posttest followups after the dissemination phase is completed.

Evaluations of future dissemination efforts most certainly should involve longitudinal data from a larger sample of experimental and control institutions. In particular, much more comprehensive pretest assessments must be made both of the institution's current policies and practices and of ongoing and proposed changes. These preliminary data can provide a base against which changes can be assessed with followup data.

NOTES

1. Everett C. Ladd and Seymour M. Lipset, Professors, Unions, and American Higher Education (New York: McGraw-Hill, 1973).
2. Michael D. Cohen and James G. March, The American College President (New York: McGraw-Hill, 1974).
3. Heinz Eulan and Harold Quinley, State Officials and Higher Education (New York: McGraw-Hill, 1970).

ANNEX A:
SAMPLE DATA PACKET
SENT TO ONE OF THE 19
PARTICIPATING INSTITUTIONS

COVERING LETTER FOR DATA PACKET

American Council on Education
One DuPont Circle
Washington, D.C. 20036

Office of Research

December 21, 1972

Cooperative Institutional
Research Program

Dear Colleague:

Here is the ACE data packet with which you will be working during the next few months. The tables and text have been kept to a minimum to shorten the reading time required. As you can see, we have given a title to the project: subsequent communications will use the abbreviated name, "ACE Data for Decisions."

After studying the tables, you may find that some of the additional data listed in Appendix B would be helpful in your analysis. We will do our best to fill requests for these data. Limitations in personnel and computer facilities will determine how promptly we can meet your needs, however, and should demand be great, you can expect some delay. We do hope you will take advantage of the exchange of data with other participating institutions and that you will perhaps extend this exchange to visits and the possible formation of institutional consortia for exchanging ideas.

Further instructions on the project are included in the Introduction. If you have any questions about the instructions or if you believe that you cannot meet the report deadline, please let us know.

Some institutions have asked for more information on the purpose of the reports and ACE's end of the project. The reports from the 19 institutions will be included in a monograph relating the results of the project. The findings from this study will serve as a guide for future feedback efforts of the ACE Office of Research and of other organizations seeking ways to effectively disseminate findings from empirical data as an aid to policy making. As you know, this is a pilot study, and we hope to apply what we learn in this project toward improving the quality of our feedback to all of the institutions in the Cooperative Institutional Research Program. By involving ourselves more intimately with the practical needs and problems confronting colleges and universities, we should be able to relate our future research efforts more directly to the needs of the academic community.

The number of institutions in the project has purposely been kept small so that we can provide personal assistance to the task forces. Please feel free to phone or write whenever you have questions. As mentioned in an earlier letter, if you do have problems that require first-hand assistance, we will try to send an ACE staff member-consultant team to meet with your task force.

We hope you will find the project and the data both enjoyable and productive for your institution. Good luck with your work!

Sincerely,

Linda D. Molm
Research Analyst

PARTICIPATING INSTITUTIONS

Name of Institution	Chairman
Allegheny College Meadville, Pennsylvania 16335	Dr. William P. Wharton Director of Counseling
Franklin and Marshall College Lancaster, Pennsylvania 17604	Dr. Keith Spalding President
Mills College Oakland, California 94613	Dr. Robert J. Wert President
Northwestern University Evanston, Illinois 60201	Mr. Jeremy R. Wilson Planning Coordinator
Ohio Dominican College Columbus, Ohio 43219	Sister Thomas Albert Corbett Director, Institutional Research
St. Louis University St. Louis, Missouri 63103	Mr. W. Patrick Dolan Assistant Academic Vice President
St. Norbert College West DePere, Wisconsin 54178	Dr. Neil J. Webb Administrative Vice President
SUNY at Oswego Oswego, New York 13126	Dr. Gubbi Sachidanandan Research Coordinator
Tulane University New Orleans, Louisiana 70118	Dr. Edward A. Rogge Assistant Provost for Academic Services
U.S. Coast Guard Academy New London, Connecticut 06320	Captain Malcolm J. Williams Director of Admissions
University of Denver Denver, Colorado 80210	Mr. Walden C. Irish Director, Admissions and Records
University of Massachusetts Amherst, Massachusetts 01002	Mr. Richard W. Story Staff Assistant, Counseling Center
University of Michigan Ann Arbor, Michigan 48104	Dr. James R. Bower Associate Director of Admissions

Name of Institution	Chairman
University of Redlands Redlands, California 92373	Dr. Richard A. Andrews Assistant Professor of American History
Vanderbilt University Nashville, Tennessee 37203	Dr. Glen Clanton Associate Provost, Dean for Academic Planning
Vassar College Poughkeepsie, New York 12601	Mr. John Duggan Vice President for Student Affairs/ Professor of Psychology
Washington State University Pullman, Washington 99163	Dr. Mark Hammer Assistant Professor of Business Administration
Western Illinois University Macomb, Illinois 61455	Dr. Charles C. Gilbert III Executive Assistant, Institutional Research and Planning
Williams College Williamstown, Massachusetts 01267	Dr. David Booth Associate Provost

AN INTRODUCTION TO THE PROJECT

The enclosed packet contains the materials that you will be working with during the next few months. While we realize that this information will by no means solve all of the many complex problems involved in running an institution of higher education, we hope it will provide a basis for making decisions and will stimulate continued use of empirical data on students.

In the belief that a structured format hinders creativity, we will offer only a few guidelines on how to work with the data and write the initial report. If you want further suggestions about the form which the project should take, let us know. Otherwise, we will assume that these guidelines were sufficient for you to complete the task successfully.

The project can be conceptualized as consisting of two phases: analysis and implementation. In the first phase, you will analyze the data in this packet (and any additional data you request) and write an initial report covering the findings and the proposed solutions for any "problem areas" on your campus. The deadline for this report, which should be a minimum of 15 pages, is March 31, 1973, or about three months from the time you receive this packet. The report should integrate the following elements: (a) an analysis, based on the ACE data and interpreted by the experience and knowledge of the task force members, of how your institution is affecting your students; (b) a statement of institutional goals (that is, how you want your institution to affect your students) for the areas of student development covered in the data; (c) a delineation of the problem areas suggested by discrepancies between (a) and (b); and (d) specific plans of action for lessening the gap between (a) and (b), again using ACE data and your own knowledge of the resources available and the potential for change on your campus.

The second phase of the project, which may overlap with the first, involves implementing the specific plans of action formulated by the task force and should continue for the remainder of the year. It is presumed that changes of most kinds can be initiated by the 1973-74 academic year. More information on this second phase will be sent to you later.

A few final suggestions may facilitate your work on the project:

1. Be aware of both the strengths and limitations of the ACE data. Most of the data can only suggest what educational problems exist at your institution; they must be supplemented by your own knowledgeability about your campus before conclusions can be drawn. In particular, some of the national data may not apply to your institution, and findings should not be accepted unless supported by your own experiences.
2. Remember that ACE data are "objective" in that they imply no value judgments. Only you can decide which institutional effects are desirable and which are undesirable. Our task is not to impose our goals but to help you to reach yours.
3. Utilize the ACE staff to answer questions about data-gathering techniques, methodological procedures, and possible interpretations or to provide "outside" opinions. Keep in contact with us by phone, letter, or whatever. You might also consider consulting other outside source persons.
4. Get the rest of the campus interested in the project. Although only a few people can work directly with the data, the rest of the college community can be informed about interesting aspects of the data and about the progress of the project through such outlets as the campus newspaper or radio. Talks and letters to alumni are other possible means of giving news about the project. In addition, your campus may offer unique opportunities for spreading the word in other ways.

5.   Get in touch with other institutions participating in the project.
     Visit or consult with schools similar to yours to exchange ideas
     on the data or to discuss common problems. Some of the greatest
     benefits of the project may come from this kind of interaction.

INTERPRETATION OF THE DATA

The data included in this packet were collected as part of the
ACE Cooperative Institutional Research Program (CIRP), a longitudinal
project which began with a pilot study in the fall of 1965 and has now
collected data from more than 500 institutions and two million students. Institutions are sampled so as to be representative of the entire population of two-year colleges, four-year colleges, and universities throughout the United States.* The general plan of the CIRP
is to collect annual input data from all entering freshmen at each of
the participating institutions in the fall and to follow up periodically
a subsample of the same students. Data on college characteristics
are derived from the followup surveys of students, special surveys
of institutions, and secondary sources such as the publications of the
U.S. Office of Education. So far we have conducted a four-year followup of each of the first three freshman classes (1966, 1967, and 1968)
and special followups of these and other classes over shorter time
intervals.
     The rationale behind the CIRP is based upon a conceptual frame-
work consisting of three components: student inputs, student outputs,
and the college environment. For a discussion of the relations among
these components and a more complete description of the CIRP, see
the enclosed manual, The ACE Office of Research: Its Purposes and
Activities.
     The material in this packet was selected specifically to aid in
the formulation of policy. Thus, for ease of reading and of comprehen-
sion, the results are given in percentage or statement form. We have
included three sets of data: (1) college impact data, based on information collected from the students who entered your college in 1966 and
graduated in 1970; (2) trend data, based on comparisons of successive

---

*For a discussion of the sampling design, see John A. Creager,
General Purpose Sampling in the Domain of Higher Education (Wash-
ington, D.C.: American Council on Education, 1968); vol. 3, no. 2,
ACE Research Reports.

classes of freshmen at your institution from 1966 to the present, and
(3) data on college environmental effects, based on national data. We
will explain briefly how these data were obtained and how they should
be interpreted for practical application.

College Impact Data

By college impact (data shown in Tables A.1-A.7) we mean those
effects of the college that bring about changes in the student that are
attributes and potentialities of the student. In other words, to assess
college impact, we must first control for the types and degrees of
change which are due to the characteristics of students themselves
at the time of college entry. The findings presented in this packet
are based on analyses of the comparative impact of different types
of institutions, rather than the comparative effects of college attendance versus nonattendance. Since the methodology is more complex
for this set of data than for the other two sets, it requires a lengthier
explanation.

Data Collection

These data were obtained from students who entered your college
as first-time freshmen in 1966, at which time (during the fall orientation and registration period), they completed the 150-item Student
Information Form (SIF) included in Appendix A. A subsample of
these students was followed up four years later (during the late
summer and fall of 1970) when, presumably, many of them had received the baccalaureate. To conserve costs, groups of 250 students
for whom we had freshman data were selected randomly from the larger institutions; at those institutions enrolling 300 or fewer students,
all students for whom we had freshman data were followed up. The final sample numbered 217 institutions. Approximately 55 percent of the
51,721 students surveyed returned the questionnaire. Their responses
to the followup questionnaire were matched with their responses to
the SIF. These students, for whom both freshman and followup data
were available, constituted the sample used for estimating college
impact. Data on the students' college grade-point average, academic
degrees completed, and scores on high school aptitude tests (SAT,
ACT, or NMSQT) were provided by the institutions during the fall
of 1970. The aptitude test scores were converted to a common scale.

Procedure of Analysis

The followup questionnaire (also in Appendix A) included many items which were repeated verbatim from the SIF, such as those on career choice and degree aspirations. In addition, the questionnaire contained items asking about satisfaction with various aspects of the college. (These items had not, of course, appeared in the freshman questionnaire.) We analyzed the impact of the college on the following student outcomes (as indicated on the followup questionnaire):

Career choice (15 measures: artist, businessman, clergyman, etc.).
Major field (17 measures: Agriculture, Biological Sciences, Business, etc.).
Degree aspirations (2 measures: planning to obtain a bachelor's degree or higher, planning to obtain a doctorate degree or the equivalent).
Religious preference (4 measures: Protestant, Catholic, Jewish, none).
Overall rating of the college. Scored on a five-point scale: very satisfied, satisfied, on the fence, dissatisfied, very dissatisfied. The percentage of students who were dissatisfied or very dissatisfied is shown in the table.
Satisfaction with specific aspects of the college enviornment (11 measures: overall quality of instruction, the variety of science courses, etc.). Scored on a five-point scale: excellent, good, satisfactory, unsatisfactory, very unsatisfactory. The percentage of students who rated an aspect as unsatisfactory or very unsatisfactory is shown in the table.
Ratings of the sufficiency of selected aspects of the college (8 measures: freedom in course selection, social life, and so on). Scored on a three-point scale: too much or too many, just about the right amount, not enough. The percentage of students who said there was too much or not enough of each aspect is shown in the table.
Persistence in college (4 measures: returned for at least a second undergraduate year; received the bachelor's degree; received the bachelor's degree or was still enrolled; received the bachelor's degree, was still enrolled, or had transcripts sent to another institution.)

Additional impact data in the form of mean scores (rather than percentages) are available on a number of other variables that may be of interest to you. (See the list in Appendix C.) Please check any of this additional information which you believe would be useful, and we will send it to you as soon as possible.

To determine the effects of individual institutions on student outcomes, as reflected in the students' responses to the various followup items (i.e., the impact of the institutions on the students), it was first necessary to correct for the fact that colleges differ with respect to the kinds of students that they initially recruit. This control was achieved by using students' responses to the 1966 freshman survey to "predict" their responses to the followup items; the means employed was a standardized statistical procedure, stepwise multiple regression.

For each of the student outcomes listed above, data on the following items from the freshman survey were considered as possible "predictors" of response: (1) demographic and background data: sex, age, parents' income, father's education, mother's education, race, religious background, type of high school attended, high school grades, extracurricular achievements in high school, and sources of financing college; (2) the freshman "pretests" of the followup items or outcomes; (3) the student's high school aptitude test scores (provided by the institutions).

The regression analyses resulted in a predictive equation for each followup item relating a particular response to the item to the freshman characteristics of the students responding in that way. The equation was then applied to the freshman data for each individual student, yielding an "expected" response for that student. The expected responses for all students at a given college were then averaged to yield an estimated percentage for that college.

As a result of this procedure, the percentage of your students who were expected to respond in a certain way (on the basis of their characteristics as freshmen) can be compared with the actual percentage of students who gave the response. In Tables A.1 through A.6,* three percentages are shown. The first is the actual percentage of freshmen giving a particular response in 1966. The second is the actual percentage of students who gave this response four years later, presumably as seniors. By comparing these first two percentages, you can see the degree of actual change in your students during the college years. The third is the percentage of students who had

---

*Tables A.5 and A.6 are exceptions. Since there can be no freshman measures of satisfaction with the college or ratings of the various aspects of the college, only comparisons of the actual and estimated percentages in 1970 are given. The estimated percentages were computed in the manner described above; the only difference was that the freshman responses used to predict response to the satisfaction items in the followup did not include freshman "pretests" of those items.

been "estimated" or expected to give the response in 1970. The last column of each table, which gives the difference between the 1970 actual and estimated percentages, indicates whether your institution's impact was greater than expected, less than expected, or equal to what was expected from the characteristics of your students as freshmen.

Therefore, the estimated percentage for your students (based on data from students at all types of colleges) is what would result if their development during the four years was similar to that of comparable students elsewhere. Thus, if your students conform to the national pattern, the actual percentage will be equal or very close to the estimated percentage; this does not mean that your college exerts no influence on the outcome in question but simply that its influence is like that of a typical college.

In effect, then, our data provide a comparative analysis of the impact of various institutions. For this reason, you may find it helpful to compare your data with those of another school. Data packets from the other 18 institutions participating in this project are available on request. Please check those institutions listed in Appendix C whose data you would like to receive and return the list to us. You may check up to three institutions.

In interpreting the tables, it is important to distinguish changes observed in students during the undergraduate years from "college impact." Certain maturational changes are likely to occur in all persons of this age regardless of where—or even whether—they go to college. The estimated percentages provide an estimate of how the students at your college would be expected to turn out if they developed and matured according to the national pattern. Thus, even if your students changed substantially between their freshman and their senior years, one cannot be sure that these changes were attributable to the college environment unless the estimated percentage deviates from the actual percentage of students responding to a follow-up item. The college environment may affect student change in three ways:

1. The college can bring about changes that ordinarily do not occur in college students.

   If, on a given item, the actual percentage for 1966 and the estimated percentage for 1970 are about the same, but the actual percentage for 1970 is larger or smaller, then your college is having this effect. (Or, the expected change may be in one direction, and the actual change in the opposite direction.) As an example, let us suppose that the percentage of freshmen who said, in 1966, that they planned to major in history was 10 percent. If the estimated percentage of seniors majoring in history in 1970

was also 10 percent, but the percentage of history majors had
actually increased to 15 percent over the four years, then your
college has brought about an increase in history majors that does
not normally occur among college students similar to those on
your campus.
2. The college can accentuate or magnify changes that occur in most
   students.
      In this case, the estimated percentage for 1970 might be larger
   or smaller than the actual percentage for 1966, but the actual percentage for 1970 would be even higher than expected, and in the
   same direction. Let us use the same basic example: In 1966, 10
   percent of the freshmen planned to major in history. Suppose that,
   according to our predictive equation, 5 percent more (or 15 percent of all students) were expected to be majoring in history as
   seniors whereas the actual increase was twice as large: 10 percent (or 20 percent of all students). In this case, even though
   some students in history majors is normal, your college has
   accentuated this effect by "recruiting" a greater number of
   students to the field of history.
3. The college can diminish or impede changes that occur in most
   students.
      Your college is having this effect if an expected change does
   not occur at all or occurs to a lesser degree than normal. If, in
   the above example of 10 percent of the freshmen planning to major
   in history with an expected increase to 15 percent by the senior
   year, only 12 percent of the seniors in 1970 were actually majoring
   in history, your college has deterred students from history majors
   even though an increase still occurred.

      To summarize, the actual percentages for 1966 and 1970 show
how much students changed between their freshman and senior years
but not necessarily whether this change (or lack of it) was uniquely
attributable to the college. Thus, the impact of the college itself can
be estimated by comparing the actual 1970 percentage with the estimated percentage based on the regression equation as applied to
the freshman data.
      Tables A.5 and A.6 require additional explanation. Both show
the estimated and the actual percentages of students who were dissatisfied with various aspects of the college experience or who said
that they received "not enough" or "too much" of some aspects.
Obviously, freshmen could not make such ratings, so student change
is not the issue. The comparison of the estimated and the actual percentages of students can still give valuable information, however,
since educational policy makers may well be concerned about whether
more or less seniors than expected are dissatisfied with aspects of
their college experience.

Persistence in College

The final table in this section on college impact data, Table A.7, gives actual and estimated percentages of persisters in your college for four different measures of persistence or dropout status. These four measures are:

1. Returned for at least a second undergraduate year
2. Received the bachelor's degree (or equivalent)
3. Received the bachelor's degree or was still enrolled for work toward the degree in fall 1970
4. Received the bachelor's degree, was still enrolled for work toward the degree, or had transcripts sent to another institution

While the use of four different measures of persistence in college may seem unnecessarily confusing, the lack of any single suitable measure makes it desirable to include several approximate measures. Actually, there can never be a wholly satisfactory definition of the term dropout until anyone who ever enrolled in college either obtains a degree or dies without obtaining one; any former student can, in theory, go back to school at any time to complete the degree.

Strictly speaking, the first measure is not an index of dropout status, since it does not relate directly to the completion of degree requirements. Rather, it provides an estimate of the rate of attrition after the freshman year relative to that of other years and to that of other institutions. The second measure is, of course, the most stringent definition of persistence, since it classifies as dropouts all students in five-year programs and all students who left your institution to complete their degree work elsewhere. The third measure is somewhat less so, in that it considers students who were still working toward a degree in the same institution as persisters. (Note also that, by this definition, students who significantly delayed their degree completion by dropping out for a time and then reenrolling are not regarded as dropouts.) The fourth definition narrows the field considerably, since it classifies as dropouts only those students who left your institution without completing a degree and who never requested that their transcripts be sent to another institution. This measure is the least stringent one, since it classifies as persisters (a) all students who requested that their transcripts be sent to, but who may never actually enrolled in, another institution, and (b) all students who may have enrolled at a second institution but subsequently dropped out. Of course, those students who left your institution and entered another without attempting to transfer credits would be classified as dropouts by this definition, but it seems likely that their numbers are far exceeded by the numbers who requested transcripts but never actually enrolled in (or subsequently dropped out of) the second institution.

While the third measure classifies as dropouts those students who left their institution and subsequently may have completed their degree at another, it treats those currently enrolled students who may eventually drop out as persisters. Since the former probably outnumber the latter, the true attrition rate for most institutions will fall somewhere between the third and fourth definitions. You are in the best position to determine which of these measures is most accurate for your institution. By comparing the different measures, you can also get some idea of how your institution compares with similar institutions in the number of students still enrolled after four years and in the number of students transferring out of your institution.*

Trend Data

The trend data, shown in Table A.8, are not new to you. They are simply a selection and compilation of the freshman data which were sent to you previously for the years 1966, 1969, and 1971. (See Appendix A for the Student Information Forms for these years.) Presenting the data in this form, however, may make it easier for you to compare successive freshman classes at your institution. To avoid overwhelming you with data, we have selected only the variables that would seem to be most useful in policy making; perhaps you will choose to do some further elimination and will give only some of these variables your close attention. If you wish to examine trends with respect to variables not included here, and if your past freshman data are not handy, we will be glad to send you additional information.

The first six columns of Table A.8 give the percentages for freshman men and women at your institution. The last six columns give the corresponding normative percentages for all institutions in the CIRP that are of the same level (two-year college, four-year college, or university) and control as yours. For any given item, therefore, you may compare trends in the responses of men and of women at your institution and trends in the responses of your male

---

*Adapted from Alexander W. Astin, College Dropouts: A National Profile (Washington, D.C.: American Council on Education, 1972), pp. 4-6; vol. 7, no. 1, ACE Research Reports.

or female students with those of male or female students at similar institutions. The absence of data on an item for a particular year is indicated in the table by dashes.

Should you find the normative categories of institutions too broad for comparative purposes, you may again wish to compare your trend data with those of another institution. As mentioned previously, data packets from the other 18 participating institutions are available on request.

Environmental Effects

The impact data should suggest to you some areas of student development on which your college exerts an unusual or atypical effect. To assist you in understanding what kinds of college characteristics or experiences may influence students, Table A.9 lists environmental factors which have statistically significant positive or negative relationships with some of the same student outcomes covered in the impact data.

These relationships were determined through multiple regression analysis, using the same student freshman and followup data used in the impact studies. Separate analyses were not conducted for each institution, however. In addition to student input items from the freshman questionnaire, three separate types of environmental factors were included as predictors of student outcomes in the followup questionnaire:

1. Factors from the Inventory of College Activities (ICA) developed by Astin.* These 33 factors—measures of the psychological "climates" or environments of collegiate institutions—are grouped into four categories: the peer environment, the classroom environment, the administrative environment, and the college image. They are denoted by the abbreviation (ICA) in the table.
2. Institutional characteristics, which presumably affect all students at an institution: level, curricular emphasis, type of control, sex, selectivity, size, percentage of Ph.D.'s on faculty.
3. Within-college experiences, which ordinarily apply only to certain students within each college: marital and parental status at the

---

*For a full discussion of the ICA factors, see Alexander W. Astin, The College Environment (Washington, D.C.: American Council on Education, 1968).

time of followup, methods of financing college, and residence during the freshman year.

Not all of these factors were included in the analysis for each outcome. Thus, the absence of a factor from the table for a particular outcome does not necessarily imply that the factor is unrelated to the outcome.

Table A.9 should help to suggest factors which may be causally related to strengths or weaknesses in your institution (as indicated by the impact data) or possible effects on students of contemplated changes in college characteristics (e.g., an increase in enrollment size). Since the findings in this table were obtained from a national sample of institutions, they do not necessarily apply to your institution and should be considered only as complementary to your own knowledge and experience.

APPLICATION OF THE DATA

The transition from interpreting the data to applying them in appropriate institutional departments and programs may present some problems. To stimulate your own thinking on the matter, we offer the two following examples of how the data might be put to practical use.

Career Choice and Major Field (Tables A.1 and A.2)

These data are, of course, most relevant to evaluation of departmental programs and curricular revision. Sharp increases or declines in the popularity of some major fields at your institution may suggest that the number of courses offered in those fields should be either expanded or cut, though such decisions will ultimately depend on the academic goals of your institution. Should the actual proportion of seniors majoring in a field which you wish to emphasize be less than expected, you will probably want to review the performance of the faculty, the course requirements, the grading system, and any other aspects of the program that might discourage students from remaining in the field. Professional clubs or other extracurricular activities might be introduced to stimulate students' interest in the field. If vocational or career training versus traditional liberal arts education is an issue at your school, the degree of student interest in technical fields should be useful in making curricular

decisions. The counseling center also might work more effectively
if it had information on the major field choices and career plans of
entering freshmen; in turn, it might draw on its experience for explanations about why some fields are less popular than expected,
and these insights might benefit the task force.

These suggestions are fairly obvious. An account of how one
school actually used its student data exemplifies an unusual application whereby the school refrained from introducing revisions and
reforms. Alarmed by the large number of students who had "de-
fected" from the major field of engineering by their senior year,
this school had considered making major changes in their engineering
program. But ACE data showed that, while a larger proportion of
students did indeed switch from engineering to another field during
their college years, the decrease was not as large as expected from
the characteristics of the students as entering freshmen. The decrease that they had noted was a national trend, and their program
was actually effective insofar as it was retarding the decline. Had
they revised the engineering program, the proportion of students
changing from an engineering major might have increased rather
than decreased. On the basis of these considerations, then, the proposed revision was dropped.

Persistence in College (Table A.7)

Increasingly, educators are recognizing that completion of the
B.A. in four years is not necessarily the optimal pattern, or even
the normal one; on some campuses, students are encouraged to take
a leave of absence or to "drop out" for a period while pursuing other
interests. Many colleges are still concerned about attrition rates,
however, and if the data on Table A.7 show that more students than
expected leave your institution before receiving a degree, you may
be interested in which approaches are most likely to be successful
in retaining students. Since the characteristics of the students are
controlled in calculating the expected proportion of persisters,
changing admissions policies (even if this were feasible at your
campus) would not solve the problem. Instead, the characteristics
of the institution itself should be taken into account. Table A.9 may
suggest some aspects of your institution that are related to attrition.
You might also consider introducing programs designed specifically
to reduce dropout rates. Some programs which have proved helpful
at other schools include special preregistration counseling sessions
with potential dropouts, flexible administrative policies, and liberal
financial assistance programs. If you would like additional information on approaches to reducing attrition rates, we will send you a

reprint from ERIC which reviews them. In addition, you might find
it helpful to get in touch with schools similar to yours that have low
attrition rates or that have successfully implemented programs to
curb attrition.

If attrition is especially high at the end of the freshman year (as
indicated by the percentage of students returning for a second year)
you might examine the orientation program, freshman course requirements and grading standards, living arrangements, student-advisor
relationships, and so forth.

Trends in Characteristics of Entering Freshmen
(Table A.8)

One of the more controversial issues in higher education has
been that of admissions policies: Should admissions be restricted
or open? Are selective admissions unfairly discriminatory? Should
institutions be selecting students they can help rather than simply
picking "winners?" As a result of these pressing questions, admissions policies in many institutions have been undergoing revision.

One example of changing policies are the current efforts of many
institutions to admit more students from minority and low-income
backgrounds. Consequently, the need for data showing the actual
trends in these characteristics of entering students has increased.
As changing policies produce a different type of student body at a
given institution, other kinds of questions become pertinent: Is the
need for financial aid increasing? Are curriculum changes necessary
to adapt to the needs and interests of the students? Does high school
preparation appear adequate? The data in Table A.8 should aid in
answering these kinds of questions.

For institutions with open admission policies, the issue of which
students to admit is nonexistent. Data on trends in freshman characteristics are no less important, however. A knowledge of the changing
backgrounds and interests of entering students is essential for any
institution concerned with how it may best educate its students. For
example, one school, noting an increase in the number of students
with interests and talent in writing, added several courses in creative
writing and composition to its curriculum. Changes in the sex or age
composition of the student body may also alert an institution to a need
for revision in administrative policies, curriculum, or facilities.

If you would like other suggestions on the application of findings
for your institution, please write or phone for assistance.

TABLE A.1

Actual and Estimated Changes in Career Choice
between the Freshman and Senior Years, 1966-70
(in percent[a])

Career Choice[b]	Actual 1966	Actual 1970	Estimated for 1970	1970 Actual Minus 1970 Estimated
Artist (including performer)	6	9	7	+2
Businessman	3	6	9	-3
Clergyman	0	2	1	+1
College Teacher	5	11	7	+4
Doctor (M.D. or D.D.S.)	12	10	8	-2
Educator (secondary)	11	10	12	2
Elementary teacher	7	6	8	-2
Engineer	3	1	2	-1
Farmer or forester	0	0	1	-1
Health professional	2	1	2	-1
Lawyer	11	6	9	-3
Nurse	1	1	2	-1
Research scientist	6	0	4	-4
Other choice	27	24	18	+6
Undecided	5	10	11	-1

[a]Percentages may not add to 100 percent due to rounding error.
[b]See Appendix B for an explanation of these categories.

TABLE A.2

Actual and Estimated Changes in Major Field
between the Freshman and Senior Years, 1966-70
(in percent[a])

Major Field[b]	Actual 1966	Actual 1970	Estimated for 1970	1970 Actual Minus 1970 Estimated
Agriculture	0	0	0	0
Biological sciences	7	5	7	-2
Business	2	2	4	-2
Education	3	1	6	-5
Engineering	3	0	3	-3
English	7	17	10	+7
Health professional	2	1	2	-1
History and political science	13	25	17	+8
Humanities (other)	8	7	7	0
Fine arts	6	8	7	+1
Mathematics and statistics	5	7	4	+3
Physical sciences	6	9	7	+2
Preprofessional	19	1	2	-1
Social sciences	12	14	16	-2
Other fields (technical)	1	1	1	0
Other fields (nontechnical)	1	1	2	-2
Undecided	3	0	0	0

[a]Percentages may not add to 100 percent due to rounding error.
[b]See Appendix B for an explanation of these categories.

Actual and Estimated Changes in Degree Aspirations
between the Freshman and Senior Years, 1966-70
(in percent)

Highest Degree Planned	Actual 1966	Actual 1970	Estimated for 1970	1970 Actual Minus 1970 Estimated
Bachelor's (B.A., B.S., or equivalent) or higher	95	91	93	-2
Doctorate (Ph.D., Ed.D., M.D., D.D.S., D.V.M., D.O., LL.B., J.D., or B.D.)	37	36	37	-1

TABLE A.4

Actual and Estimated Changes in Religious Preference
between the Freshman and Senior Years, 1966-70
(in percent*)

Religious Preference	1966	1970	Estimated for 1970	1970 Actual Minus 1970 Estimated
Protestant	73	54	54	0
Catholic	9	5	6	-1
Jewish	3	2	2	0
None	9	27	27	0

*The percentage of respondents choosing "other religion" is omitted from the table.

TABLE A.5

Actual and Estimated Dissatisfaction with Selected
Aspects of College in the Senior Year
(percentage of dissatisfied students)

Aspect Evaluated	Actual for 1970	Estimated for 1970	1970 Actual Minus 1970 Estimated
Overall rating of college	6	5	+1
Overall quality of instruction	0	3	-3
The variety of science* courses	6	6	0
The variety of courses in humanities	5	10	-5
Opportunities for undergraduate scientific research	12	11	+1
Undergraduate training as preparation for future career	19	14	+5
The quality of science* instruction	3	3	0
The quality of instruction in the humanities	0	6	-6
Opportunities for discussion of work with professors in major field	3	9	-6
Science equipment and facilities	6	5	+1
Facilities for library research	18	14	+4
Opportunities for extracurricular science activities and projects	10	8	+2

*Science refers to both the natural and social sciences.

TABLE A.6

Actual and Estimated Senior Ratings of the Sufficiency
of Selected Aspects of College
(percentage of students receiving "not enough"*of aspect evaluated).

Aspect Evaluated	Actual for 1970	Estimated for 1970	1970 Actual Minus 1970 Estimated
Freedom in course selection	11	25	-14
Social life	21	20	+1
Personal contacts with classmates	9	7	+2
Work required in courses	16	10	+6
Outlets for creative activities	32	24	+8
Personal contacts with faculty	19	21	-2
Personal contacts with family	33	40	-7
Advice and guidance from faculty and staff	18	23	-5

*For "work required in courses," the percentage of students reporting "too much" is given.

TABLE A.7

Persistence in College

Status	Women	Men	All Students
Returned for a second undergraduate year			
Number of students for whom followup data were provided	91	142	233
Actual percentage returning for a second year	94.5	89.4	91.4
Estimated Percentage from freshman data	88.5	85.7	86.8
Difference between actual and estimated percentages	+6.0	+3.6	+4.6
Received bachelors degree			
Number of students for whom followup data were provided	91	142	233
Actual percentage receiving degree	81.3	69.7	74.2
Estimated percentage from freshman data	65.9	62.9	64.0
Difference between actual and estimated percentages	+15.3	+6.6	+10.1
Received bachelors degree or still enrolled			
Number of students for whom followup data were provided	91	142	233
Actual percentage receiving degree or still enrolled	82.4	71.8	75.9
Estimated percentage from freshman data	70.0	72.8	71.7
Difference between actual and estimated percentages	+12.3	-1.0	+4.1
Received bachelors degree, still enrolled, or had a transcript sent to another institution			
Number of students for whom followup data were provided	91	142	233
Actual percentage receiving degree, still enrolled, or requesting transcript	97.8	93.6	95.2
Estimated percentage from freshman data	92.0	93.0	92.6
Difference between actual and estimated percentages	+5.0	+.6	+2.6

TABLE A.8

Trends in Characteristics of Entering Freshmen, 1966-71
(in percent)

	Class of 1970		Class of 1973		Class of 1975		4-year Private Nonsectarian Colleges Class of 1970		Class of 1973		Class of 1975	
Item	Men	Women	Men	Women	Men	Women	Men	Women	Men	Women	Men	Women
Class composition by sex	60.9	39.1	59.4	40.6	53.0	47.0	55.6	44.4	47.2	52.8	49.1	50.9
Age, in years, as of December 31, 1966, 1969, 1971												
16 or younger	—	—	0.0	0.6	0.0	0.0	—	—	0.2	0.2	0.2	0.3
17	—	—	3.8	9.0	1.1	5.2	—	—	5.3	8.1	5.0	8.5
18	—	—	87.3	84.3	89.7	87.9	—	—	74.4	80.4	75.4	80.5
19*	12.8	4.1	8.5	6.2	8.8	6.9	19.1	9.7	14.8	9.3	15.6	9.1
20	—	—	0.0	0.0	0.4	0.0	—	—	2.1	0.9	1.6	0.7
21	—	—	0.4	0.0	0.0	0.0	—	—	0.9	0.5	0.4	0.2
Older than 21	—	—	0.0	0.0	0.0	0.0	—	—	2.2	0.6	1.8	0.6
Average grade in high school												
A or A+	6.4	31.1	6.9	26.4	8.4	25.1	6.5	11.2	6.0	9.2	7.1	10.9
A-	12.8	34.4	15.8	29.2	14.8	29.5	10.9	16.2	9.9	16.2	10.8	17.2
B+	26.9	21.9	28.8	30.9	26.8	30.0	16.8	23.3	16.7	24.1	18.5	26.1
B	28.6	8.6	25.4	12.4	35.2	12.8	20.6	23.6	22.5	24.9	24.9	25.2
B-	15.4	3.3	17.3	1.0	10.0	2.2	15.5	10.6	16.6	12.6	16.2	10.5
C+	6.0	0.7	4.2	0.0	3.6	0.4	17.0	9.1	15.2	8.7	13.2	6.5
C	3.8	0.0	1.5	0.0	0.8	0.0	11.8	5.7	12.3	4.1	8.6	3.3
D	0.0	0.0	0.0	0.0	0.4	0.0	0.7	0.3	0.7	0.2	0.6	0.2

(continued)

TABLE A.8 (continued)

							4-year Private Nonsectarian Colleges					
	Class of 1970		Class of 1973		Class of 1975		Class of 1970		Class of 1973		Class of 1975	
Item	Men	Women	Men	Women	Men	Women	Men	Women	Men	Women	Men	Women
Secondary school achievement												
Elected president student organization	34.5	32.5	30.0	23.0	24.0	23.8	31.0	27.5	26.1	26.0	24.2	23.0
High rating state music contest	7.7	11.9	6.9	11.8	5.4	7.8	8.9	9.6	9.1	12.3	8.3	12.1
State/regional speech contest	9.8	4.6	8.5	10.1	7.3	8.2	7.3	7.7	7.0	7.0	5.6	5.7
Major part in a play	23.4	22.5	22.7	21.9	16.9	23.4	22.0	22.9	20.4	21.6	17.4	19.5
Varsity letter (sports)	53.6	8.6	50.8	16.9	51.0	16.5	53.2	22.1	52.4	17.1	50.9	16.8
Award in art competition	6.4	9.9	3.8	9.6	1.9	7.4	4.8	7.0	4.8	7.9	5.5	8.3
Edited school paper or year- book	16.2	37.1	16.2	30.3	13.8	26.0	13.5	22.2	13.0	21.7	13.1	19.5
Had original writing published	21.3	26.5	26.2	29.2	24.9	29.0	21.2	28.3	20.1	27.5	20.1	25.2
NSF summer program	3.4	0.7	1.5	1.7	1.5	0.4	3.8	2.0	1.6	1.0	1.3	1.0
State/regional science contest	2.6	4.0	3.1	2.2	3.1	5.2	4.2	3.3	2.7	2.2	2.4	1.9
Scholastic honor society	42.1	78.1	38.5	77.5	43.7	70.6	32.0	45.3	27.0	41.7	27.0	39.7
National merit recognition	—	—	19.6	34.3	15.3	21.6	—	—	12.7	14.6	16.3	18.6
Highest degree planned												
None	1.8	0.7	0.4	2.2	2.4	0.9	3.9	2.1	0.9	1.7	3.9	4.1
Associate (or equivalent)	0.9	0.0	0.0	0.6	0.0	0.0	0.2	2.6	0.8	1.9	0.4	1.2
Bachelor's degree (B.A., B.S.)	16.3	29.9	14.1	25.8	13.8	21.5	22.3	40.7	26.8	40.1	28.7	37.9
Master's degree (M.A., M.S.)	25.1	59.9	29.3	52.8	24.5	49.6	32.0	39.2	33.9	39.1	26.2	35.5
Ph.D. or Ed.D.	26.4	5.4	28.9	12.9	21.3	13.2	22.8	10.2	20.8	12.3	15.6	11.6
M.D., D.D.S., or D.V.M.	23.3	2.0	18.4	4.5	27.3	9.6	12.5	3.7	9.7	2.6	11.3	4.5
LL.B. or J.D.	5.3	0.0	8.2	1.1	10.3	5.3	4.9	0.8	4.5	0.9	10.8	3.2
B.D.	0.0	0.0	0.0	0.0	0.0	0.0	0.2	0.0	0.7	0.2	1.0	0.1
Other	0.9	2.0	0.8	0.0	0.4	0.0	1.2	0.6	1.9	1.3	2.0	2.0

Probable major field of study

Agriculture (including forestry)	0.0	0.0	0.4	0.0	0.4	0.0	2.3	0.0	2.5	0.1	2.7	0.3
Biological sciences	6.0	12.9	5.6	7.1	6.6	8.3	7.0	5.1	5.2	4.3	5.7	4.4
Business	3.0	0.7	2.8	0.0	3.5	0.0	15.3	5.4	16.3	4.3	14.7	4.7
Education	0.9	4.1	0.8	4.8	1.2	10.5	5.1	13.4	5.6	11.8	3.6	10.5
Engineering	3.9	0.0	1.2	0.0	3.5	0.9	5.5	0.1	5.2	0.2	4.3	0.2
English	4.7	10.9	4.8	11.9	3.1	7.9	3.8	10.3	3.0	7.3	2.5	4.9
Health professions (non-M.D.)	0.9	2.7	0.0	3.6	0.4	2.6	0.8	4.8	0.9	4.6	4.0	9.1
History and political science	15.5	9.5	15.5	9.5	8.9	4.4	11.8	10.4	10.8	7.3	9.0	6.3
Humanities (other)	3.9	17.0	3.6	13.1	1.9	7.9	3.4	10.7	5.8	9.1	4.6	7.4
Fine arts	3.4	11.6	6.4	11.3	5.0	11.0	4.8	10.5	7.9	15.2	8.0	15.5
Mathematics and statistics	5.2	4.8	7.2	10.7	5.4	4.4	6.3	5.4	4.5	4.7	2.9	3.6
Physical sciences	9.5	3.4	10.4	3.6	5.4	1.8	7.1	1.8	5.2	1.4	3.5	1.1
Preprofessional	30.6	1.4	26.7	6.0	39.5	14.9	15.4	3.7	13.6	3.1	18.6	6.3
Social sciences	8.6	17.7	10.4	15.5	7.8	19.3	8.6	15.4	8.8	20.4	9.3	18.9
Other fields (technical)	0.4	0.7	0.4	0.0	2.7	3.1	0.9	0.3	2.1	1.1	3.8	2.0
Other fields (nontechnical)	0.4	0.7	0.4	0.6	0.4	0.4	0.1	1.1	0.3	2.6	0.5	2.3
Undecided	3.0	2.0	3.6	2.4	4.7	2.6	1.8	1.4	2.4	2.5	2.4	2.4

Probable career occupation

Artist (including performer)	7.3	8.7	7.1	13.6	4.7	7.9	5.3	9.7	5.8	12.3	7.1	11.9
Businessman	9.9	0.7	5.9	1.1	3.9	0.0	18.8	2.1	16.1	2.1	13.9	2.7
Clergyman	1.3	0.7	0.0	0.0	0.0	0.0	0.8	0.3	4.3	0.5	2.3	0.3
College teacher	5.2	2.0	4.0	2.8	2.3	1.8	4.0	2.7	2.3	1.4	1.5	1.1
Doctor (M.D. or D.D.S.)	21.9	2.7	17.4	2.8	23.8	7.9	12.7	3.4	8.3	2.1	11.1	3.8
Educator (secondary)	3.9	14.8	5.1	14.2	2.0	8.8	10.3	18.6	11.0	14.1	5.7	9.5
Elementary teacher	0.0	12.1	0.4	7.4	0.4	11.5	0.5	10.1	0.6	11.9	0.8	8.9
Engineer	4.3	0.7	2.0	0.0	1.6	0.4	6.4	0.1	4.9	0.2	3.6	0.1
Farmer or forester	0.4	0.7	0.8	0.0	1.2	0.4	2.0	0.3	2.0	0.4	2.8	0.8
Health professional (non-M.D.)	1.7	2.0	1.6	3.4	2.0	5.3	2.5	4.2	2.7	4.0	4.7	8.1
Lawyer	15.5	1.3	15.4	1.7	12.5	4.8	10.4	1.6	9.3	1.7	12.5	3.4
Nurse	0.0	2.7	0.0	1.1	0.0	0.0	0.0	2.3	0.0	2.5	0.1	2.9

(continued)

TABLE A.8 (continued)

| Item | Class of 1970 | | Class of 1973 | | Class of 1975 | | 4-Year Private Nonsectarian Colleges | | | | | |
| | | | | | | | Class of 1970 | | Class of 1973 | | Class of 1975 | |
	Men	Women	Men	Women	Men	Women	Men	Women	Men	Women	Men	Women
Research scientist	8.6	8.1	7.9	5.1	10.5	6.2	7.0	3.9	4.5	2.4	4.2	2.8
Other choice	13.3	39.6	11.9	25.0	10.5	18.1	14.1	35.8	13.9	28.2	12.6	24.0
Undecided	6.9	3.4	20.6	21.6	24.6	26.9	5.2	4.9	14.1	16.3	17.1	19.8
Objectives considered to be essential or very important												
Becoming accomplished in one of the performing arts	11.1	17.2	12.0	18.1	15.7	23.0	11.8	16.2	13.6	19.1	14.0	21.4
Becoming an authority in my subject field	72.6	59.3	62.0	52.8	66.2	60.6	72.2	64.6	64.4	57.1	63.8	56.8
Obtaining recognition from my colleagues	52.2	34.7	47.9	39.0	42.9	34.3	50.8	38.2	46.0	35.2	42.3	34.2
Becoming an expert in finance and commerce	14.2	0.7	11.3	2.3	6.5	1.3	20.1	3.8	21.4	6.8	15.9	5.3
Having administrative responsibility	29.9	19.9	18.2	9.0	13.1	7.8	34.4	18.4	27.2	12.7	22.4	10.6
Being very well off financially	52.3	22.0	46.7	23.7	39.5	15.7	53.0	32.3	47.1	27.4	43.4	24.1
Helping others who are in difficulty	66.2	86.7	65.4	82.5	61.4	70.0	64.3	78.8	66.4	77.1	61.8	73.3
Participating in organization like Peace Corps	18.8	44.0	—	—	18.0	31.7	18.6	33.6	—	—	14.6	25.2
Becoming a community leader	34.2	19.5	25.5	13.6	15.7	11.7	35.5	22.2	25.3	16.8	19.2	11.6
Making a theoretical contribution to science	22.6	8.7	18.9	11.4	17.2	8.3	21.0	8.9	13.7	6.3	12.6	7.0
Writing original works	22.2	30.5	22.0	29.9	23.0	29.1	18.2	23.3	17.3	22.4	18.2	22.4
Never being obligated to people	26.5	21.2	26.3	24.3	22.0	17.5	29.1	28.5	24.9	22.9	22.3	20.3

Creating artistic work	11.5	26.0	16.6	26.0	12.7	27.0	11.5	23.5	13.3	26.2	14.1	26.4
Keeping up to date with political affairs	63.7	58.0	60.7	55.9	54.2	55.0	64.6	59.1	58.9	55.0	51.7	48.1
Being successful in a business of my own	51.9	23.8	42.6	15.2	40.4	17.5	60.0	33.8	49.8	28.7	48.3	26.4
Developing a meaningful philosophy of life	—	—	82.7	89.3	74.3	87.8	—	—	82.9	89.0	73.3	80.2
Father's education												
Grammar school or less	2.1	3.3	1.9	1.1	2.3	0.9	7.5	5.6	7.5	6.0	5.2	4.8
Some high school	7.7	5.3	3.1	7.9	5.4	5.7	11.2	9.6	12.2	9.6	11.2	9.5
High school graduate	17.5	10.0	20.0	14.7	22.0	18.3	21.0	19.5	24.4	19.3	23.2	20.4
Some college	14.1	14.0	18.5	19.2	11.6	14.4	16.4	19.1	17.2	16.8	15.6	16.3
College degree	33.3	40.0	31.5	32.8	34.0	34.5	22.6	24.9	22.0	25.6	25.1	26.6
Postgraduate degree	25.2	27.3	25.0	24.3	24.7	26.2	21.4	21.3	16.7	22.7	19.6	22.3
Mother's education												
Grammar school or less	0.9	1.3	0.8	0.0	0.8	0.0	4.4	3.1	4.0	2.9	3.4	2.6
Some high school	5.1	2.0	5.0	4.5	3.8	4.4	9.9	8.1	11.6	8.7	9.6	7.8
High school graduate	35.7	27.2	35.4	38.4	32.3	34.2	34.3	31.0	38.9	30.6	37.1	32.0
Some college	19.6	22.5	19.6	20.9	24.2	21.1	19.6	23.1	19.3	23.3	19.2	22.3
College degree	32.3	41.1	30.4	27.1	30.4	32.5	25.0	26.8	20.7	25.9	23.6	25.8
Postgraduate degree	6.4	6.0	8.8	9.0	8.5	7.9	6.8	7.9	5.5	8.7	7.2	9.4
Racial background												
White/Caucasian	99.1	98.7	98.8	98.4	98.1	95.2	82.5	87.4	87.6	82.8	87.6	84.3
Black/Negro/Afro-American	0.4	0.7	0.4	0.9	1.9	4.3	15.1	10.1	10.6	15.6	10.4	14.1
American Indian	0.0	0.0	0.4	0.2	0.4	2.2	0.2	0.3	0.2	0.3	1.0	1.1
Oriental	0.0	0.0	0.0	0.0	0.0	0.0	0.5	0.7	0.8	0.9	0.7	0.9
Other	0.4	0.7	0.4	0.6	0.8	1.3	1.6	1.5	0.8	0.5	1.9	1.9
Religious background												
Protestant	71.1	83.4	66.9	64.0	58.0	70.2	60.5	64.9	57.8	61.9	47.8	51.6
Roman Catholic	18.1	10.6	24.6	25.8	30.0	20.2	19.9	18.8	22.6	19.4	28.0	22.8

(continued)

153

TABLE A.8 (continued)

| | Class of 1970 | | Class of 1973 | | Class of 1975 | | 4-year Private Nonsectarian Colleges | | | | | |
| | | | | | | | Class of 1970 | | Class of 1973 | | Class of 1975 | |
Item	Men	Women	Men	Women	Men	Women	Men	Women	Men	Women	Men	Women
Jewish	4.3	1.3	3.5	1.1	6.2	1.8	10.7	9.2	8.0	7.4	11.3	10.6
Other	5.6	3.3	2.8	5.6	4.3	4.8	6.2	4.7	8.5	8.0	9.7	11.4
None	0.9	1.3	2.3	3.4	1.6	3.1	2.6	2.4	3.1	3.4	3.2	3.6
Present religious preference												
Protestant	62.2	74.2	42.3	51.7	46.5	57.1	51.9	57.7	45.7	51.2	34.6	39.1
Roman Catholic	17.2	9.3	19.9	22.2	23.4	15.5	19.0	18.9	19.4	16.4	20.6	16.9
Jewish	4.3	1.3	2.0	1.1	3.1	1.8	9.1	8.5	6.4	5.3	8.2	7.7
Other	5.2	6.6	7.4	8.5	7.4	6.2	7.3	5.6	11.2	10.6	13.4	14.8
None	11.2	8.6	28.5	16.5	19.5	19.5	12.6	9.4	17.3	16.4	23.2	21.5
Father's occupation												
Artist (including performer)	—	—	0.8	2.3	0.4	0.4	—	—	1.1	1.7	1.2	1.4
Businessman	—	—	44.2	39.5	43.8	42.2	—	—	34.3	34.1	38.1	36.5
Clergyman	—	—	0.0	1.2	0.8	1.3	—	—	2.3	2.2	1.5	1.7
College teacher	—	—	0.4	2.3	2.3	2.2	—	—	1.5	2.1	1.3	1.9
Doctor (M.D. or D.D.S.)	—	—	5.8	6.4	7.0	3.6	—	—	4.1	5.2	4.7	5.0
Educator (secondary)	—	—	4.3	2.9	2.3	2.2	—	—	3.0	3.2	2.6	2.8
Elementary teacher	—	—	0.0	0.0	0.0	1.3	—	—	0.2	0.4	0.4	0.4
Engineer	—	—	10.1	11.0	9.3	11.1	—	—	6.2	7.2	7.1	7.9

154

Farmer or forester	—	—	1.6	0.6	1.2	1.8	—	—	3.3	3.1	2.2	2.3
Health professional (non-M.D.)	—	—	2.3	0.0	0.8	1.8	—	—	1.2	1.5	1.5	1.4
Lawyer	—	—	3.9	2.3	2.7	2.2	—	—	2.3	3.2	3.0	3.1
Military career	—	—	1.6	2.9	0.0	0.4	—	—	1.3	1.7	1.0	1.3
Research scientist	—	—	1.9	1.7	0.4	2.7	—	—	0.9	1.1	1.0	0.9
Skilled worker	—	—	5.4	9.9	8.1	6.7	—	—	11.0	7.6	9.2	7.6
Semi-skilled worker	—	—	3.1	2.9	7.4	3.6	—	—	6.6	5.1	6.0	4.1
Unskilled worker	—	—	0.8	0.0	1.6	2.2	—	—	3.8	3.1	2.6	2.6
Unemployed	—	—	0.4	1.7	1.2	0.0	—	—	1.2	1.2	1.0	1.5
Other	—	—	13.6	12.2	10.9	14.2	—	—	15.7	16.2	15.6	17.8
Estimated parental income												
Less than $4,000	1.3	1.5	1.2	1.7	1.2	1.0	6.8	5.7	5.3	5.5	4.2	4.4
$4,000–$5,999	5.4	7.4	3.1	3.4	2.1	1.6	10.2	8.4	8.0	7.4	4.8	5.8
$6,000–$7,999	8.5	8.8	4.7	5.7	3.3	7.3	12.7	11.6	9.9	9.3	6.7	7.6
$8,000–$9,999	10.8	11.0	10.5	8.6	5.8	4.2	12.7	12.4	13.4	10.5	8.5	8.8
$10,000–$14,999	29.1	30.9	25.0	30.3	32.5	22.4	23.5	25.1	25.3	22.6	26.0	23.5
$15,000–$19,999	18.8	16.2	19.1	20.6	17.7	16.7	11.9	14.2	13.6	14.2	15.0	14.5
$20,000–$24,999	11.2	8.8	14.8	12.6	11.9	24.0	7.1	7.8	8.2	10.2	10.6	11.1
$25,000–$29,999	1.8	6.6	8.2	8.0	7.4	8.3	4.5	5.2	4.4	6.6	6.6	6.5
$30,000 or more	13.0	8.8	13.3	9.1	18.1	14.6	10.6	9.6	11.8	13.6	17.7	17.8
Concern about financing education												
None	46.8	47.7	35.0	33.1	34.9	29.3	38.9	42.0	33.6	36.8	34.8	33.7
Some concern	49.8	49.7	57.7	59.0	55.2	60.3	53.0	50.0	56.0	52.3	54.2	53.5
Major concern	3.4	2.6	7.3	7.9	10.0	10.5	8.1	8.0	10.4	10.8	11.0	12.8

*Although this item was detailed in the 1966 SIF, the institutional report and 1966 national norms indicated only those students 19 years or older as of December 31, 1966.

TABLE A.9

Institutional and Environmental Factors
Associated with Various Student Outcomes

| Outcome | Institutional and Environmental Factors Which Have: | |
	Positive Effect	Negative Effect
Career Choice:		
Artist	Verbal aggressiveness in class (ICA)	Married at time of followup
	Degree of informal dating (ICA)	Had children at time of followup
	Administrative permissiveness (ICA)	Lived with parents as freshman
	Degree of musical and artistic activity (ICA)	
Businessman	Highly organized classes (ICA)	
	Severe policies on student aggression (ICA)	
	Severe policies on cheating (ICA)	
	Emphasis on social activities (ICA)	
	At least 21 percent of expenses paid by earnings from employment	
Engineer	Lived with parents as freshman	
Lawyer	Independence of student body (ICA)	
Physician	Flexible curriculum (ICA)*	Married at time of followup
Teacher	Severe policies on student drinking (ICA)	Academic competitiveness (ICA)*
	Cohesiveness of student body (ICA)	Had children at time of followup
	Severe policies on heterosexual activities (ICA)	
	At least 21 percent of expenses paid by spouse	
	At least 21 percent of expenses paid by loan	
	Lived with parents as freshman	
Degree aspirations:		
Planning to obtain doctorate	Independence of student body (ICA)	Married at time of followup
	Familiarity between instructors and students (ICA)	At least 21 percent of expenses paid by spouse
	At least 21 percent of expenses paid by scholarship	
Applied for admission to graduate school	Lived in dorm as freshman	Married at time of followup
	At least 41 percent of expenses paid by parents	
	At least 21 percent of expenses paid by scholarship	

156

| Outcome | Institutional and Environmental Factors Which Have: | |
	Positive Effect	Negative Effect
Religious preference:		
Protestant	Married at time of followup	Women's college
	At least 41 percent of expenses paid by parents	Private-nonsectarian institution
	Lived with parents as freshman	Roman Catholic institution
	Technological institution	
	Public institution	
	Sectarian institution	
Catholic	Lived with parents as freshman	Coeducational institution
	Women's college	Public institution
	Roman Catholic institution	Private-nonsectarian institution
Jewish	—	—
None	Administrative permissiveness (ICA)	Classes highly organized
	Frequent student drinking (ICA)	Severe policies against student sexual activity (ICA)
	At least 21 percent of expenses paid by loan	Roman Catholic institution
	Private-nonsectarian institution	Sectarian institution
	Selective institution	
Satisfaction with:		
Total college experience	Extroverted instructors (ICA)	Lived with parents as freshman
	Administrative permissiveness (ICA)	At least 21 percent of expenses paid by loan
	Flexible curriculum (ICA)*	Coeducational institution
	At least 21 percent of expenses paid by spouse	Large institution
	Lived in dorm as freshman	
	Men's college	
	Private-nonsectarian institution	
	Selective institution	
	Institution with high percentage of Ph.D.'s on faculty	
Quality of instruction	At least 21 percent of expenses paid by scholarship	At least 21 percent of expenses paid by earnings from employment
	Private-nonsectarian college	Public institution
	Four-year college	University
	Men's college	Coeducational institution
	Women's college	Teachers college
	Liberal arts college	Large institution
	Selective college	
	Institution with high percentage of Ph.D.'s on faculty	

(continued)

157

| Outcome | Institutional and Environmental Factors Which Have: | |
	Positive Effect	Negative Effect
Preparation for career	Men's college Technological institution	At least 21 percent of expenses paid by loan Coeducation institution Large institution
Opportunities to discuss work with professors	At least 21 percent of expenses paid by scholarship Private institution Four-year college Men's college Women's college Liberal arts college	Had children at time of followup At least 21 percent of expenses paid by spouse Lived with parents as freshman Public institution University Coeducation institution Teachers college Technological institu- tion Large institution
Facilities for library research	Married at time of followup Had children at time of followup Lived with parents as freshman University Men's college Theological institution Public institution Private-nonsectarian institution Large institution Selective institution Institution with high percentage of Ph.D.'s on faculty	At least 21 percent of expenses paid by scholarship At least 21 percent of expenses paid by loan Four-year college Coeducation institution Liberal arts college Teachers college Roman Catholic insti- tution Sectarian institution
Students have enough: Social life	Married at time of followup Had children at time of followup University Coeducation institution Public institution Large institution	At least 21 percent of expenses paid by scholarship Lived with parents as freshman Four-year college Men's college Technological institu- tion Private-nonsectarian institution Selective institution

| Outcome | Institutional and Environmental Factors Which Have: | |
	Positive Effect	Negative Effect
Personal contacts with classmates	Married at time of followup Four-year college Women's college	Lived with parents as freshman Lived in other private home as freshman
Personal contacts with family	Lived with parents as freshman	Married at time of followup At least 21 percent of expenses paid by earnings from employment
Advice and guidance from faculty and staff	Private institution Four-year college Men's college Women's college Liberal arts college	At least 41 percent of expenses paid by parents Lived with parents as freshman Lived in other private home as freshman Public institution University Coeducational institution Large institution Institution with high percentage of Ph.D.'s on faculty
Freedom in course selection	Liberal arts college Private-nonsectarian institution Sectarian institution	Teachers college Technological institution Public institution Roman Catholic institution Large institution University Coeducational institution Selective institution Institution with high percentage of Ph.D.'s on faculty
Outlets for creative activities		Technological institution
Personal contacts with faculty	Private institution	Lived with parents as freshman

(continued)

159

TABLE A.9 (continued)

Outcome	Institutional and Environmental Factors Which Have:	
	Positive Effect	Negative Effect
Personal contacts with faculty (continued)	Four-year college Men's college Women's college Liberal arts college	Public institution University Coeducational institution Teachers college Large institution Institution with high percentage of Ph.D.'s on faculty
Too much work required in courses	Men's college Technological institution Private-nonsectarian institution Selective college	Coeducational institution Theological institution Roman Catholic institution Sectarian institution
Persistence in College: Dropped out for a while	Married at time of followup Had children at time of follow-up At least 21 percent of expenses paid by spouse Lived with parents as freshman Lived in other private home as freshman Coeducational institution Public institution Large institution	At least 41 percent of expenses paid by parents At least 21 percent of expenses paid by scholarship Private institution Four-year college Women's college Liberal arts college Roman Catholic institution Sectarian institution Selective college
Completed the baccalaureate	Administrative concern for the individual student (ICA) Frequent musical and artistic activity (ICA)	Flexible curriculum (ICA) Frequent use of automobiles (ICA)

| Outcome | Institutional and Environmental Factors Which Have: | |
	Positive Effect	Negative Effect
Completed the baccalaureate (continued)	Cooperative student inter- actions (ICA) At least 41 percent of ex- penses paid by parents At least 21 percent of ex- penses paid by scholar- ship Lived in dormitory as freshman	Competitive student interactions (ICA) Married at time of followup Had children at time of followup At least 21 percent of expenses paid by spouse

*Few requirements; changes easy to make.

APPENDIX A: QUESTIONNAIRES

1966 Student Information Form

YOUR NAME(please print)_____
               First   Middle or Maiden   Last

HOME STREET ADDRESS_____

CITY   STATE   ZIP CODE (if known)

Note: The information in this report is being collected through the American Council on Education as part of a study of this year's entering class. Please complete all items. Your name and address has been requested in order to facilitate mail follow-up studies. Your responses will be used only in group summaries for research purposes, and will <u>not</u> be identified with you individually.

Social Security Number (if known)

If you recently took any of the national achievement tests and happen to remember your score, fill in the appropriate information:

	Score		Score
SAT Verbal		ACT Composite	
SAT Math		NMSC Selection Score	

Date of Birth _____ _____ _____
         Month Day Year

DIRECTIONS: Your responses will be read by an automatic scanning device. Your careful observance of these few simple rules will be most appreciated.

Use only black lead pencil (No. 2½ or softer). Make heavy black marks that fill the circle. Erase cleanly any answer you wish to change. Make no stray markings of any kind.

                              Yes No
Example: Will marks made with ball pen or ○ ●
fountain pen be properly read?

1. Your Sex: Male ○   Female ○

2. From what kind of secondary school did you graduate? (Mark one)

Public .... ○
Private (denominational) .... ○
Private (nondenominational) ..... ○
Other .... ○

3. What was your average grade in secondary school? (Mark one)

A or A+ .. ○   B− ... ○
A− ..... ○   C+ ... ○
B+ ..... ○   C .... ○
B ...... ○   D .... ○

4. What is the highest academic degree that you intend to obtain? (Mark one)

None .... ○
Associate (or equivalent) .... ○
Bachelor's degree (B.A., B.S., etc.) .. ○
Master's degree (M.A., M.S., etc.) .... ○
Ph.D. or Ed.D. .... ○
M.D., D.D.S., or D.V.M. .... ○
LL.B. or J.D .... ○
B.D. .... ○
Other .... ○

5. The following questions deal with accomplishments that might possibly apply to your high school years. Do not be discouraged by this list; it covers many areas of interest and few students will be able to say "yes" to many items. (Mark all that apply)

Was elected president of one or more student organizations (recognized by the school) .... ○
Received a high rating (Good, Excellent) in a <u>state</u> or <u>regional</u> music contest ○
Participated in a <u>state</u> or <u>regional</u> speech or debate contest .... ○
Had a major part in a play...................................... ○
Won a varsity letter (sports) .... ○
Won a prize or award in an art competition .... ○
Edited the school paper, yearbook, or literary magazine .... ○
Had poems, stories, essays, or articles published .... ○
Participated in a National Science Foundation summer program .... ○
Placed (first, second, or third) in a <u>state</u> or <u>regional</u> science contest ...... ○
Was a member of a scholastic honor society .... ○
Won a Certificate of Merit or Letter of Commendation in the National Merit Program .... ○

162

6. Do you have any concern about your ability to finance your college education? (Mark one)

None (I am confident that I will have sufficient funds)............... ○
Some concern (but I will probably have enough funds)................. ○
Major concern (not sure I will be able to complete college)............. ○

7. Through what source do you intend to finance the first year of your undergraduate education?
(Mark one for each item)

Major Source / Minor Source / Not a Source

Employment during college ...... ○○○
Employment during summer ...... ○○○
Scholarship .... ○○○
G. I. Bill .... ○○○
Personal savings .... ○○○
Tuition deferment loan from college ○○○
Parental aid.................. ○○○
Federal government .... ○○○
Commercial loan .... ○○○

8. What is your racial background? (Mark one)

Caucasian .... ○
Negro............... ○
American Indian .... ○
Oriental .... ○
Other............... ○

9. What is the highest level of formal education obtained by your parents? (Mark one in each column)

	Father	Mother
Grammar school or less ..	○	○
Some high school.......	○	○
High school graduate....	○	○
Some college.........	○	○
College degree	○	○
Postgraduate degree	○	○

10. What is your best estimate of the total income last year of your parental family (not your own family if you are married)? Consider annual income from all sources before taxes.

Less than $4,000..○ $15,000–$19,999..○
$4,000–$5,999....○ $20,000–$24,999...○
$6,000–$7,999....○ $25,000–$29,999...○
$8,000–$9,999....○ $30,000 or more ...○
$10,000–$14,999..○

11. Mark one in each column below:

	Religion in Which You Were Reared	Your Present Religious Preference
Protestant	○	○
Roman Catholic.....	○	○
Jewish	○	○
Other	○	○
None	○	○

12. In deciding where to go to college, through what source did this college first come to your attention?
(Mark one)

Relative .... ○
Friend...................... ○
High school counselor or teacher... ○
Professional counseling or college placement service .... ○
This college or a representative from this college .... ○
Other source .... ○
I cannot recall............... ○

13. To what extent do you think each of the following describes the psychological climate or atmosphere at this college?
(Mark one answer for each item)

Very Descriptive / In Between / Not at all Descriptive

Intellectual...... ○○○
Snobbish .... ○○○
Social .... ○○○
Victorian ...... ○○○
Practical-minded.. ○○○
Warm .... ○○○
Realistic .... ○○○
Liberal......... ○○○

14. Answer each of the following as you think it applies to this college:

	Yes	No
The students are under a great deal of pressure to get high grades.....	○	○
The student body is apathetic and has little "school spirit".........	○	○
Most of the students are of a very high calibre academically.........	○	○
There is a keen competition among most of the students for high grades ..	○	○
Freshmen have to take orders from upperclassmen for a period of time ...	○	○
There isn't much to do except to go to class and study	○	○
I felt "lost" when I first came to the campus	○	○
Being in this college builds poise and maturity....................	○	○
Athletics are overemphasized	○	○
The classes are usually run in a very informal manner	○	○
Most students are more like "numbers in a book"..................	○	○

15. Are you:

An only child (Mark and skip to number 20) ○
The first-born (but not an only child) .... ○
The second-born.................. ○
The third-born .... ○
Fourth (or later) born .... ○

16. How many brothers and sisters now living do you have? (Mark one)

None (Mark and skip to number 20)......... ○

1 2 3 4 5 6 7 8 or more
○ ○ ○ ○ ○ ○ ○ ○

17. Mark one circle for each of your brothers and sisters between the ages of 13 and 23

	13	14	15	16	17	18	19	20	21	22	23
Brothers	○	○	○	○	○	○	○	○	○	○	○
Sisters	○	○	○	○	○	○	○	○	○	○	○

18. Are you a twin? (Mark one)

No, (Mark and skip to number 20).. ○
Yes, identical............... ○
Yes, fraternal same sex .... ○
Yes, fraternal opposite sex ..... ○

19. Is your twin attending college?

No .... ○
Yes, the same college..... ○
Yes, a different college ... ○

163

20.
Mark one in
each column:

Your current home state
Your birthplace
Your father's birthplace
Your mother's birthplace

Alabama	O	O O O
Alaska	O	O O O
Arizona	O	O O O
Arkansas	O	O O O
California	O	O O O
Colorado	O	O O O
Connecticut	O	O O O
Delaware	O	O O O
D. C.	O	O O O
Florida	O	O O O
Georgia	O	O O O
Hawaii	O	O O O
Idaho	O	O O O
Illinois	O	O O O
Indiana	O	O O O
Iowa	O	O O O
Kansas	O	O O O
Kentucky	O	O O O
Louisiana	O	O O O
Maine	O	O O O
Maryland	O	O O O
Massachusetts	O	O O O
Michigan	O	O O O
Minnesota	O	O O O
Mississippi	O	O O O
Missouri	O	O O O
Montana	O	O O O
Nebraska	O	O O O
Nevada	O	O O O
New Hampshire	O	O O O
New Jersey	O	O O O
New Mexico	O	O O O
New York	O	O O O
North Carolina	O	O O O
North Dakota	O	O O O
Ohio	O	O O O
Oklahoma	O	O O O
Oregon	O	O O O
Pennsylvania	O	O O O
Rhode Island	O	O O O
South Carolina	O	O O O
South Dakota	O	O O O
Tennessee	O	O O O
Texas	O	O O O
Utah	O	O O O
Vermont	O	O O O
Virginia	O	O O O
Washington	O	O O O
West Virginia	O	O O O
Wisconsin	O	O O O
Wyoming	O	O O O
Latin America	O	O O O
Europe	O	O O O
Africa	O	O O O
Asia	O	O O O
Other	O	O O O

21. Below is a list of 66 different undergraduate major
fields grouped into general categories.
Mark only three of the 66 fields as follows:

① First choice (your probable major field of study).
② Second choice.
Ⓛ The field of study which is least appealing to you.

Arts and Humanities

Architecture ① ② Ⓛ
English (literature) ① ② Ⓛ
Fine arts ① ② Ⓛ
History ① ② Ⓛ
Journalism (writing) ① ② Ⓛ
Language (modern) ① ② Ⓛ
Language (other) ① ② Ⓛ
Music ① ② Ⓛ
Philosophy ① ② Ⓛ
Speech and drama ① ② Ⓛ
Theology ① ② Ⓛ
Other ① ② Ⓛ

Biological Science

Biology (general) ① ② Ⓛ
Biochemistry ① ② Ⓛ
Biophysics ① ② Ⓛ
Botany ① ② Ⓛ
Zoology ① ② Ⓛ
Other ① ② Ⓛ

Business

Accounting ① ② Ⓛ
Business admin. ① ② Ⓛ
Electronic data
processing ① ② Ⓛ
Secretarial studies ① ② Ⓛ
Other ① ② Ⓛ

Engineering

Aeronautical ① ② Ⓛ
Civil ① ② Ⓛ
Chemical ① ② Ⓛ
Electrical ① ② Ⓛ
Industrial ① ② Ⓛ
Mechanical ① ② Ⓛ
Other ① ② Ⓛ

Physical Science

Chemistry ① ② Ⓛ
Earth science ① ② Ⓛ
Mathematics ① ② Ⓛ
Physics ① ② Ⓛ
Statistics ① ② Ⓛ
Other ① ② Ⓛ

Professional

Health Technology
(medical, dental,
laboratory) ① ② Ⓛ
Nursing ① ② Ⓛ
Pharmacy ① ② Ⓛ
Predentistry ① ② Ⓛ
Prelaw ① ② Ⓛ
Premedical ① ② Ⓛ
Preveterinary ① ② Ⓛ
Therapy (occupat.,
physical, speech) ① ② Ⓛ
Other ① ② Ⓛ

Social Science

Anthropology ① ② Ⓛ
Economics ① ② Ⓛ
Education ① ② Ⓛ
History ① ② Ⓛ
Political science
(government,
int. relations) ① ② Ⓛ
Psychology ① ② Ⓛ
Social work ① ② Ⓛ
Sociology ① ② Ⓛ
Other ① ② Ⓛ

Other Fields

Agriculture ① ② Ⓛ
Communications
(radio, T. V., etc.) ① ② Ⓛ
Electronics
(technology) ① ② Ⓛ
Forestry ① ② Ⓛ
Home economics ① ② Ⓛ
Industrial arts ① ② Ⓛ
Library science ① ② Ⓛ
Military science ① ② Ⓛ
Physical education
and recreation ① ② Ⓛ
Other (technical) ① ② Ⓛ
Other (nontechnical) ① ② Ⓛ
Undecided ① ② Ⓛ

Please be sure that only three circles have been marked in the
above list.

22. Probable Career Occupation

Note:
Make only three responses, one in each column { ① First Choice ② Second Choice Ⓛ Least Appealing

Accountant or actuary ① ② Ⓛ
Actor or entertainer ① ② Ⓛ
Architect ① ② Ⓛ
Artist ① ② Ⓛ
Business (clerical) ① ② Ⓛ
Business executive
(management, administrator) ① ② Ⓛ
Business owner or proprietor ① ② Ⓛ
Business salesman or buyer ① ② Ⓛ
Clergyman (minister, priest) ① ② Ⓛ
Clergy (other religious) ① ② Ⓛ
Clinical psychologist ① ② Ⓛ
College teacher ① ② Ⓛ
Computer programmer ① ② Ⓛ
Conservationist or forester ① ② Ⓛ
Dentist (including orthodontist) ① ② Ⓛ
Dietitian or home economist ① ② Ⓛ
Engineer ① ② Ⓛ
Farmer or rancher ① ② Ⓛ
Foreign service worker
(including diplomat) ① ② Ⓛ
Housewife ① ② Ⓛ
Interior decorator
(including designer) ① ② Ⓛ
Interpretor (translator) ① ② Ⓛ
Lab technician or hygienist ① ② Ⓛ
Law enforcement officer ① ② Ⓛ
Lawyer (attorney) ① ② Ⓛ
Military service (career) ① ② Ⓛ
Musician (performer, composer) ① ② Ⓛ
Nurse ① ② Ⓛ
Optometrist ① ② Ⓛ
Pharmacist ① ② Ⓛ
Physician ① ② Ⓛ
School counselor ① ② Ⓛ
School principal or superintendant ① ② Ⓛ
Scientific researcher ① ② Ⓛ
Social worker ① ② Ⓛ
Statistician ① ② Ⓛ
Therapist (physical,
occupational, speech) ① ② Ⓛ
Teacher (elementary) ① ② Ⓛ
Teacher (secondary) ① ② Ⓛ
Veterinarian ① ② Ⓛ
Writer or journalist ① ② Ⓛ
Skilled trades ① ② Ⓛ
Other ① ② Ⓛ
Undecided ① ② Ⓛ

23. Below is a general list of things that students sometimes do. Indicate which of these things you did during the past year in school. If you engaged in an activity frequently, Mark "f." If you engaged in an activity one or more times, but not frequently, Mark "o"(occasionally). Mark "n"(not at all) if you have not performed the activity during the past year.
(Mark one for each item)

Frequently / *Occasionally* / *Not at all*

Voted in a student election .... Ⓕ Ⓞ Ⓝ
Came late to class .... Ⓕ Ⓞ Ⓝ
Listened to New Orlean's (Dixieland) jazz .... Ⓕ Ⓞ Ⓝ
Gambled with cards or dice .... Ⓕ Ⓞ Ⓝ
Played a musical instrument .... Ⓕ Ⓞ Ⓝ
Took a nap or rest during the day .... Ⓕ Ⓞ Ⓝ
Drove a car .... Ⓕ Ⓞ Ⓝ
Stayed up all night .... Ⓕ Ⓞ Ⓝ
Studied in the library .... Ⓕ Ⓞ Ⓝ
Attended a ballet performance .... Ⓕ Ⓞ Ⓝ
Participated on the speech or debate team .... Ⓕ Ⓞ Ⓝ
Acted in plays .... Ⓕ Ⓞ Ⓝ
Sang in a choir or glee club .... Ⓕ Ⓞ Ⓝ
Argued with other students .... Ⓕ Ⓞ Ⓝ
Called a teacher by his or her first name .... Ⓕ Ⓞ Ⓝ
Wrote an article for the school paper or literary magazine Ⓕ Ⓞ Ⓝ
Had a blind date .... Ⓕ Ⓞ Ⓝ
Wrote a short story or poem (not for a class) ...... Ⓕ Ⓞ Ⓝ
Played in a school band .... Ⓕ Ⓞ Ⓝ
Played in a school orchestra .... Ⓕ Ⓞ Ⓝ
Smoked cigarettes .... Ⓕ Ⓞ Ⓝ
Attended Sunday school .... Ⓕ Ⓞ Ⓝ
Checked out a book or journal from the school library .... Ⓕ Ⓞ Ⓝ
Went to the movies .... Ⓕ Ⓞ Ⓝ
Discussed how to make money with other students ...... Ⓕ Ⓞ Ⓝ
Said grace before meals .... Ⓕ Ⓞ Ⓝ
Prayed (not including grace before meals) .... Ⓕ Ⓞ Ⓝ
Listened to folk music .... Ⓕ Ⓞ Ⓝ
Attended a public recital or concert .... Ⓕ Ⓞ Ⓝ
Made wisecracks in class .... Ⓕ Ⓞ Ⓝ
Arranged a date for another student .... Ⓕ Ⓞ Ⓝ
Went to an over-night or week-end party .... Ⓕ Ⓞ Ⓝ
Took weight-reducing or dietary formula .... Ⓕ Ⓞ Ⓝ
Drank beer .... Ⓕ Ⓞ Ⓝ
Overslept and missed a class or appointment .... Ⓕ Ⓞ Ⓝ
Typed a homework assignment .... Ⓕ Ⓞ Ⓝ
Participated in an informal group sing .... Ⓕ Ⓞ Ⓝ
Drank wine .... Ⓕ Ⓞ Ⓝ
Cribbed on an examination .... Ⓕ Ⓞ Ⓝ
Turned in a paper or theme late .... Ⓕ Ⓞ Ⓝ
Tried on clothes in a store without buying anything .... Ⓕ Ⓞ Ⓝ
Asked questions in class .... Ⓕ Ⓞ Ⓝ
Attended church .... Ⓕ Ⓞ Ⓝ
Participated in organized demonstrations .... Ⓕ Ⓞ Ⓝ

24. Indicate the importance to you personally of each of the following:
(Mark one for each item)

Essential / *Very Important* / *Somewhat Important* / *Not Important*

Becoming accomplished in one of the performing arts (acting, dancing, etc.).. Ⓔ Ⓥ Ⓢ Ⓝ
Becoming an authority on a special subject in my subject field... Ⓔ Ⓥ Ⓢ Ⓝ
Obtaining recognition from my colleagues for contributions in my special field .... Ⓔ Ⓥ Ⓢ Ⓝ
Becoming an accomplished musician (performer or composer) .... Ⓔ Ⓥ Ⓢ Ⓝ
Becoming an expert in finance and commerce .... Ⓔ Ⓥ Ⓢ Ⓝ
Having administrative responsibility for the work of others .... Ⓔ Ⓥ Ⓢ Ⓝ
Being very well-off financially .... Ⓔ Ⓥ Ⓢ Ⓝ
Helping others who are in difficulty .... Ⓔ Ⓥ Ⓢ Ⓝ
Participating in an organization like the Peace Corps or Vista ... Ⓔ Ⓥ Ⓢ Ⓝ
Becoming an outstanding athlete .... Ⓔ Ⓥ Ⓢ Ⓝ
Becoming a community leader................................. Ⓔ Ⓥ Ⓢ Ⓝ
Making a theoretical contribution to science .... Ⓔ Ⓥ Ⓢ Ⓝ
Writing original works (poems, novels, short stories, etc.)....... Ⓔ Ⓥ Ⓢ Ⓝ
Never being obligated to people .... Ⓔ Ⓥ Ⓢ Ⓝ
Creating artistic work (painting, sculpture, decorating, etc.)...... Ⓔ Ⓥ Ⓢ Ⓝ
Keeping up to date with political affairs .... Ⓔ Ⓥ Ⓢ Ⓝ
Being successful in a business of my own····················· Ⓔ Ⓥ Ⓢ Ⓝ

25. Rate yourself on each of the following traits as you really think you are when compared with the average student of your own age. We want the most accurate estimate of how you see yourself. (Mark one for each item)

Trait	Highest 10 Percent	Above Average	Average	Below Average	Lowest 10 Percent
Academic ability	O	O	O	O	O
Athletic ability	O	O	O	O	O
Artistic ability	O	O	O	O	O
Cheerfulness	O	O	O	O	O
Defensiveness	O	O	O	O	O
Drive to achieve	O	O	O	O	O
Leadership ability	O	O	O	O	O
Mathematical ability	O	O	O	O	O
Mechanical ability	O	O	O	O	O
Originality	O	O	O	O	O
Political conservatism	O	O	O	O	O
Political liberalism	O	O	O	O	O
Popularity	O	O	O	O	O
Popularity with the opposite sex	O	O	O	O	O
Public speaking ability	O	O	O	O	O
Self-confidence (intellectual)	O	O	O	O	O
Self-confidence (social)	O	O	O	O	O
Sensitivity to criticism	O	O	O	O	O
Stubbornness	O	O	O	O	O
Understanding of others	O	O	O	O	O
Writing ability	O	O	O	O	O

26. How old will you be on December 31 of this year?
(Mark one)

16 or younger	O	20	O
17	O	21	O
18	O	Older than 21	O
19	O		

27. (If you are married, omit the following question)
What is your best guess as to the chances that you will marry

	While in College?	Within a Year after College?
Very good chance	O	O
Some chance	O	O
Very little chance	O	O
No chance	O	O

165

1969 Student Information Form

YOUR NAME (please print) _____

First · Middle or Maiden · Last

HOME STREET ADDRESS _____

City · State · Zip Code (if known)

When were you born?

Month (01-12)	Day (01-31)	Year

Dear Student:

The information in this report is being collected as part of a continuing study of higher education by the American Council on Education. The Council, which is a non-governmental association of colleges and educational organizations, is soliciting your cooperation in this research in order to achieve a better understanding of how students are affected by their college experiences. Identifying information has been requested in order to make subsequent mail follow-up studies possible. Your response will be held in the strictest professional confidence, and will be used only in group summaries for research purposes.

Sincerely yours,

Logan Wilson

Logan Wilson   President

DIRECTIONS: Your responses will be read by an optical mark reader. Your careful observance of these few simple rules will be most appreciated.

Use only black lead pencil (No. 2½ or softer). Make heavy black marks that fill the circle. Erase cleanly any answer you wish to change. Make no stray markings of any kind.

EXAMPLE: Will marks made with ball pen or fountain pen be properly read?   Yes ○   No ●

1. Your Sex: Male ○ .... Female ○

2. How old will you be on December 31 of this year? (Mark one)

16 or younger ...... ○	20 .... ○
17 .... ○	21 .... ○
18 .... ○	Older than 21 ...... ○
19 .... ○	

3. What was your average grade in secondary school? (Mark one)

A or A+ ..... ○	B- ..... ○
A- .... ○	C+ ...... ○
B+ .... ○	C ...... ○
B .... ○	D ...... ○

4. To how many colleges other than this one did you actually apply for admission? From how many did you receive acceptances? (Mark one in each column)

	Applications	Acceptances
No other .... ○	.... ○
One .... ○	.... ○
Two .... ○	.... ○
Three .... ○	.... ○
Four .... ○	.... ○
Five .... ○	.... ○
Six or more .... ○	.... ○

5. Mark one:

This is the first time I have enrolled in college as a freshman .... ○

I came to this college from a junior college .... ○

I came to this college from a four-year college or university .. .. ○

6. The following questions deal with accomplishments that might possibly apply to your high school years. Do not be discouraged by this list; it covers many areas of interest and few students will be able to say "yes" to many items. (Mark all that apply)

Yes

Was elected president of one or more student organizations (recognized by the school). .... ○

Received a high rating (Good, Excellent) in a state or regional music contest .... ○

Participated in a state or regional speech or debate contest .... ○

Had a major part in a play .... ○

Won a varsity letter (sports) .... ○

Won a prize or award in an art competition .... ○

Edited the school paper, yearbook, or literary magazine .... ○

Had poems, stories, essays, or articles published .... ○

Participated in a National Science Foundation summer program .... ○

Placed (first, second, or third) in a state or regional science contest .... ○

Was a member of a scholastic honor society .... ○

Won a Certificate of Merit or Letter of Commendation in the National Merit Program .... ○

7. What is the highest academic degree that you intend to obtain? That your parents hope you will obtain? (Mark one in each column)

You Intend / Your Parents Hope

None	○○
Associate (or equivalent)	○○
Bachelor's degree (B.A., B.S., etc.)	○○
Master's degree (M.A., M.S. etc.)	○○
Ph.D or Ed.D	○○
M.D., D.D.S., or D.V.M.	○○
LL.B. or J.D.	○○
B.D.	○○
Other	○○

8. Do you have any concern about your ability to finance your college education? (Mark one)

None (I am confident that I will have sufficient funds) .... ○

Some concern (but I will probably have enough funds) .... ○

Major concern (not sure I will be able to complete college) ..... ○

9. Are you a U.S. Citizen? (Mark one)

Yes, native born	○
Yes, naturalized	○
No	○

10. Through what source do you intend to finance the first year of your undergraduate education? (Mark one in each row)

Major Source / Minor Source / Not a Source

Personal savings and/or employment . ○○○
Parental or other family aid . . . . ○○○
Repayable loan . . . . ○○○
Scholarship, grant, or other gift . . . . ○○○

11. What is the highest level of formal education obtained by your parents? (Mark one in each column)

	Father	Mother
Grammar school or less	○	○
Some high school	○	○
High school graduate	○	○
Some college	○	○
College degree	○	○
Postgraduate degree	○	○

12. What is your best estimate of the total income last year of your parental family (not your own family if you are married)? Consider annual income from all sources before taxes. (Mark one)

Less than $4,000 . . ○ $15,000-$19,999 . ○
$4,000-$5,999 . . . . ○ $20,000-$24,999 . ○
$6,000-$7,999 . . . . ○ $25,000-$29,999 . ○
$8,000-$9,999 . . . . ○ $30,000 or more . . ○
$10,000-$14,999 . . . ○

13. What is your racial background? (Mark one)

White/Caucasian . . . . ○
Black/Negro/Afro-American . . . . ○
American Indian . . . . ○
Oriental . . . . ○
Other . . . . ○

14. Mark one in each column:

	Religion in Which you Were Reared	Your Present Religious Preference
Baptist	○	○
Congregational (United Church of Christ)	○	○
Episcopal	○	○
Jewish	○	○
Latter Day Saints (Mormon)	○	○
Lutheran	○	○
Methodist	○	○
Muslim	○	○
Presbyterian	○	○
Quaker (Society of Friends)	○	○
Roman Catholic	○	○
Seventh Day Adventist	○	○
Unitarian-Universalist	○	○
Other Protestant	○	○
Other Religions	○	○
None	○	○

15. Where did you rank academically in your high school graduating class? (Mark one)

Top 1% . . . ○   Top 10% . . ○   Top Quarter . ○
2nd Quarter ○   3rd Quarter ○   4th Quarter . ○

16. During the next few years, to what extent do you think the Federal Government should be involved in each of the following national issues? (Mark one in each row)

1. Eliminate any existing programs or remain uninvolved
2. Decrease involvement from current levels
3. Maintain current level of involvement
4. Increase involvement from current level
5. Initiate new crash program

① ② ③ ④ ⑤ Control of cigarette advertising
① ② ③ ④ ⑤ Elimination of violence from T.V.
① ② ③ ④ ⑤ Control of environmental pollution
① ② ③ ④ ⑤ Use of tax incentives to control the birth rate
① ② ③ ④ ⑤ Protection of the consumer from faulty goods and services
① ② ③ ④ ⑤ Compensatory education for the disadvantaged
① ② ③ ④ ⑤ Special benefits for veterans
① ② ③ ④ ⑤ Control of firearms
① ② ③ ④ ⑤ Elimination of poverty
① ② ③ ④ ⑤ Crime prevention
① ② ③ ④ ⑤ School desegregation
① ② ③ ④ ⑤ Compensatory financial aid for the disadvantaged
① ② ③ ④ ⑤ Control of student activists

17. Where did you live for most of the time while you were growing up?

On a farm . . . . ○
In a small town . . . . ○
In a moderate size town or city . . . . ○
In a suburb of a large city . . . . ○
In a large city . . . . ○

MAKE SURE YOU HAVE ANSWERED ITEMS 18-21

18. Mark one in each row:

1. Left
2. Liberal
3. Middle-of-the-road
4. Moderately conservative
5. Strongly conservative

① ② ③ ④ ⑤ How would you characterize yourself politically at the present time?
① ② ③ ④ ⑤ How do you think you will characterize yourself politically four years from now?

19. How many miles is this college from your home?

10 or less ○   101-500 . . . . ○
11-50 . . . . ○   501-1000 . . . . . . ○
51-100 . . . ○   More than 1000 . ○

20. From what kind of secondary school did you graduate? (Mark one)

Public . . . . ○
Private (denominational) . . . . ○
Private (non-denominational) . . . ○
Other . . . . ○

21. How many brothers and sisters now living do you have? (Mark one in each row)

None / 1 / 2 / 3 or more

Number of older brothers . . ○○○○
Number of older sisters . . . ○○○○
Number of younger brothers ○○○○
Number of younger sisters . ○○○○

22. What is your best guess as to the chances that you will: (Mark one in each row)

	Very Good Chance	Some Chance	Very Little Chance	No Chance
Get married while in college?	○	○	○	○
Get married within a year after college?	○	○	○	○
Obtain an A– or better over-all grade point average?	○	○	○	○
Change major field?	○	○	○	○
Change career choice?	○	○	○	○
Fail one or more courses?	○	○	○	○
Graduate with honors?	○	○	○	○
Be elected to a student office?	○	○	○	○
Join a social fraternity, sorority, or club?	○	○	○	○
Author or co-author a published article?	○	○	○	○
Be drafted while I am in college?	○	○	○	○
Be elected to an academic honor society?	○	○	○	○
Protest against U.S. military policy?	○	○	○	○
Protest against administrative policy at this college?	○	○	○	○
Protest against existing racial or ethnic policies?	○	○	○	○
Drop out of this college temporarily (exclude transferring)?	○	○	○	○
Enlist in the Armed Services before graduating?	○	○	○	○
Be more successful after graduation than most students attending this college?	○	○	○	○
Drop out permanently (exclude transferring)?	○	○	○	○
Transfer to another college before graduating?	○	○	○	○

23. Mark one in each column:

Your current home state / Your birthplace / Father's birthplace / Mother's birthplace

State		
Alabama	O	Ⓥ Ⓕ Ⓜ
Alaska	O	Ⓥ Ⓕ Ⓜ
Arizona	O	Ⓥ Ⓕ Ⓜ
Arkansas	O	Ⓥ Ⓕ Ⓜ
California	O	Ⓥ Ⓕ Ⓜ
Colorado	O	Ⓥ Ⓕ Ⓜ
Connecticut	O	Ⓥ Ⓕ Ⓜ
Delaware	O	Ⓥ Ⓕ Ⓜ
D.C.	O	Ⓥ Ⓕ Ⓜ
Florida	O	Ⓥ Ⓕ Ⓜ
Georgia	O	Ⓥ Ⓕ Ⓜ
Hawaii	O	Ⓥ Ⓕ Ⓜ
Idaho	O	Ⓥ Ⓕ Ⓜ
Illinois	O	Ⓥ Ⓕ Ⓜ
Indiana	O	Ⓥ Ⓕ Ⓜ
Iowa	O	Ⓥ Ⓕ Ⓜ
Kansas	O	Ⓥ Ⓕ Ⓜ
Kentucky	O	Ⓥ Ⓕ Ⓜ
Louisiana	O	Ⓥ Ⓕ Ⓜ
Maine	O	Ⓥ Ⓕ Ⓜ
Maryland	O	Ⓥ Ⓕ Ⓜ
Massachusetts	O	Ⓥ Ⓕ Ⓜ
Michigan	O	Ⓥ Ⓕ Ⓜ
Minnesota	O	Ⓥ Ⓕ Ⓜ
Mississippi	O	Ⓥ Ⓕ Ⓜ
Missouri	O	Ⓥ Ⓕ Ⓜ
Montana	O	Ⓥ Ⓕ Ⓜ
Nebraska	O	Ⓥ Ⓕ Ⓜ
Nevada	O	Ⓥ Ⓕ Ⓜ
New Hampshire	O	Ⓥ Ⓕ Ⓜ
New Jersey	O	Ⓥ Ⓕ Ⓜ
New Mexico	O	Ⓥ Ⓕ Ⓜ
New York	O	Ⓥ Ⓕ Ⓜ
North Carolina	O	Ⓥ Ⓕ Ⓜ
North Dakota	O	Ⓥ Ⓕ Ⓜ
Ohio	O	Ⓥ Ⓕ Ⓜ
Oklahoma	O	Ⓥ Ⓕ Ⓜ
Oregon	O	Ⓥ Ⓕ Ⓜ
Pennsylvania	O	Ⓥ Ⓕ Ⓜ
Rhode Island	O	Ⓥ Ⓕ Ⓜ
South Carolina	O	Ⓥ Ⓕ Ⓜ
South Dakota	O	Ⓥ Ⓕ Ⓜ
Tennessee	O	Ⓥ Ⓕ Ⓜ
Texas	O	Ⓥ Ⓕ Ⓜ
Utah	O	Ⓥ Ⓕ Ⓜ
Vermont	O	Ⓥ Ⓕ Ⓜ
Virginia	O	Ⓥ Ⓕ Ⓜ
Washington	O	Ⓥ Ⓕ Ⓜ
West Virginia	O	Ⓥ Ⓕ Ⓜ
Wisconsin	O	Ⓥ Ⓕ Ⓜ
Wyoming	O	Ⓥ Ⓕ Ⓜ
Canada	O	Ⓥ Ⓕ Ⓜ
Mexico	O	Ⓥ Ⓕ Ⓜ
Puerto Rico	O	Ⓥ Ⓕ Ⓜ
Other Latin America	O	Ⓥ Ⓕ Ⓜ
Europe	O	Ⓥ Ⓕ Ⓜ
Asia	O	Ⓥ Ⓕ Ⓜ
Other	O	Ⓥ Ⓕ Ⓜ

24. Mark only three responses, one in each column.

Your probable career occupation.
Your father's occupation.
Your mother's occupation.
Ⓥ Ⓕ Ⓜ

NOTE: If your father (or mother) is deceased, please indicate his (her) last occupation.

Accountant or actuary	Ⓥ Ⓕ Ⓜ
Actor or entertainer	Ⓥ Ⓕ Ⓜ
Architect	Ⓥ Ⓕ Ⓜ
Artist	Ⓥ Ⓕ Ⓜ
Business (clerical)	Ⓥ Ⓕ Ⓜ
Business executive (management, administrator)	Ⓥ Ⓕ Ⓜ
Business owner or proprietor	Ⓥ Ⓕ Ⓜ
Business salesman or buyer	Ⓥ Ⓕ Ⓜ
Clergyman (minister, priest)	Ⓥ Ⓕ Ⓜ
Clergy (other religious)	Ⓥ Ⓕ Ⓜ
Clinical psychologist	Ⓥ Ⓕ Ⓜ
College teacher	Ⓥ Ⓕ Ⓜ
Computer programmer	Ⓥ Ⓕ Ⓜ
Conservationist or forester	Ⓥ Ⓕ Ⓜ
Dentist (including orthodontist)	Ⓥ Ⓕ Ⓜ
Dietitian or home economist	Ⓥ Ⓕ Ⓜ
Engineer	Ⓥ Ⓕ Ⓜ
Farmer or rancher	Ⓥ Ⓕ Ⓜ
Foreign service worker (including diplomat)	Ⓥ Ⓕ Ⓜ
Housewife	Ⓥ Ⓕ Ⓜ
Interior decorator (including designer)	Ⓥ Ⓕ Ⓜ
Interpreter (translator)	Ⓥ Ⓕ Ⓜ
Lab technician or hygienist	Ⓥ Ⓕ Ⓜ
Law enforcement officer	Ⓥ Ⓕ Ⓜ
Lawyer (attorney)	Ⓥ Ⓕ Ⓜ
Military service (career)	Ⓥ Ⓕ Ⓜ
Musician (performer, composer)	Ⓥ Ⓕ Ⓜ
Nurse	Ⓥ Ⓕ Ⓜ
Optometrist	Ⓥ Ⓕ Ⓜ
Pharmacist	Ⓥ Ⓕ Ⓜ
Physician	Ⓥ Ⓕ Ⓜ
School counselor	Ⓥ Ⓕ Ⓜ
School principal or superintendent	Ⓥ Ⓕ Ⓜ
Scientific researcher	Ⓥ Ⓕ Ⓜ
Social worker	Ⓥ Ⓕ Ⓜ
Statistician	Ⓥ Ⓕ Ⓜ
Therapist (physical, occupational, speech)	Ⓥ Ⓕ Ⓜ
Teacher (elementary)	Ⓥ Ⓕ Ⓜ
Teacher (secondary)	Ⓥ Ⓕ Ⓜ
Veterinarian	Ⓥ Ⓕ Ⓜ
Writer or journalist	Ⓥ Ⓕ Ⓜ
Skilled trades	Ⓥ Ⓕ Ⓜ
Other	Ⓥ
Undecided	
Laborer (unskilled)	Ⓕ Ⓜ
Semi-skilled worker	Ⓕ Ⓜ
Other occupation	Ⓕ Ⓜ
Unemployed	Ⓕ

25. In general, my parents could be characterized as:
(Mark one circle in each row)

1. Strongly agree
2. Agree
3. Disagree
4. Strongly disagree
①②③④

Interested in intellectual pursuits	①②③④
Interested in cultural pursuits	①②③④
Deeply religious	①②③④
Interested in politics	①②③④
Deeply concerned about their children	①②③④
Financially comfortable	①②③④
Having high aspirations for me	①②③④

26.

Below is a general list of things that students sometimes do. Indicate which of these things you did during the past year in school. If you engaged in an activity frequently, mark "F". If you engaged in an activity one or more times, but not frequently, mark "O" (occasionally). Mark "N" (not at all) if you have not performed the activity during the past year. (Mark one for each item)

Frequently / Occasionally / Not at all

Voted in a student election	Ⓕ Ⓞ Ⓝ
Came late to class	Ⓕ Ⓞ Ⓝ
Played a musical instrument	Ⓕ Ⓞ Ⓝ
Studied in the library	Ⓕ Ⓞ Ⓝ
Checked out a book or journal from the school library	Ⓕ Ⓞ Ⓝ
Arranged a date for another student	Ⓕ Ⓞ Ⓝ
Overslept and missed a class or appointment	Ⓕ Ⓞ Ⓝ
Typed a homework assignment	Ⓕ Ⓞ Ⓝ
Discussed my future with my parents	Ⓕ Ⓞ Ⓝ
Failed to complete a homework assignment on time	Ⓕ Ⓞ Ⓝ
Argued with a teacher in class	Ⓕ Ⓞ Ⓝ
Attended a religious service	Ⓕ Ⓞ Ⓝ
Demonstrated for a change in some racial or ethnic policy	Ⓕ Ⓞ Ⓝ
Demonstrated for a change in some military policy	Ⓕ Ⓞ Ⓝ
Demonstrated for a change in some administrative policy of my high school	Ⓕ Ⓞ Ⓝ
Did extra (unassigned) reading for a course	Ⓕ Ⓞ Ⓝ
Took sleeping pills	Ⓕ Ⓞ Ⓝ
Tutored another student	Ⓕ Ⓞ Ⓝ
Played chess	Ⓕ Ⓞ Ⓝ
Read poetry not connected with a course	Ⓕ Ⓞ Ⓝ
Took a tranquilizing pill	Ⓕ Ⓞ Ⓝ
Discussed religion	Ⓕ Ⓞ Ⓝ
Took vitamins	Ⓕ Ⓞ Ⓝ
Visited an art gallery or museum	Ⓕ Ⓞ Ⓝ
Worked in a school political campaign	Ⓕ Ⓞ Ⓝ
Worked in a local, state, or national political campaign	Ⓕ Ⓞ Ⓝ
Missed school because of illness	Ⓕ Ⓞ Ⓝ
Smoked cigarettes	Ⓕ Ⓞ Ⓝ
Discussed politics	Ⓕ Ⓞ Ⓝ
Drank beer	Ⓕ Ⓞ Ⓝ
Discussed sports	Ⓕ Ⓞ Ⓝ
Asked a teacher for advice after class	Ⓕ Ⓞ Ⓝ
Had vocational counseling	Ⓕ Ⓞ Ⓝ
Stayed up all night	Ⓕ Ⓞ Ⓝ

27. Below is a list of 66 different undergraduate major fields grouped into general categories. <u>Mark only three</u> of the 66 fields as follows:

① <u>First</u> choice (your probable major field of study).
② <u>Second</u> choice.
Ⓛ The field of study which is <u>least</u> appealing to you.

ARTS AND HUMANITIES

Architecture ....①②Ⓛ
English (literature) ...①②Ⓛ
Fine arts.............①②Ⓛ
History ....①②Ⓛ
Journalism (writing) ..①②Ⓛ
Language (modern) ...①②Ⓛ
Language (other) .....①②Ⓛ
Music................①②Ⓛ
Philosophy ....①②Ⓛ
Speech and drama ....①②Ⓛ
Theology............①②Ⓛ
Other ....①②Ⓛ

BIOLOGICAL SCIENCE

Biology (general).....①②Ⓛ
Biochemistry ....①②Ⓛ
Biophysics ....①②Ⓛ
Botany..............①②Ⓛ
Zoology.............①②Ⓛ
Other ....①②Ⓛ

BUSINESS

Accounting ....①②Ⓛ
Business admin ......①②Ⓛ
Electronic data
  processing ....①②Ⓛ
Secretarial studies ...①②Ⓛ
Other ....①②Ⓛ

ENGINEERING

Aeronautical..........①②Ⓛ
Civil ....①②Ⓛ
Chemical............①②Ⓛ
Electrical ....①②Ⓛ
Industrial ....①②Ⓛ
Mechanical ....①②Ⓛ
Other ....①②Ⓛ

PHYSICAL SCIENCE

Chemistry ....①②Ⓛ
Earth science........①②Ⓛ
Mathematics ....①②Ⓛ
Physics..............①②Ⓛ
Statistics ....①②Ⓛ
Other ....①②Ⓛ

PROFESSIONAL

Health Technology
  (medical, dental,
  laboratory) ....①②Ⓛ
Nursing............①②Ⓛ
Pharmacy ....①②Ⓛ
Predentistry........①②Ⓛ
Prelaw ....①②Ⓛ
Premedical ....①②Ⓛ
Preveterinary......①②Ⓛ
Therapy (occupat.,
  physical, speech)..①②Ⓛ
Other..............①②Ⓛ

SOCIAL SCIENCE

Anthropology ......①②Ⓛ
Economics ....①②Ⓛ
Education ....①②Ⓛ
History ....①②Ⓛ
Political science
  (government,
  int. relations) ....①②Ⓛ
Psychology ....①②Ⓛ
Social work ....①②Ⓛ
Sociology ....①②Ⓛ
Other ....①②Ⓛ

OTHER FIELDS

Agriculture........①②Ⓛ
Communications
  (radio, T.V., etc.)..①②Ⓛ
Electronics
  (technology)......①②Ⓛ
Forestry ....①②Ⓛ
Home economics ....①②Ⓛ
Industrial arts ....①②Ⓛ
Library science.....①②Ⓛ
Military science ...①②Ⓛ
Physical education
  and recreation ....①②Ⓛ
Other (technical)...①②Ⓛ
Other (nontechnical).①②Ⓛ
Undecided ....①②Ⓛ

Please be sure that <u>only three</u> circles have been marked in the above list.

28. Indicate the importance to you personally of each of the following: (Mark one for each item)

Column headers: Essential / Very Important / Somewhat Important / Not Important

Becoming accomplished in one of the performing arts (acting, dancing, etc.)............Ⓔ Ⓥ Ⓢ Ⓝ
Becoming an authority on a special subject in my subject field .Ⓔ Ⓥ Ⓢ Ⓝ
Obtaining recognition from my colleagues for contributions in my special field............Ⓔ Ⓥ Ⓢ Ⓝ
Influencing the political structure.......................Ⓔ Ⓥ Ⓢ Ⓝ
Influencing social values.................................Ⓔ Ⓥ Ⓢ Ⓝ
Raising a family ....Ⓔ Ⓥ Ⓢ Ⓝ
Having an active social life ....Ⓔ Ⓥ Ⓢ Ⓝ
Having friends with different backgrounds and interests from mine.......................................Ⓔ Ⓥ Ⓢ Ⓝ
Becoming an expert in finance and commerce................Ⓔ Ⓥ Ⓢ Ⓝ
Having administrative responsibility for the work of others.....Ⓔ Ⓥ Ⓢ Ⓝ
Being very well-off financially..........................Ⓔ Ⓥ Ⓢ Ⓝ
Helping others who are in difficulty.....................Ⓔ Ⓥ Ⓢ Ⓝ
Becoming a community leader ....Ⓔ Ⓥ Ⓢ Ⓝ
Making a theoretical contribution to science ....Ⓔ Ⓥ Ⓢ Ⓝ
Writing original works (poems, novels, short stories, etc.) .....Ⓔ Ⓥ Ⓢ Ⓝ
Never being obligated to people ....Ⓔ Ⓥ Ⓢ Ⓝ
Creating artistic work (painting, sculpture, decorating, etc.)...Ⓔ Ⓥ Ⓢ Ⓝ
Keeping up to date with political affairs..................Ⓔ Ⓥ Ⓢ Ⓝ
Being successful in a business of my own..................Ⓔ Ⓥ Ⓢ Ⓝ
Developing a meaningful philosophy of life ....Ⓔ Ⓥ Ⓢ Ⓝ

29. Mark one in each row:

{ Agree strongly
  Agree somewhat
  Disagree somewhat
  Disagree strongly

Column headers: Agree strongly / Agree somewhat / Disagree somewhat / Disagree strongly

Students should have a major role in specifying the college curriculum .... O O O O
Scientists should publish their findings regardless of the possible consequences .... O O O O
Realistically, an individual person can do little to bring about changes in our society .... O O O O
College officials have the right to regulate student behavior off campus .... O O O O
The chief benefit of a college education is that it increases one's earning power .... O O O O
Faculty promotions should be based in part on student evaluations .... O O O O
My beliefs and attitudes are similar to those of most other students .... O O O O
Student publications should be cleared by college officials .... O O O O
Marijuana should be legalized .... O O O O
College officials have the right to ban persons with extreme views from speaking on campus................ O O O O
Only volunteers should serve in the armed forces.....O O O O
Students from disadvantaged social backgrounds should be given preferential treatment in college admissions O O O O
Most college officials have been too lax in dealing with student protests on campus .... O O O O
Divorce laws should be liberalized................. O O O O
Under some conditions, abortions should be legalized O O O O
There is too much concern in the courts for the rights of criminals.................................... O O O O
Capital punishment (the death penalty) should be abolished..................................... O O O O

1971 Student Information Form

YOUR NAME _____
(please print) First Middle or Maiden Last

HOME STREET ADDRESS _____
(print)

CITY _____ STATE _____
(print)   (print)   Zip Code (if known)

When were you born?

Month (01-12)	Day (01-31)	Year

Dear Student:

The information in this report is being collected as part of a continuing study of higher education by the American Council on Education. The Council, which is a non-governmental association of colleges and educational organizations, encourages and solicits your cooperation in this research in order to achieve a better understanding of how students are affected by their college experiences. Detailed information on the goals and design of this research program are furnished in research reports available from the Council. Identifying information has been requested in order to make subsequent mail follow-up studies possible. Your response will be held in the strictest professional confidence.

Sincerely yours,

Logan Wilson

Logan Wilson, President

GRP.

(grid of numbered circles 0–9)

DIRECTIONS: Your responses will be read by an optical mark reader. Your careful observance of these few simple rules will be most appreciated:

Use only black lead pencil (No. 2½ or less).
Make heavy black marks that fill the circle.
Erase cleanly any answer you wish to change.
Make no stray markings of any kind.

          Yes No

EXAMPLE: Will marks made with ball pen or fountain pen be properly read? ○ ●

1. Your Sex:
Male ... ○
Female .. ○

2. Are you presently married?
Yes .. ○
No ... ○

3. How old will you be on December 31 of this year? (Mark one)
16 or younger .. ○
17 .... ○
18 .... ○
19 .... ○
20 .... ○
21 .... ○
22-25 .... ○
26 or older ..... ○

4. What was your average grade in secondary school? (Mark one)
A or A+ . ○
A- ..... ○
B+ ..... ○
B ...... ○
B- ..... ○
C+ ..... ○
C ...... ○
D ...... ○

5. Where did you rank academically in your high school graduating class? (Mark one)
Top Quarter ○ 3rd Quarter ○
2nd Quarter ○ 4th Quarter ○

6. Did you graduate from secondary school in the class of 1971?
Yes .... ○ No .... ○

7. Are you a veteran? (Mark one)
No .... ○
Yes, I served in Southeast Asia .... ○
Yes, but I did not serve in Southeast Asia .... ○

8. Mark one: This is the first time I have enrolled in college as a freshman .... ○
I have attended this college before .... ○
I came to this college from a junior college .... ○
I came to this college from a four-year college or university .... ○

9. The following questions deal with accomplishments that might possibly apply to your high school years. Do not be discouraged by this list; it covers many areas of interest and few students will be able to say "yes" to many items.
(Mark all that apply)   Yes

Was elected president of one or more student organizations (recognized by the school) .... ○
Received a high rating (Good, Excellent) in a state or regional music contest .... ○
Participated in a state or regional speech or debate contest .... ○
Had a major part in a play .... ○
Won a varsity letter (sports) .... ○
Won a prize or award in an art competition .... ○
Edited the school paper, yearbook, or literary magazine .... ○
Had poems, stories, essays, or articles published .... ○
Participated in a National Science Foundation summer program .... ○
Placed (first, second, or third) in a state or regional science contest .... ○
Was a member of a scholastic honor society .... ○
Won a Certificate of Merit or Letter of Commendation in the National Merit Program ... ○

10. What is the highest academic degree that you intend to obtain? (Mark one)
None .... ○
Associate (A.A. or equivalent) .. ○
Bachelor's degree (B.A.,B.S.,etc.) ○
Master's degree (M.A.,M.S.,etc.) . ○
Ph.D. or Ed.D. .... ○
M.D.,D.O.,D.D.S., or D.V.M. ... ○
LL.B. or J.D. (Law) .... ○
B.D. (Divinity) .... ○
Other .... ○

11. How many miles is this college from your home? (Mark one)
5 or less ○ 51-100 .... ○
6-10 ... ○ 101-500 ..... ○
11-50 .. ○ More than 500 ○

12. What is the highest level of formal education obtained by your parents? (Mark one in each column) Father Mother
Grammar school or less ○ .... ○
Some high school ..... ○ .... ○
High school graduate .. ○ .... ○
Some college .... ○ .... ○
College degree .... ○ .... ○
Postgraduate degree ... ○ .... ○

13. Do you have any concern about your ability to finance your college education?
  (Mark one)
None (I am confident that I will have sufficient funds) ..... ○
Some concern (but I will probably have enough funds) .. ○
Major concern (not sure I will be able to complete college) ... ○

170

14. For each item indicate if it is a source for financing your education. (Mark one in each row)

Major Source / Minor Source / Not a Source

	Major Source	Minor Source	Not a Source
Part-time or summer work	○	○	○
Savings from full-time employment	○	○	○
Parental or family aid or gifts	○	○	○
Federal benefits from parent's military service	○	○	○
G.I. benefits from your military service	○	○	○
Scholarships and grants	○	○	○
NDEA loans, federally insured loans or college loans	○	○	○
Other repayable loans.	○	○	○

15. What is your best estimate of the total income last year of your parental family (not your own family if you are married)? Consider annual income from all sources before taxes. (Mark one)

Less than $4,000 . . ○	$15,000-$19,999 . . . ○
$4,000-$5,999 . . . . ○	$20,000-$24,999 . . . ○
$6,000-$7,999 . . . . ○	$25,000-$29,999 . . . ○
$8,000-$9,999 . . . . ○	$30,000-$34,999 . . . ○
$10,000-$12,499 . . ○	$35,000-$39,999 . . . ○
$12,500-$14,999 . . ○	$40,000 or more . . . ○

16. Are you: (Mark all that apply.)

White/Caucasian	○
Black/Negro/Afro-American	○
American Indian	○
Oriental	○
Mexican-American/Chicano	○
Puerto Rican-American	○
Other	○

17. Mark one in each column:

	Religion in Which You Were Reared	Your Present Religious Preference
Protestant	○	○
Roman Catholic	○	○
Jewish	○	○
Other	○	○
None	○	○

18. In deciding to go to college, how important to you was each of the following reasons? (Mark one answer for each reason)

Very important / Somewhat important / Not important

	V	S	N
My parents wanted me to go	Ⓥ	Ⓢ	Ⓝ
To be able to contribute more to my community	Ⓥ	Ⓢ	Ⓝ
To be able to get a better job	Ⓥ	Ⓢ	Ⓝ
To gain a general education and appreciation of ideas	Ⓥ	Ⓢ	Ⓝ
To improve my reading and study skills	Ⓥ	Ⓢ	Ⓝ
There was nothing better to do	Ⓥ	Ⓢ	Ⓝ
To make me a more cultured person	Ⓥ	Ⓢ	Ⓝ
To be able to make more money	Ⓥ	Ⓢ	Ⓝ
To learn more about things that interest me	Ⓥ	Ⓢ	Ⓝ
To meet new and interesting people	Ⓥ	Ⓢ	Ⓝ
To prepare myself for graduate or professional school	Ⓥ	Ⓢ	Ⓝ

19. Below is a general list of things that students sometimes do. Indicate which of these things you did during the past year in school. If you engaged in an activity frequently, mark Ⓕ. If you engaged in an activity one or more times, but not frequently, mark Ⓞ (occasionally). Mark Ⓝ (not at all) if you have not performed the activity during the past year. (Mark one for each item)

Frequently / Occasionally / Not at all

	F	O	N
Voted in a student election	Ⓕ	Ⓞ	Ⓝ
Came late to class	Ⓕ	Ⓞ	Ⓝ
Played a musical instrument	Ⓕ	Ⓞ	Ⓝ
Studied in the library	Ⓕ	Ⓞ	Ⓝ
Checked out a book or journal from the school library	Ⓕ	Ⓞ	Ⓝ
Arranged a date for another student	Ⓕ	Ⓞ	Ⓝ
Overslept and missed a class or appointment	Ⓕ	Ⓞ	Ⓝ
Read about collegiate rights and responsibilities of students	Ⓕ	Ⓞ	Ⓝ
Typed a homework assignment	Ⓕ	Ⓞ	Ⓝ
Discussed my future with my parents	Ⓕ	Ⓞ	Ⓝ
Failed to complete a homework assignment on time	Ⓕ	Ⓞ	Ⓝ
Argued with a teacher in class	Ⓕ	Ⓞ	Ⓝ
Attended a religious service	Ⓕ	Ⓞ	Ⓝ
Demonstrated for a change in some racial or ethnic policy	Ⓕ	Ⓞ	Ⓝ
Demonstrated for a change in some military policy	Ⓕ	Ⓞ	Ⓝ
Demonstrated for a change in some administrative policy of my high school	Ⓕ	Ⓞ	Ⓝ
Did extra (unassigned) reading for a course	Ⓕ	Ⓞ	Ⓝ
Took sleeping pills	Ⓕ	Ⓞ	Ⓝ
Tutored another student	Ⓕ	Ⓞ	Ⓝ
Played chess	Ⓕ	Ⓞ	Ⓝ
Read poetry not connected with a course	Ⓕ	Ⓞ	Ⓝ
Took a tranquilizing pill	Ⓕ	Ⓞ	Ⓝ
Discussed religion	Ⓕ	Ⓞ	Ⓝ
Took vitamins	Ⓕ	Ⓞ	Ⓝ
Visited an art gallery or museum	Ⓕ	Ⓞ	Ⓝ
Worked in a school political campaign	Ⓕ	Ⓞ	Ⓝ
Worked in a local, state, or national political campaign	Ⓕ	Ⓞ	Ⓝ
Missed school because of illness	Ⓕ	Ⓞ	Ⓝ
Smoked cigarettes	Ⓕ	Ⓞ	Ⓝ
Discussed politics	Ⓕ	Ⓞ	Ⓝ
Drank beer	Ⓕ	Ⓞ	Ⓝ
Discussed sports	Ⓕ	Ⓞ	Ⓝ
Read about civil rights and liberties	Ⓕ	Ⓞ	Ⓝ
Asked a teacher for advice after class	Ⓕ	Ⓞ	Ⓝ
Had vocational counseling	Ⓕ	Ⓞ	Ⓝ
Stayed up all night	Ⓕ	Ⓞ	Ⓝ

20. How would you characterize your political views? (Mark one)

Far left	○
Liberal	○
Middle-of-the-road	○
Conservative	○
Far right	○

21. Mark only three responses, one in each column.

- Your probable career occupation.
- Your father's occupation.
- Your mother's occupation.

Ⓨ Ⓕ Ⓜ

NOTE: If your father (or mother) is deceased please indicate his (her) last occupation.

	Y	F	M
Accountant or actuary	Ⓨ	Ⓕ	Ⓜ
Actor or entertainer	Ⓨ	Ⓕ	Ⓜ
Architect	Ⓨ	Ⓕ	Ⓜ
Artist	Ⓨ	Ⓕ	Ⓜ
Business (clerical)	Ⓨ	Ⓕ	Ⓜ
Business executive (management, administrator)	Ⓨ	Ⓕ	Ⓜ
Business owner or proprietor	Ⓨ	Ⓕ	Ⓜ
Business salesman or buyer	Ⓨ	Ⓕ	Ⓜ
Clergyman (minister, priest)	Ⓨ	Ⓕ	Ⓜ
Clergy (other religious)	Ⓨ	Ⓕ	Ⓜ
Clinical psychologist	Ⓨ	Ⓕ	Ⓜ
College teacher	Ⓨ	Ⓕ	Ⓜ
Computer programmer	Ⓨ	Ⓕ	Ⓜ
Conservationist or forester	Ⓨ	Ⓕ	Ⓜ
Dentist (including orthodontist)	Ⓨ	Ⓕ	Ⓜ
Dietitian or home economist	Ⓨ	Ⓕ	Ⓜ
Engineer	Ⓨ	Ⓕ	Ⓜ
Farmer or rancher	Ⓨ	Ⓕ	Ⓜ
Foreign service worker (including diplomat)	Ⓨ	Ⓕ	Ⓜ
Housewife	Ⓨ	Ⓕ	Ⓜ
Interior decorator (including designer)	Ⓨ	Ⓕ	Ⓜ
Interpreter (translator)	Ⓨ	Ⓕ	Ⓜ
Lab technician or hygienist	Ⓨ	Ⓕ	Ⓜ
Law enforcement officer	Ⓨ	Ⓕ	Ⓜ
Lawyer (attorney)	Ⓨ	Ⓕ	Ⓜ
Military service (career)	Ⓨ	Ⓕ	Ⓜ
Musician (performer, composer)	Ⓨ	Ⓕ	Ⓜ
Nurse	Ⓨ	Ⓕ	Ⓜ
Optometrist	Ⓨ	Ⓕ	Ⓜ
Pharmacist	Ⓨ	Ⓕ	Ⓜ
Physician	Ⓨ	Ⓕ	Ⓜ
School counselor	Ⓨ	Ⓕ	Ⓜ
School principal or superintendent	Ⓨ	Ⓕ	Ⓜ
Scientific researcher	Ⓨ	Ⓕ	Ⓜ
Social worker	Ⓨ	Ⓕ	Ⓜ
Statistician	Ⓨ	Ⓕ	Ⓜ
Therapist (physical, occupational, speech)	Ⓨ	Ⓕ	Ⓜ
Teacher (elementary)	Ⓨ	Ⓕ	Ⓜ
Teacher (secondary)	Ⓨ	Ⓕ	Ⓜ
Veterinarian	Ⓨ	Ⓕ	Ⓜ
Writer or journalist	Ⓨ	Ⓕ	Ⓜ
Skilled trades	Ⓨ	Ⓕ	Ⓜ
Other	Ⓨ		
Undecided	Ⓨ		
Laborer (unskilled)		Ⓕ	Ⓜ
Semi-skilled worker		Ⓕ	Ⓜ
Other occupation		Ⓕ	Ⓜ
Unemployed		Ⓕ	Ⓜ

22. Rate yourself on each of the following traits as you really think you are when compared with the average student of your own age. We want the most accurate estimate of how you see yourself. (Mark one for each item)

Trait	Highest 10 Percent	Above Average	Average	Below Average	Lowest 10 Percent
Academic ability	O	O	O	O	O
Athletic ability	O	O	O	O	O
Artistic ability	O	O	O	O	O
Cheerfulness	O	O	O	O	O
Defensiveness	O	O	O	O	O
Drive to achieve	O	O	O	O	O
Leadership ability	O	O	O	O	O
Mathematical ability	O	O	O	O	O
Mechanical ability	O	O	O	O	O
Originality	O	O	O	O	O
Political conservatism	O	O	O	O	O
Political liberalism	O	O	O	O	O
Popularity	O	O	O	O	O
Popularity with the opposite sex	O	O	O	O	O
Public speaking ability	O	O	O	O	O
Self-confidence (intellectual)	O	O	O	O	O
Self-confidence (social)	O	O	O	O	O
Sensitivity to criticism	O	O	O	O	O
Stubbornness	O	O	O	O	O
Understanding of others	O	O	O	O	O
Writing ability	O	O	O	O	O

23. Mark one in each row:
Agree Strongly
Agree somewhat
Disagree somewhat
Disagree strongly

	Agree strongly	Agree somewhat	Disagree somewhat	Disagree strongly
The Federal government is not doing enough to control environmental pollution	O	O	O	O
The Federal government is not doing enough to protect the consumer from faulty goods and services	O	O	O	O
The Federal government is not doing enough to promote school desegregation	O	O	O	O
There is too much concern in the courts for the rights of criminals	O	O	O	O
The death penalty should be abolished.	O	O	O	O
The activities of married women are best confined to the home and family	O	O	O	O
The "generation gap" between me and my parents is so great that we can barely communicate.	O	O	O	O
Marijuana should be legalized	O	O	O	O
Parents should be discouraged from having large families.	O	O	O	O
Women should receive the same salary and opportunities for advancement as men in comparable positions	O	O	O	O
Everybody should be given an opportunity to go to college regardless of past performance or aptitude test scores	O	O	O	O
Realistically, an individual person can do little to bring about changes in our society	O	O	O	O

24. Mark one in each row:
Agree strongly
Agree somewhat
Disagree somewhat
Disagree strongly

	Agree strongly	Agree somewhat	Disagree somewhat	Disagree strongly
College officials have the right to regulate student behavior off campus	O	O	O	O
The chief benefit of a college education is that it increases one's earning power	O	O	O	O
Faculty promotions should be based in part on student evaluations	O	O	O	O
College grades should be abolished	O	O	O	O
Colleges would be improved if organized sports were de-emphasized	O	O	O	O
Student publications should be cleared by college officials	O	O	O	O
College officials have the right to ban persons with extreme views from speaking on campus	O	O	O	O
Students from disadvantaged social backgrounds should be given preferential treatment in college admissions	O	O	O	O
Most college officials have been too lax in dealing with student protests on campus	O	O	O	O
Open admissions (admitting anyone who applies) should be adopted by all publicly-supported colleges	O	O	O	O
Even if it employs open admissions, a college should use the same performance standards in awarding degrees to all students.	O	O	O	O

25. What is your best guess as to the chances that you will: (Mark one for each item)

	Very Good Chance	Some Chance	Very Little Chance	No Chance
Get married while in college?	O	O	O	O
Get married within a year after college?	O	O	O	O
Vote in the 1972 presidential election?	O	O	O	O
Enlist in the armed services before graduating?	O	O	O	O
Change major field?	O	O	O	O
Change career choice?	O	O	O	O
Fail one or more courses?	O	O	O	O
Graduate with honors?	O	O	O	O
Be elected to a student office?	O	O	O	O
Join a social fraternity, sorority, or club?	O	O	O	O
Be elected to an academic honor society?	O	O	O	O
Make at least a "B" average?	O	O	O	O
Need extra time to complete your degree requirements?	O	O	O	O
Have to work at an outside job?	O	O	O	O
Seek vocational counseling?	O	O	O	O
Seek individual counseling on personal problems?	O	O	O	O
Enroll in honors courses?	O	O	O	O
Get tutoring help in specific courses?	O	O	O	O
Author or co-author a published article?	O	O	O	O
Be more successful after graduation than most students attending this college?	O	O	O	O
Drop out of this college temporarily (exclude transferring)?	O	O	O	O
Drop out permanently (exclude transferring)?	O	O	O	O
Transfer to another college before graduating?	O	O	O	O
Be satisfied with your college?	O	O	O	O

26. Do you feel that you will need any special tutoring or remedial work in any of the following subjects? (Mark all that apply)

English ... O   Mathematics ... O   Science ... O

Reading ... O   Social studies ... O   Foreign language ... O

27. Below is a list of 68 different undergraduate major fields grouped into general categories. Mark only three of the 68 fields as follows:

①First choice (your probable major field of study).
②Second choice.
ⓁThe field of study which is least appealing to you.

ARTS AND HUMANITIES

Architecture	①②Ⓛ
English (literature)	①②Ⓛ
Fine arts	①②Ⓛ
History	①②Ⓛ
Journalism (writing)	①②Ⓛ
Language (modern)	①②Ⓛ
Language (other)	①②Ⓛ
Music	①②Ⓛ
Philosophy	①②Ⓛ
Speech and drama	①②Ⓛ
Theology	①②Ⓛ
Other	①②Ⓛ

BIOLOGICAL SCIENCE

Biology (general)	①②Ⓛ
Biochemistry	①②Ⓛ
Biophysics	①②Ⓛ
Botany	①②Ⓛ
Zoology	①②Ⓛ
Other	①②Ⓛ

BUSINESS

Accounting	①②Ⓛ
Business admin.	①②Ⓛ
Electronic data processing	①②Ⓛ
Secretarial studies	①②Ⓛ
Other	①②Ⓛ

ENGINEERING

Aeronautical	①②Ⓛ
Civil	①②Ⓛ
Chemical	①②Ⓛ
Electrical	①②Ⓛ
Industrial	①②Ⓛ
Mechanical	①②Ⓛ
Other	①②Ⓛ

PHYSICAL SCIENCE

Chemistry	①②Ⓛ
Earth science	①②Ⓛ
Mathematics	①②Ⓛ
Physics	①②Ⓛ
Statistics	①②Ⓛ
Other	①②Ⓛ

PROFESSIONAL

Health Technology (medical, dental, laboratory)	①②Ⓛ
Nursing	①②Ⓛ
Pharmacy	①②Ⓛ
Predentistry	①②Ⓛ
Prelaw	①②Ⓛ
Premedical	①②Ⓛ
Preveterinary	①②Ⓛ
Therapy (occupat., physical, speech)	①②Ⓛ
Other	①②Ⓛ

SOCIAL SCIENCE

Anthropology	①②Ⓛ
Economics	①②Ⓛ
Education	①②Ⓛ
History	①②Ⓛ
Political Science (government, int. relations)	①②Ⓛ
Psychology	①②Ⓛ
Social work	①②Ⓛ
Sociology	①②Ⓛ
Other	①②Ⓛ

OTHER FIELDS

Agriculture	①②Ⓛ
Communications (radio, T.V., etc.)	①②Ⓛ
Computer Science	①②Ⓛ
Environmental Science	①②Ⓛ
Electronics (technology)	①②Ⓛ
Forestry	①②Ⓛ
Home economics	①②Ⓛ
Industrial arts	①②Ⓛ
Library science	①②Ⓛ
Military science	①②Ⓛ
Physical education and recreation	①②Ⓛ
Other (technical)	①②Ⓛ
Other (nontechnical)	①②Ⓛ
Undecided	①②Ⓛ

Please be sure that only three circles have been marked in the above list.

28. Indicate the importance to you personally of each of the following: (Mark one for each item)

Columns: Essential / Very Important / Somewhat Important / Not Important

	ⒺⓋⓈⓃ
Becoming accomplished in one of the performing arts (acting, dancing, etc.)	ⒺⓋⓈⓃ
Becoming an authority in my field	ⒺⓋⓈⓃ
Obtaining recognition from my colleagues for contributions in my special field	ⒺⓋⓈⓃ
Influencing the political structure	ⒺⓋⓈⓃ
Influencing social values	ⒺⓋⓈⓃ
Raising a family	ⒺⓋⓈⓃ
Having an active social life	ⒺⓋⓈⓃ
Having friends with different backgrounds and interests from mine	ⒺⓋⓈⓃ
Becoming an expert in finance and commerce	ⒺⓋⓈⓃ
Having administrative responsibility for the work of others	ⒺⓋⓈⓃ
Being very well-off financially	ⒺⓋⓈⓃ
Helping others who are in difficulty	ⒺⓋⓈⓃ
Participating in an organization like the Peace Corps or Vista	ⒺⓋⓈⓃ
Becoming a community leader	ⒺⓋⓈⓃ
Making a theoretical contribution to science	ⒺⓋⓈⓃ
Writing original works (poems, novels, short stories,etc.)	ⒺⓋⓈⓃ
Never being obligated to people	ⒺⓋⓈⓃ
Creating artistic work (painting, sculpture, decorating,etc.)	ⒺⓋⓈⓃ
Keeping up to date with political affairs	ⒺⓋⓈⓃ
Being successful in a business of my own	ⒺⓋⓈⓃ
Becoming involved in programs to clean up the environment	ⒺⓋⓈⓃ
Developing a meaningful philosophy of life	ⒺⓋⓈⓃ
Participating in a community action program	ⒺⓋⓈⓃ
Getting married within the next five years	ⒺⓋⓈⓃ

29. Below are some of the reasons that might have influenced your decision to attend this particular college. How important was each reason in deciding to come here? (Mark one answer for each statement.)

Columns: Very important / Somewhat important / Not important

	ⓋⓈⓃ
My relatives wanted me to come here	ⓋⓈⓃ
This college has a very good reputation	ⓋⓈⓃ
Most of my friends are going to this college	ⓋⓈⓃ
Because of low tuition	ⓋⓈⓃ
Someone who had been here before advised me to go	ⓋⓈⓃ
Because of the special educational programs offered	ⓋⓈⓃ
I was not accepted anywhere else	ⓋⓈⓃ
My guidance counselor advised me to go	ⓋⓈⓃ
I wanted to live at home	ⓋⓈⓃ

DIRECTIONS:

The remaining circles are provided for items specifically designed by your college, rather than by the American Council on Education. If your college has chosen to use the circles, observe carefully the supplemental directions given you.

	DO NOT MARK
30. ⒶⒷⒸⒹⒺ	⓪⓪⓪⓪
31. ⒶⒷⒸⒹⒺ	①①①①
32. ⒶⒷⒸⒹⒺ	②②②②
33. ⒶⒷⒸⒹⒺ	③③③③
34. ⒶⒷⒸⒹⒺ	④④④④
35. ⒶⒷⒸⒹⒺ	⑤⑤⑤⑤
36. ⒶⒷⒸⒹⒺ	⑥⑥⑥⑥
37. ⒶⒷⒸⒹⒺ	⑦⑦⑦⑦
38. ⒶⒷⒸⒹⒺ	⑧⑧⑧⑧
39. ⒶⒷⒸⒹⒺ	⑨⑨⑨⑨
	①②③④Ⓐ

1970 Followup Questionnaire

AMERICAN COUNCIL ON EDUCATION

WASHINGTON, D. C. 20036

AUGUST, 1970

If there are any errors in the address label to the left, mark this circle ➔ ○
and enter your correct name and address in the spaces below.

Student Last Name   First Name   Init.

Street Address

Dear Student:

City & State   Zip Code

You may remember that when you first entered college in 1966 you completed a brief information form in which you indicated your educational and career plans. Our research staff is now engaged in several studies that are intended to contribute to an understanding of how students are affected by their college experiences. Such studies will yield useful information for re-examining educational policy and practice.

We should greatly appreciate your completing this brief questionnaire and returning it to us in the enclosed envelope. All of the information is to be coded and used in group comparisons for research purposes only, so your responses will be held in the strictest professional confidence.

Since we are following up only a limited sample of students, it is important to secure as complete a response as possible. We hope that you will be able to participate.

Thank you for your consideration.

Sincerely yours,

Logan Wilson

Logan Wilson, President

DIRECTIONS: Your responses will be read by an automatic scanning device. Your careful observance of these few simple rules will be most appreciated.
Use only black lead pencil (No. 2½ or softer).
Make heavy black marks that fill the circle.
Erase cleanly any answer you wish to change.
Make no stray markings of any kind.   Yes   No
Example: Will marks made with ball point pen or fountain pen be properly read? ○   ●

---

1. Please mark one answer in each column:

┌── A. Highest Degree now held
│ ┌── B. Highest Degree planned

Ⓐ Ⓑ None
Ⓐ Ⓑ Associate (or equivalent) (A.A., A.S., etc.)
Ⓐ Ⓑ Bachelor's Degree (A.B., B.A., B.S., etc.)
Ⓐ Ⓑ Master's Degree (M.A., M.S., etc.)
Ⓐ Ⓑ Ph.D. or Ed.D.
Ⓐ Ⓑ M.D., D.D.S., D.V.M. or D.O.
Ⓐ Ⓑ LL.B. or J.D. (Law)
Ⓐ Ⓑ B.D. (Divinity)
Ⓐ Ⓑ Other

---

2. Have you ever been married? (Mark one)

○ No
○ Yes, now living with spouse
○ Yes — separated
○ Yes — divorced
○ Yes — widowed

How many children do you have?

○ None
○ One
○ Two
○ Three or more

---

3. Who is your current employer? Whom do you expect to be your long-run future employer? (If you are still a student, answer in terms of your expectations after you complete your studies.) (Mark one in each column.)

┌── A. Current (or first) employer
│ ┌── B. Long-run career employer

Government:
Ⓐ Ⓑ Federal
Ⓐ Ⓑ State and local
Education:
Ⓐ Ⓑ Elementary
Ⓐ Ⓑ Secondary
Ⓐ Ⓑ Higher education
Other non-profit organizations:
Ⓐ Ⓑ Hospitals, clinics
Ⓐ Ⓑ Social welfare
Ⓐ Ⓑ Church
Ⓐ Ⓑ Other non-profit organization
Business, industry and services:
Ⓐ Ⓑ Self-employed, or family business
Ⓐ Ⓑ Private company
Ⓐ Ⓑ Professional partnership
Ⓐ Ⓑ Other

4. How have you financed your college and living expenses during your undergraduate years? (Mark the appropriate percentage in each row below.)

Columns: None / 1-20% / 21-40% / 41-60% / 61-80% / 81-100%

- ○ ○ ○ ○ ○ ○ Support from your parents
- ○ ○ ○ ○ ○ ○ Support from your spouse
- ○ ○ ○ ○ ○ ○ Scholarship or fellowship
- ○ ○ ○ ○ ○ ○ Earnings from your own employment
- ○ ○ ○ ○ ○ ○ Loan
- ○ ○ ○ ○ ○ ○ Other sources (savings, etc.)

5. Below is a general list of things that people sometimes do. Indicate which of these things you did during the past year. If you engaged in an activity frequently, Mark "F." If you engaged in an activity one or more times, but not frequently, Mark "O" (occasionally). Mark "N" (not at all) if you have not performed the activity during the past year. (Mark one for each item.)

Columns: Frequently / Occasionally / Not at all

- Ⓕ Ⓞ Ⓝ Listened to rock music
- Ⓕ Ⓞ Ⓝ Listened to soul music
- Ⓕ Ⓞ Ⓝ Listened to New Orlean's (Dixieland) jazz
- Ⓕ Ⓞ Ⓝ Gambled with cards or dice
- Ⓕ Ⓞ Ⓝ Played a musical instrument
- Ⓕ Ⓞ Ⓝ Took a nap or rest during the day
- Ⓕ Ⓞ Ⓝ Drove a car
- Ⓕ Ⓞ Ⓝ Stayed up all night
- Ⓕ Ⓞ Ⓝ Attended a ballet performance
- Ⓕ Ⓞ Ⓝ Argued with friends
- Ⓕ Ⓞ Ⓝ Had a blind date
- Ⓕ Ⓞ Ⓝ Wrote a short story or poem
- Ⓕ Ⓞ Ⓝ Smoked cigarettes
- Ⓕ Ⓞ Ⓝ Attended Sunday School
- Ⓕ Ⓞ Ⓝ Went to the movies
- Ⓕ Ⓞ Ⓝ Discussed how to make money with friends
- Ⓕ Ⓞ Ⓝ Said grace before meals
- Ⓕ Ⓞ Ⓝ Prayed (not including grace before meals)
- Ⓕ Ⓞ Ⓝ Listened to folk music
- Ⓕ Ⓞ Ⓝ Attended a public recital or concert
- Ⓕ Ⓞ Ⓝ Arranged a date for a friend
- Ⓕ Ⓞ Ⓝ Went to an over-night or week-end party
- Ⓕ Ⓞ Ⓝ Took weight-reducing or dietary formula
- Ⓕ Ⓞ Ⓝ Drank beer
- Ⓕ Ⓞ Ⓝ Overslept and missed a class or appointment
- Ⓕ Ⓞ Ⓝ Participated in an informal group sing
- Ⓕ Ⓞ Ⓝ Drank wine
- Ⓕ Ⓞ Ⓝ Attended church
- Ⓕ Ⓞ Ⓝ Participated in organized demonstrations

6. What is the name of your current (or most recently attended) undergraduate college?
(Please do not write outside designated area)

NAME _____
LOCATION (STATE) _____

7. Where have you lived since entering college in 1966? (Exclude vacations; if you lived several places during any year, indicate the place you lived the majority of the time.) (Mark one in each column.)

Columns: 1966-1967 / 1967-1968 / 1968-1969 / 1969-1970

- ○ ○ ○ ○ With parents
- ○ ○ ○ ○ Other private home, apartment or room
- ○ ○ ○ ○ College dormitory
- ○ ○ ○ ○ Fraternity or sorority house
- ○ ○ ○ ○ Other student housing
- ○ ○ ○ ○ Other

8. Mark one in each column below:
— A. Religion in which you were reared
— B. Your present religious preference

- Ⓐ Ⓑ Protestant   Ⓐ Ⓑ Other
- Ⓐ Ⓑ Roman Catholic   Ⓐ Ⓑ None
- Ⓐ Ⓑ Jewish

9. What other language besides English is spoken in your home? (Mark one.)

- ○ None
- ○ Spanish (Puerto Rican)
- ○ Spanish (Mexican)
- ○ Spanish (other)
- ○ Chinese
- ○ German
- ○ Greek
- ○ Italian
- ○ Polish
- ○ Other foreign language

10. What is your average undergraduate grade (or grade point average) so far?
— A. Over-all
— B. In major subject

- Ⓐ Ⓑ 3.75 – 4.00 (A or A+)
- Ⓐ Ⓑ 3.25 – 3.74 (A- or B+)
- Ⓐ Ⓑ 2.75 – 3.24 (B)
- Ⓐ Ⓑ 2.25 – 2.74 (B- or C+)
- Ⓐ Ⓑ 1.75 – 2.24 (C)
- Ⓐ Ⓑ 1.25 – 1.74 (C- or D+)
- Ⓐ Ⓑ Less than 1.25 (D or less)

11. What is your over-all evaluation of your undergraduate college? (The one most recently attended)

- Very satisfied with my college ....○
- Satisfied with my college ....○
- On the fence ....○
- Dissatisfied with my college ....○
- Very dissatisfied with my college .....○

12. What is your probable career occupation? (Mark one)

- ○ Accountant or actuary
- ○ Actor or entertainer
- ○ Architect
- ○ Artist
- ○ Business (clerical)
- ○ Business executive (management, administrator)
- ○ Business owner or proprietor
- ○ Business salesman or buyer
- ○ Clergyman (minister, priest)
- ○ Clergy (other religious)
- ○ Clinical psychologist
- ○ College teacher
- ○ Computer programmer
- ○ Conservationist or forester
- ○ Dentist (including orthodontist)
- ○ Dietitian or home economist
- ○ Engineer
- ○ Farmer or rancher
- ○ Foreign Service worker (including diplomat)
- ○ Housewife
- ○ Interior decorator (including designer)
- ○ Interpreter (translator)
- ○ Lab technician or hygienist
- ○ Law enforcement officer
- ○ Lawyer (attorney)
- ○ Military service (career)
- ○ Musician (performer, composer)
- ○ Nurse
- ○ Optometrist
- ○ Pharmacist
- ○ Physician
- ○ School counselor
- ○ School principal/superintendent
- ○ Scientific researcher
- ○ Social worker
- ○ Statistician
- ○ Therapist (physical, occupational, speech)
- ○ Teacher (elementary)
- ○ Teacher (secondary)
- ○ Veterinarian
- ○ Writer or journalist
- ○ Skilled trades
- ○ Other
- ○ Undecided

13. **Indicate the importance to you personally of each of the following: (Mark one for each item)**

Essential	Very important	Somewhat important	Not important	
○	○	○	○	Becoming accomplished in one of the performing arts (acting, dancing, etc.)
○	○	○	○	Becoming an authority on a special subject in my subject field
○	○	○	○	Obtaining recognition from my colleagues for contributions in my special field
○	○	○	○	Becoming an accomplished musician (performer or composer)
○	○	○	○	Becoming an expert in finance and commerce
○	○	○	○	Having administrative responsibility for the work of others
○	○	○	○	Being very well off financially
○	○	○	○	Helping others who are in difficulty
○	○	○	○	Participating in an organization like the Peace Corps or Vista
○	○	○	○	Becoming an outstanding athlete
○	○	○	○	Becoming a community leader
○	○	○	○	Making a theoretical contribution to science
○	○	○	○	Writing original works (poems, novels, short stories, etc.)
○	○	○	○	Never being obligated to people
○	○	○	○	Creating artistic work (painting, sculpture, decorating, etc.)
○	○	○	○	Keeping up to date with political affairs
○	○	○	○	Being successful in a business of my own

14. **Rate yourself on each of the following traits as <u>you really think you are</u> when compared with the average person of your own age. We want the most accurate estimate of <u>how you see yourself.</u> (Mark one for each item.)**

Highest 10 percent	Above average	Average	Below average	Lowest 10 percent	
○	○	○	○	○	Academic ability
○	○	○	○	○	Athletic ability
○	○	○	○	○	Artistic ability
○	○	○	○	○	Cheerfulness
○	○	○	○	○	Defensiveness
○	○	○	○	○	Drive to achieve
○	○	○	○	○	Leadership ability
○	○	○	○	○	Mathematical ability
○	○	○	○	○	Mechanical ability
○	○	○	○	○	Originality
○	○	○	○	○	Political conservatism
○	○	○	○	○	Political liberalism
○	○	○	○	○	Popularity
○	○	○	○	○	Popularity with the opposite sex
○	○	○	○	○	Public speaking ability
○	○	○	○	○	Self-confidence (intellectual)
○	○	○	○	○	Self-confidence (social)
○	○	○	○	○	Sensitivity to criticism
○	○	○	○	○	Stubbornness
○	○	○	○	○	Understanding of others
○	○	○	○	○	Writing ability

15. **Below is a list of 66 different undergraduate major fields grouped into general categories. Mark <u>only three</u> of the 66 fields as follows:**

① Undergraduate <u>major</u> field of study
② Undergraduate <u>minor</u> field of study
③ Graduate major field (complete if you are enrolled, or plan to enroll, in graduate studies; otherwise, omit)

Arts and Humanities

①②③ Architecture
①②③ English (literature)
①②③ Fine arts
①②③ History
①②③ Journalism (writing)
①②③ Language (modern)
①②③ Language (other)
①②③ Music
①②③ Philosophy
①②③ Speech and drama
①②③ Theology
①②③ Other

Biological Science

①②③ Biology (general)
①②③ Biochemistry
①②③ Biophysics
①②③ Botany
①②③ Zoology
①②③ Other

Business

①②③ Accounting
①②③ Business Admin.
①②③ Electronic Data Processing
①②③ Secretarial studies
①②③ Other

Engineering

①②③ Aeronautical
①②③ Civil
①②③ Chemical
①②③ Electrical
①②③ Industrial
①②③ Mechanical
①②③ Other

Physical Science

①②③ Chemistry
①②③ Earth Science
①②③ Mathematics
①②③ Physics
①②③ Statistics
①②③ Other

Professional

①②③ Health Technology (medical, dental, laboratory)
①②③ Nursihg
①②③ Pharmacy
①②③ Predentistry
①②③ Prelaw
①②③ Premedical
①②③ Preveterinary
①②③ Therapy (occupat., physical, speech)
①②③ Other

Social Science

①②③ Anthropology
①②③ Economics
①②③ Education
①②③ History
①②③ Political science (government, int. relations)
①②③ Psychology
①②③ Social work
①②③ Sociology
①②③ Other

Other Fields

①②③ Agriculture
①②③ Communications (radio, T.V., etc.)
①②③ Electronics (technology)
①②③ Forestry
①②③ Home economics
①②③ Industrial arts
①②③ Library science
①②③ Military science
①②③ Physical education and recreation
①②③ Other (technical)
①②③ Other (nontechnical)
①②③ Undecided

Please be sure that <u>only three</u> circles have been marked in the above list.

16. Rate the following at your <u>most recently attended</u> college. (Mark one in each row)

Columns: Excellent / Good / Satisfactory / Unsatisfactory / Very unsatisfactory / Not applicable or no opinion

- ○○○○○○ The over-all quality of instruction
- ○○○○○○ The <u>variety</u> of science* courses
- ○○○○○○ The <u>variety</u> of courses in humanities
- ○○○○○○ The opportunities you had to do scientific research as an undergraduate
- ○○○○○○ How well your undergraduate training has prepared you for your future career
- ○○○○○○ The <u>quality</u> of science* instruction
- ○○○○○○ The <u>quality</u> of instruction in the humanities
- ○○○○○○ Opportunities to discuss your work outside the class-room with professors in your major field of study
- ○○○○○○ The science equipment and facilities at your school
- ○○○○○○ The facilities for library research
- ○○○○○○ Opportunities for extracurricular science activities and projects at your school

*"Science" refers to both natural and social science.

17. Please answer each of the following:

Yes No
- ○ ○ Since entering college in 1966 I dropped out for a period of time (exclude summers or graduation)
- ○ ○ I have attended only one undergraduate college since 1966
- ○ ○ I have applied for admission to graduate or professional school

18. Since entering college in 1966, which of the following applies to you? (Mark "yes" or "no" for each):

Yes No
- ○ ○ Been placed on academic probation
- ○ ○ Assisted on a professor's research project
- ○ ○ Worked on an independent research project
- ○ ○ Been elected to "Who's Who in American Colleges"
- ○ ○ Been elected to Phi Beta Kappa (or comparable academic honorary society)
- ○ ○ Graduated (or expect to graduate) with honors
- ○ ○ Served as a laboratory assistant
- ○ ○ Participated in departmental honors program
- ○ ○ Participated in general honors program
- ○ ○ Was an active member of a fraternity or sorority
- ○ ○ Participated in a demonstration against U. S. involvement in Cambodia (Spring, 1970)
- ○ ○ Participated in other demonstrations against the war in Southeast Asia
- ○ ○ Participated in a demonstration against an administrative policy of the college
- ○ ○ Was author or co-author of an article in a scientific publication
- ○ ○ Was author or co-author of an article in other scholarly or literary publication

19. <u>Impressions of your undergraduate college:</u> Answer each of the following as it applies to your college (the one most recently attended)

Yes No
- ○ ○ The students are under a great deal of pressure to get high grades
- ○ ○ The student body is apathetic and has little "school spirit"
- ○ ○ Most of the students are of a very high calibre academically
- ○ ○ There is a keen competition among most of the students for high grades
- ○ ○ Freshmen have to take orders from upperclassmen for a period of time
- ○ ○ There isn't much to do except to go to class and study
- ○ ○ I felt "lost" when I first came to the campus
- ○ ○ Being in the college builds poise and maturity
- ○ ○ Athletics are overemphasized
- ○ ○ The classes are usually run in a very informal manner
- ○ ○ Most students are more like "numbers in a book"

20. To what extent does each of the following describe the psychological climate or atmosphere at your college (the one most recently attended)? (Mark one column for each)

Columns: Very descriptive / In-between / Not at all descriptive

- ○○○ Intellectual
- ○○○ Snobbish
- ○○○ Social
- ○○○ Victorian
- ○○○ Practical--minded
- ○○○ Warm
- ○○○ Realistic
- ○○○ Liberal

21. All in all, in terms of your own needs and desires, how much of the following did you receive from your undergraduate college? (Mark the appropriate column after each item)

Columns: Too much or too many / Just about the right amount / Not enough

- ○○○ Freedom in course selection
- ○○○ Social life
- ○○○ Personal contacts with classmates
- ○○○ Work required of you in courses
- ○○○ Outlets for creative activities
- ○○○ Sleep
- ○○○ Exercise
- ○○○ Personal contacts with faculty
- ○○○ Personal contacts with family
- ○○○ Advice and guidance from faculty and staff

177

APPENDIX B: CODING SCHEME FOR
COLLAPSED ITEMS

Probable Major Field of Study

Collapsed Category	Item Response Alternatives
Agriculture	Agriculture; forestry
Biological sciences	Biology (general); biochemistry; biophysics; botany; zoology; other biological sciences
Business	Accounting; business administration; data processing; secretarial studies; other business
Education	Education; physical education and recreation
Engineering	Aeronautical; civil; chemical; electrical; industrial; mechanical; other engineering
English	English (literature)
Health professional	Health technology; nursing; pharmacy; therapy
History and political science	History (arts and humanities); history (social science); political science
Humanities (other)	Language (modern); language (other); philosophy; theology; other arts and humanities
Fine arts	Architecture; fine arts; journalism; music; speech and drama
Mathematics and statistics	Mathematics; statistics
Physical sciences	Chemistry; earth science; physics; other physical science

Collapsed Category	Item Response Alternatives
Preprofessional	Predentistry; prelaw; premedical; preveterinary
Social sciences	Anthropology; economics; psychology; social work; sociology; other social science
Other fields (technical)	Other professional; communications; electronics; industrial arts; other technical
Other fields (nontechnical)	Home economics; library science; military science; other nontechnical
Undecided	Undecided

Probable Occupation

Artist (including performer)	Actor or entertainer; artist; interior decorator; musician; writer or journalist
Businessman	Accountant or actuary; business executive; business owner or proprietor; business salesman or buyer
Clergyman	Clergyman; clergy (other religious)
College teacher	College teacher
Doctor (M.D. or D.D.S.)	Dentist (including orthodontist); physician
Educator (secondary)	School counselor; school principal or superintendant; teacher (secondary)
Elementary teacher	Teacher (elementary)
Engineer	Engineer
Farmer or forester	Conservationist or forester; farmer or rancher

Collapsed Category	Item Response Alternatives
Health professional	Dietician or home economist; lab technician or hygienist; optometrist; pharmacist; therapist; veterinarian
Lawyer	Lawyer (attorney)
Nurse	Nurse
Research scientist	Scientific researcher
Other choice	Architect; business (clerical); clinical psychologist; computer programmer; foreign service worker; housewife; interpreter; law enforcement officer; military service; social worker; statistician; skilled trades; other
Undecided	Undecided

APPENDIX C: ADDITIONAL DATA AVAILABLE UPON REQUEST

Data from Other Participating Institutions

The 19 institutions participating in this project have expressed agreement with an exchange of data. We are now in the processing of securing formal permission for the release of data from each school. You may request the data packets of up to three of the institutions listed below, with receipt contingent upon their permission. Please check those institutions for which you would like to receive data and send your request to the Office of Research.

Check Here	Name of Institution
_____	Mills College, Oakland, California
_____	University of Redlands, Redlands, California
_____	University of Denver, Denver, Colorado
_____	U.S. Coast Guard Academy, New London, Connecticut

_____ Northwestern University, Evanston, Illinois

_____ Western Illinois University, Macomb, Illinois

_____ Tulane University, New Orleans, Louisiana

_____ University of Massachusetts, Amherst

_____ Williams College, Williamstown, Massachusetts

_____ University of Michigan, Ann Arbor, Michigan

_____ Saint Louis University, St. Louis, Missouri

_____ SUNY at Oswego, Oswego, New York

_____ Vassar College, Poughkeepsie, New York

_____ Ohio Dominican College, Columbus, Ohio

_____ Allegheny College, Meadville, Pennsylvania

_____ Franklin and Marshall College, Lancaster, Pennsylvania

_____ Vanderbilt University, Nashville, Tennessee

_____ Washington State University, Pullman, Washington

_____ St. Norbert College, West DePere, Wisconsin

Additional College Impact Data

Actual and estimated mean scores on a number of additional student outcomes are available at your request. Please check any of the following variables which you believe would be helpful in an analysis of your students. Return the checklist to the Office of Research.

_____ Life Goals
(17 measures: Becoming accomplished in one of the performing arts; becoming an authority in my subject field; obtaining recognition from my colleagues; becoming an expert in finance

and commerce; having administrative responsibility; being very
well off financially; helping others who are in difficulty; participating in an organization like the Peace Corps; being an outstanding athlete; becoming a community leader; making a theoretical contribution to science; writing original works; never
being obligated to people; creating artistic work; keeping up to
date with political affairs; being successful in a business of my
own.) Each scored on a four-point scale: essential, very important, somewhat important, of little or no importance.

Student Self-ratings
(21 measures: Academic ability; athletic ability; artistic ability;
cheerfulness; defensiveness; drive to achieve; leadership ability;
mathematical ability; mechanical ability; originality; political
conservatism; political liberalism; popularity; popularity with
opposite sex; public speaking ability; self-confidence (intellectual; self-confidence (social); sensitivity to criticism; stubborn-
ness; understanding of others; writing ability.) Scored on a five-
point scale: "Rate yourself on each of the following traits as you
really think you are when compared with the average person of
your own age: highest 10 percent, above average, average, below average, lowest 10 percent."

Behaviors
(29 measures: Listened to rock music; listened to soul music;
listened to jazz; gambled; played a musical instrument; took a
nap; drove a car; stayed up all night; attended a ballet; argued
with friends; had a blind date; wrote a short story or poem;
smoked cigarettes; attended Sunday school; went to the movies;
discussed how to make money; said grace before meals; prayed;
listened to folk music; attended a public recital; arranged a
date; went to an overnight party; took dietary formula; drank
beer; overslept and missed a class or appointment; participated
in a group sing; drank wine; attended church; participated in an
organized demonstration.) Scored on a three-point scale: "Indicate which of these things you did during the past year: frequently, occasionally, not at all."

Freshman Characteristics Predicting Senior Outcomes
(National Sample Only)

Table A.9 lists institutional characteristics that are related to
various student outcomes for a national sample. You also may request data on characteristics of students at the time of college entry
that are related nationally to the outcomes of the impact data.

We regret that we are unable to supply similar data for individual institutions. Please check any of the outcomes listed below for which you would like to receive student predictors and return the checklist to the Office of Research.

____	Career choice
____	Major field
____	Degree aspirations
____	Religious preference
____	Satisfaction with selected aspects
	of college
____	Student ratings of the sufficiency of
	selected aspects of college
____	Persistence in college
____	Life goals
____	Self-ratings
____	Behaviors

Crosstabulations of Variables
From Freshman Surveys

It is possible that we may be able to provide you with crosstabulations of variables from the freshman surveys for your institution (e.g., career choice by race and parental income for 1966). You may wish to study the questionnaires in Appendix A for the variables available. Our ability to meet requests will depend upon the amount of demand and our limited computer facilities. If such crosstabulations would be helpful in your institutional analysis, please send for our evaluation a description of the breakouts you need.

The smaller number of students in the followup sample limits the probability of doing similar breakouts for the followup or impact data. Data on any subgroup of less than 50 students will be unreliable. If you can estimate from your freshman data the percentage of students in each desired breakout category, we can evaluate the feasibility of your request.

Higher Education Panel Reports

An information service to higher education within the ACE Office of Research, HEP conducts surveys on various topics of general interest to the academic community and feeds back results rapidly.

Assisting HEP in its surveys are permanent representatives on 520 college campuses who respond to HEP's inquiries. The data received from these representatives are then weighted to represent the population of U.S. colleges and universities.

The surveys listed below have been conducted to date. Please check any of the reports which you are interested in receiving and return this checklist to the Office of Research.

		Check Here
Survey No. 1	Survey of first-year graduate and post-doctoral enrollment in science and engineering; August 19, 1971	___
Survey No. 2	Research support for science faculty; November 4, 1971	___
Survey No. 3	Freshman class vacancies in Fall 1971 and recent trends in enrollments of minority freshmen; February 29, 1972	___
Survey No. 4	Changes in graduate programs in science and engineering 1970-72 and 1972-74; July 21, 1972	___
Survey No. 5	Enrollment of junior-year students (1970 and 1971); April 21, 1972	___
Survey No. 6	What college presidents are reading; March 1, 1972	___
Survey No. 7	Commercial theme-writing services; June 15, 1972	___
Survey No. 8	Faculty tenure and contract systems: current practice; July 27, 1972	___
Survey No. 9	War protest on U.S. campuses during April, 1972; May 9, 1972	___
Survey No. 10	Expected first-year graduate enrollment in science and engineering, Fall 1972; August 11, 1972	___
Survey No. 11	Student participation on institutional governing boards; September, 1972	___

ORIGINAL LETTER OF INVITATION

American Council on Education
One DuPont Circle
Washington, D.C. 20036

Office of Research

Cooperative Institutional
 Research Program   September 25, 1972

Dear   :
     For the past seven years, you and your colleagues at   have been participants in
the Cooperative Institutional Research Program, the ongoing longitudinal study being conducted by our Office of Research. Your cooperation—and that of hundreds of other persons across
the country—has resulted in our collecting a massive array of data on undergraduates, data
that has provided the raw material for a variety of studies on the college environment, trends
in undergraduate career choice, studies of minority students, and so forth. The results of
such studies have proved valuable not only to the Council but also to organizations engaged
in national and local planning.
     From the outset of the CIRP, it has been our hope that the participating institutions
too would use these data as an aid in policy making and planning. Thus, we have returned
to the institution an annual report on the overall characteristics of their entering freshman
classes; on occasion, we have fed back information in other forms as well. Unfortunately,
this feedback has been neither as extensive nor as effective as we would like. Consequently,
we are about to launch an intensive and systematic dissemination project, limited to approximately twenty institutions. In view of your continued cooperation and support and the consistently good data provided by your institution, it has been selected as a possible participant in this pilot project to study the effects of expanded feedback.
     At this point, we would appreciate your answers to several questions. Do you feel that
your institution could benefit from having more feedback about your students? If so, what
kinds of information would be most helpful to you in terms of problems you now face?
Finally, do you think that your institution has the potential for implementing whatever
policy recommendations are implied by the research findings?
     In addition, we are hoping that a number of the participating institutions will agree
to exchange data with other participating institutions, thus enabling them to compare
the development of their students with that of students at similar institutions. Would
you be interested in such an exchange?
     We will be phoning you later in the week to find out whether you are interested in
participating in this feedback project and to discuss your responses to these specific
questions.

                                        Sincerely,

                                        Alexander W. Astin
                                        Director

185

American Council on Education
One DuPont Circle
Washington, D.C. 20036

Office of Research   October 19, 1972

Dear   :
     We're pleased that you will be participating in our pilot feedback project.
At this point further information about the project is no doubt needed to clarify
any questions you may have. Let me begin by explaining the rationale behind
the project.
     For a number of years there has been considerable discussion of the need
for research applied to practical problems. Nowhere is this need greater than
in higher education. Decisions are made and new programs planned yearly in
our colleges and universities, often with little knowledge of how the principle
clients—the students—will be affected. It has long been our belief at the ACE
that an institution will be in a better position to make constructive changes in
its policies and programs if it has some understanding of (a) how its current
program affects students, and (b) how institutional impact might be modified
by certain changes in policy and programs. For the past seven years we have
been collecting data on college students—the background characteristics which
they bring to college, their changes in behaviors and goals as they participate
in the college experience, and the extent to which the college itself influences
their development. Annually, we have been feeding back data on each entering
freshman class to the institutions in our research program. But in spite of this
effort, we do not feel that we have met our obligation to the nation's colleges and
universities as effectively as possible, nor do we feel that we have adequately
helped college personnel to meet their obligations to their students.
     As a result of this belief the present project was formulated. We began with
the assumption that the feedback effort had to be "activated" in some way—and
that receiving a finished research report to file on one's shelf is not particularly
conducive to action. Consequently, we decided to let your school write your own
report. Empirical data on your students can suggest educational problems, but
an intimate knowledge of your campus and students is necessary for an interpretation of the data which will lead to workable solutions for your college.
     We have asked you to suggest four or five active, innovative persons who
are interested in new educational polcies to serve as "change catalysts" to
translate ACE's data into guidelines for policy making on your campus. In a
few weeks you will receive a packet of data for your institution. These data have
been carefully selected from a vast array of variables to focus on those aspects
of students' development which should be most amenable to change and most
relevant to the present concerns of colleges and universities. They will include
trends of characteristics of entering freshmen at your institution from 1966
to the present, and a comparison of actual and expected changes (or what we call
"college impact" on students) from the freshman year to the senior year for the
class of 1970. National data on college characteristics which affect student development will be included also. It is possible that some additional data analyses
can be provided during the year, but this will depend on available computer time
and resources.
     Your committee of five (with you or someone you appoint as chairman) will
be working with this data. Over a period of several months, we would like you to
analyze the data, interpret it in terms of your knowledge of your school's strengths
and weaknesses, and finally apply the results to practical needs and decisions.
The result of this group analysis and synthesis should be a written report of how
ACE data on your school can be used to guide policy planning at the administrative,
faculty, or student level. At this point, committee reports often end up buried on
dusty shelves or President's desks. We do not want this to happen, and we're
certain that you do not either. The most vital part of the report, therefore, should
be specific proposals for changes and innovations with plans of action that can be

put into motion by the group members. For this reason it is very important that the people whom you suggest as group members be individuals who are at the fore-front of innovation on your campus—people who are concerned about the welfare of the institution and who are willing to devote time and effort to implement change where it is needed. They may be faculty, administrators, students, alumni directors, or whatever—we do not want persons chosen on the basis of the positions they hold, but rather on their personal reputations as dynamic individuals. We do suggest that you include a writer in the group, perhaps a member of your English or jour-nalism department, to "translate" statistical results and their application to your school into a prose summary.

We will be available to you by phone at any time to offer our assistance, an-swer any questions you may have, and discuss the progress you are making. After considering the data, if you do find that you have a number of problems and ques-tions with which you need first-hand assistance, please send us a write-up of your questions for our evaluation. Although our capability for campus visits is limited, we will send a team to your college if we conclude that our assistance is necessary.

If you need some support to help defray costs, we can provide up to $500 for clerical work, writer's fees, and so forth. In the event that you elect to take advantage of this option, we hope you will be willing to match this amount should additional funds be needed.

We are excited about the potential impact of the project on higher education, and we hope you share our enthusiasm. Please let us know the names of your group members within a week. If you have any questions now or at any time in the future, don't hesitate to call me at (202) 833-4749. If I'm not available Jeannie Royer can assist you (202) 833-4753. We look forward to working with you in the coming months.

Sincerely,

Linda D. Molm
Project Director

LETTER TO INSTITUTIONS
NOT IN FINAL SAMPLE

American Council on Education
One DuPont Circle
Washington, D.C. 20036

Office of Research   October 17, 1973

Dear   :
As I indicated in both my recent letter and our telephone call, the Council is launching an intensive dissemination effort this year with a limited number of in-stitutions. We initially contacted a large pool of institutions from which a smaller sample was to be selected. The size of the larger group relative to that of the smaller sample meant that most of the schools originally contacted inevitably would have to be excluded from the project. The criteria for selection of the schools included their willingness to participate, the possibility of affecting real policy change in the school, our ability to provide the school with the kind of data they desire, geo-graphical considerations, and a more general concern with selecting a fairly diverse group of institutions.

Unfortunately, your institution was not selected in light of these criteria. One of the major purposes behind this limited pilot effort, however, was a general con-cern with improving the quality of our feedback to all institutions in our research program. Hopefully, your school and other schools in the data bank will profit from what we will learn in the course of this project. In addition, of course, we will make a special effort to keep you and the other schools which were not selected up to date on the progress of the project and will send you a copy of the final report.

Sincerely yours,

Alexander W. Astin
Director

187

LETTER TO INSTITUTIONAL PRESIDENTS
OF PARTICIPATING INSTITUTIONS
(Long Form)

American Council on Education
One DuPont Circle
Washington, D.C. 20036

Office of the President   December 1, 1972

Dear   :

For the past seven years, you and your colleagues have been participants in the Cooperative Institutional Research Program (CIRP) of the American Council on Education. Your cooperation—and that of hundreds of other persons across the country—has resulted in our collecting a massive array of data on undergraduates, data that have provided the basis for a variety of studies on the college environment, trends in undergraduate enrollment, student subgroups, and so forth. These studies have proved valuable not only to the Council itself but also to other national and local planning agencies.

From the outset of the CIRP, it has been our hope that the participating institutions also would find these data useful in policy making and planning. We believe than an institution will be in a better position to make constructive changes if it has some understanding of how its current program affects students and how institutional impact may be modified by certain changes in policy and programs. An annual report is sent to the participating institutions on the characteristics of their entering freshman classes; on occasion, information in other forms has been fed back as well. Unfortunately, this feedback has been neither as extensive nor as useful to the institution as it might be. Consequently, the Office of Research is now launching an intensive and systematic dissemination project with a pilot group of twenty institutions. The goal of this project is to develop a means of reporting the results of our research program so that decision making in higher education will be more firmly based on data that indicate how students will be affected by the decisions.

The research staff initially got in touch with a large number of institutions who have provided cooperation, support, and consistently good data in the past. From those institutions who expressed interest in participating, twenty institutions were selected according to several criteria: the interest of the institution in using the results to affect real policy change in the school, the Council's ability to provide the school with the kind of data they desire, geographical considerations, and a more general concern with selecting a fairly diverse group of institutions.

[Name of institution] is one of the twenty institutions chosen as participants in the project. The Office of Research has contacted [name of committee chairman] on your campus, and he/ she has agreed to head a task force to work with selected student data for your institution and to develop proposals for action based on the findings. To work with him/her on this effort, he/she has suggested [names of committee members].

We expect that work on this project will continue through the remainder of the academic year. The first few months will be devoted to data analysis and to the writing of a report which will include a statement of institutional goals, findings from the data suggesting [name of institution]'s effect on its students, and proposals for change to close any existing gaps between institutional goals and actual institutional effects. The remaining months should see the implementation of the group's plans for action.

Your interest and support are vital to the success of this project. We hope that you will find the suggested task force satisfactory as a group to study academic problems and solutions with the aid of data and that the necessary time and institutional facilities will be provided for the completion of its task. Should you wish to make any changes in its composition, please contact [name of committee chairman]. We believe that the potential benefits for your school will more than balance the resources required.

In addition to the staff assistance and consultation which ACE will provide, we can supply up to $500 if some support is needed to help defray costs. Should you elect to take advantage of this option, we hope that [name of institution] will be willing to match this amount if necessary.

We are pleased to welcome you to this joint venture with ACE, and we look forward to your continued support and cooperation in our efforts to improve higher education. You may address all future correspondence and inquiries to the dissemination project director, Linda D. Molm, at the Office of Research.

Sincerely,

Roger W. Heyns
President

188

LETTER TO INSTITUTIONAL PRESIDENTS
OF PARTICIPATING INSTITUTIONS
(Short Form)

American Council on Education
One DuPont Circle
Washington, D.C. 20036

Office of the President   December 1, 1972

Dear   :
    As you know, [name of institution] is one of twenty institutions
chosen to participate in an intensive pilot feedback project being conducted by the Office of Research. We are pleased to welcome you to
this joint venture with ACE.
    The support and commitment which you have already demonstrated
should contribute greatly to the success of the project. We believe that
the potential benefits for your school will more than balance the resources and personnel commitment required. By increasing our own
awareness of the practical needs and problems confronting colleges
and universities today, we hope to shape the future direction of our
research and feedback so that it will better serve all of the institutions
in the Cooperative Institutional Research Program.
    Our sincere thanks for your continued cooperation.

                                        Sincerely,

                                        Roger W. Heyns
                                        President

DATA RELEASE FORM

    The American Council on Education has our permission to release
summary data on (name of institution) , which have been been collected through the Cooperative Institutional Research Program, to any of
the project chairmen at the other institutions listed below who are
participants in the pilot feedback project sponsored by the Office of
Research.
    We understand that these data will be used only for the purpose
of comparing institutional differences in student development, and that
individual student data will not be released.

                        _____
                                (Signature)

                        _____
                                (Name)

                        _____
                                (Title)

189

ANNEX C:
SPECIFICATIONS FOR CONSULTANTS'
REVIEW OF INSTITUTIONAL
REPORTS FROM THE NIMH
DISSEMINATION PROJECT

We should like your review of these reports to cover three basic areas: a taxonomy of institutional responses to the project, generalizations about feedback procedures, and predictions and recommendations for the second year of the project.

I. Taxonomy of Institutional Responses

Hopefully, reading through the 15-17 reports will suggest to you a taxonomic scheme within which the various forms of institutional response can be classified. Obviously, the scheme ought to have at least two categories, but probably not more than six (considering the total number of participants). We should like a brief description of each category that you come up with and your judgment as to which category each of the institutions should be sorted into. I would rather not be too leading in my suggestions about what form the taxonomy should take, but you might want to consider dimensions such as the following: degree of receptivity to change, quality of analysis and interpretation of the data, degree of receptivity to outside "experts," role of the committee vis-a-vis the institution, nature of proposed changes (if any), and so forth.

II. Generalizations about Feedback Procedures

This will probably be the largest section of your report. Basically what we would like to determine is whether your impressions from the reports suggest any rules of thumb or other generalizations concerning the whole process of attempting to bring about data-based change in institutions. There are at least six categories that we would like you to cover:

A. Initial Approach to Institutions. Was our approach effective? What changes would you suggest, if any, in future attempts to solicit institutional cooperation?

B. ACE Monitoring and Followup of Institutional Activities During the First Year. Were we too aggressive or too passive? What things might we have done differently to elicit greater involvement on the part of some of the committees and to better guide the committee's activities toward meaningful change?

C. General Dissemination Plan. What were the pluses and minuses of our strategy (initial contact with an individual, formation of a committee, and writing of a report)? Can you suggest any improvements, or possibly, radically different plans?

D. Presentation of Data. We have already discussed this in several earlier meetings, but we would still like to solicit your specific suggestions regarding the format and style of presentation of the data. Would there be any advantage to considering a more personal style of presentation (perhaps with audio-visual aids)?

E. Substance of the Data. We would like any comments you have concerning the amount and type of data that we fed back, including any ideas about what have might been redundant or unnecessary and what other kinds of data would have been desirable.

F. Your Views about Environmental Conditions in the Institution that Facilitate or Inhibit Its Ability to Utilize the Data in a Productive Way. I am thinking here of such things as the types of institution, the style of administration, the role of the faculty, the characteristics of the initial contact person, the composition of the committee, the personalities of the ACE staff and consultants, and so forth.

III. Predictions and Recommendations for the Second Year of the Project

For each of the participating institutions, we should like you to go out on a limb with certain predictions about what you think will happen during the next year (and possibly later). Specifically, we would like to know your views of what, if anything, you expect to happen to the institution as a result of the project and, more specifically, the activities of the committee at the institution. Do you expect any changes to be instituted? If so, what types of changes and when would they be likely to appear? If you see nothing substantive as resulting from the project, some observations as to why would be helpful. We should also like to get your ideas and recommendations for the remainder of the project with respect to the following:

A. Followup Evaluation. What outcomes or criteria do you think are most likely to be affected by the committee's activities? Do you have any suggestions as to how we might collect information with respect to these criteria?

B. Do you see any significant value to institutional visits? If we undertake such visits, what should we be looking for? With whom should we talk?

C. Use of Consultants. What specific ways can the talents of the consultants be utilized during the second year?

D. Should we look to NIMH for additional support beyond the summer of 1974? If so, what kind of project would be desirable?

In attempting to treat each of the above questions, we should greatly appreciate your attempting to do the following:

A. Please try to document your conclusions and recommendations, insofar as it is possible, by references to specific institutions in the study (their report, their data, etc.).

B. In drawing out your conclusions and recommendations, do you have specific suggestions about <u>interaction effects</u>? That is, should our approach to institutions vary in some systematic way? If so, how? Are certain approaches more likely to work with some kinds of institutions rather than with others? Try to be as specific as possible.

Name of Institution _____ Rater_____

Receptivity to Participation: |_____|_____|_____|

Critical or   Mixed or   Highly Receptive
Rejecting   Neutral   or Favorable

Depth of Understanding: |_____|_____|_____|

Descriptive   Interpretive   Insightful

Willingness to Change: |_____|_____|_____|

No Changes   Vague, Overly General-   Concrete,
Proposed   ized, or Trivial Changes   Meaningful
                  Only   Proposals
                                     for Change

Data Relatedness: |_____|_____|_____|

No Changes   Some Changes Based   Most or All
Based on Data   on Data   Changes Based
                                on Data

Constructive Suggestions
for Improvement of NIMH
Project: |_____|_____|_____|

None   A Few   Many

(count) number of separately identifiable proposals for change:_____

ANNEX E:
FOLLOWUP INTERVIEW
INSTRUMENT

Please record your answers by number on a separate sheet of paper and return in envelope provided.

Name _____ Age _____ Sex _____ Race _____

Your Position in Institution _____

Academic Discipline _____

Highest Degree Earned _____ Year Earned _____

Number of Years at Institution _____

Individual Committee Members: Interview Schedule

1. What was your original understanding as to the purposes of the project?

2. How did you feel about being asked to serve on the committee? (Enthusiastic? Neutral? Cautious? Resentful? Curious?) Please explain.

3. How did the committee approach the assignment? Was it a group effort, or were there one or two people who made most of the decisions or did most of the work?

4. Do you think your institution has made, or will make, any changes based in whole or in part on the data from this project? Please explain. Try to be specific.

5. Were the actual outcomes of your committee's efforts different from those that you originally expected? Please explain.

6. Do you think that the committee's efforts were productive? Please explain your answer. (If not, why? Or, if yes, how?)

7. What might have made the committee more productive in your opinion?

8. Do you think the personalities of the individuals on the committee significantly influenced the outcome?

9. In your opinion, how do changes get made on this campus—that is, what are the mechanisms for effecting change?

10. What do you see as the main problems on your campus in getting information communicated to key policymakers so that they can take it into account in making plans or decisions?

11. What are your own views about the usefulness of data in formulating policy decisions?

12. What do you see as the most important student data that your institution needs for policy and planning purposes? How do you think such data should actually be utilized in the decision-making process?

13. Would you be interested in seeing additional longitudinal data from more recent classes of students?

14. Below is a list of changes suggested in your report. Please indicate for each whether any action has been taken so far toward implementation of the recommended change. If any action has been initiated, please describe. Use a separate sheet if necessary, and give us your opinion as to the extent to which the action can be attributable to the dissemination project.

    1. definitely not attributable to the project
    2. probably not attributable to the project
    3. possibly attributable to the project
    4. partially attributable to the project
    5. totally or primarily attributable to the project

If a change was definitely or probably not attributable to the project (1 or 2), then please indicate to what you would attribute that change.

Proposed Change	Page in Report	Describe Action Taken So Far	Degree to Which Action Is Attributable to Project (1-5)	Other Factors Contrib- uting to Change
1. Adding more minority and older students.	9			
2. Greater liaison between the Placement Office and faculty departments.	10			
3. Student evaluation of faculty advising with influence on pay raises.	11			
4. Carbon copy of student grades sent to faculty advisor.	11			
5. Pay for faculty advisors to take advisees to lunch.	11			
6. More interaction be- tween advisors and the Counseling Center.	12			
7. More publicity for the Placement Office.	12			
8. Invite outsiders to campus to discuss careers.	12			
9. Provide workshops in conjunction with local placement agencies.	12			

Proposed Change	Page in Report	Describe Action Taken So Far	Degree to Which Action Is Attributable to Project (1-5)	Other Factors Contributing to Change
10. Followup studies of vocational pursuits of graduates.	12			
11. Departmental lists of occupations and brochure describing them.	12			
12. Greater reliance on internships and work-study programs.	13			
14. Provide more career information to students.	13			
15. Listing of courses of value to students in the job market.	13			
16. Implementing the list (i.e., by offering more career-oriented programs).	13			
17. Provide evening courses for towns-people and students.	13			
18. Seminars for women returning to college by the Alumni Office.	14			
19. Increase the visibility and support for student research opportunities.	14			

Proposed Change	Page in Report	Describe Action Taken So Far	Degree to Which Action Is Attributable to Project (1-5)	Other Factors Contributing to Change
20. Provide more inter-disciplinary offerings.	14			
21. Encourage more intern-ships with local paper and other agencies.	14			
22. Involve students in making up their own syllabi.	15			
23. Collect more data from students which pinpoint their dissatisfaction.	15			

INSTITUTIONAL SURVEY OF SELECTED POLICIES
AND PRACTICES IN HIGHER EDUCATION
Laboratory of Higher Education
Graduate School of Education
University of California, Los Angeles
Los Angeles, Ca. 90024

_____
Name of person completing form

_____
Position

1. For which of the following does your institution grant academic credit toward a degree and/or advanced placement without credit?

	Mark as many as apply in each column	
	Credit Toward Degree	Advanced Placement
College-level work completed in secondary school		
College-level work completed in a nonaccredited institution with accreditation pending	____	____
College-level work completed in an institution whose accreditation has been refused or rescinded	____	____
Education or training in industry or military service	____	____
Work experience in industry or military service	____	____
Successful completion of standardized achievement test (e.g., CLEP or AP)	____	____
Correspondence courses given by your institution	____	____
Correspondence courses given by other institutions	____	____
Course credit by examination without taking the course	____	____
Extension, continuing education, or adult education courses	____	____
Extensive travel and/or overseas living experience	____	____
Remedial courses given by your institution	____	____

2. Which of the following admissions policies are currently practiced by your institution?

	Mark as many as apply
Stated minimum admissions requirements for all first-year, nontransfer students	
Special selection standards to control the proportion of women students	____
Special selection standards to control the proportion of black students	____
Special selection standards to control the proportion of students from other ethnic groups	
Special admissions policies to control the proportion of students by geographic origin	____
Special efforts to recruit students from specific ethnic groups	____
Preferential admissions to spouses of matriculed students	____
Preferential admissions to veterans	____

199

Enrollment in some undergraduate courses by high school
  students (exclude extension, correspondence, or
  adult education) _____

Highly individualized admissions decisions based on
  appraisal of total applicant dossier _____

Open admissions by lottery _____

Open admissions on a first-come, first-served basis _____

Open admissions to any high school graduate _____

Open admissions, other _____

3. How are formal student evaluations of teaching effectiveness
    handled at your institution?

Made in all or nearly all departments _____

Made only in some departments _____

Made only in some courses _____

Used in faculty promotions or salary increases _____

Made generally available to campus community _____

Fed back only to individual faculty member _____

Selectively disseminated under administrative control _____

4. Which of the following policies or practices concerning student
    behavior or student services are in effect at your institution?

Student publications subject to the advice of administration or faculty _____

Student publications subject to the consent of administration or faculty _____

Procedures available for the discipline of students by students
  (e.g., student judiciary committee) _____

Students required to attend religious services _____

Health service permitted to issue contraceptives _____

Special policies for health-related guidance in sexual matters
  (e.g., abortion referral) _____

Special policies for guidance in drug usage _____

Coed dormitories, with sexes segregated by floors or wings _____

Coed dormitories, with sexes segregated by rooms, same floor or wing _____

Extensive academic and cultural programming in residence halls _____

Regular faculty involvement in residence halls _____

Living learning centers in residence halls _____

5. In what proportion of courses are each of the following grading practices used at your
    institution?

	In All Courses	In Most Courses	In a Few Courses	In No Courses
Letter grades	_____	_____	_____	_____
Numerical grades	_____	_____	_____	_____
Pass-fail	_____	_____	_____	_____
Satisfactory-unsatisfactory	_____	_____	_____	_____
Pass-no record	_____	_____	_____	_____
Honors—pass-fail	_____	_____	_____	_____
Completed-incomplete	_____	_____	_____	_____
Descriptive reports by faculty	_____	_____	_____	_____
Faculty evaluation of self-evaluative report by student	_____	_____	_____	_____
Student self-grading	_____	_____	_____	_____
No record kept of individual course grades	_____	_____	_____	_____

Other (specify)

_____

_____

_____

_____

6. Indicate whether each of the following special undergraduate programs is in effect at your institution, has been tried but abandoned, or is planned, and estimate the largest percentage of undergraduates involved in a single academic year since 1965. Unless otherwise indicated, the program need not lead to a specific degree but only provide opportunities for meeting special student needs.

Mark One in Each Row

PROGRAM	In Effect	Tried but Abandoned	Planned	No Plans	Largest Percentage of Undergraduates Involved
Ethnic studies	___	___	___	___	___
Women's studies	___	___	___	___	___
Honors program	___	___	___	___	___
Career-related work/study	___	___	___	___	___
Interdepartment/interdisciplinary (e.g., urban, environmental)	___	___	___	___	___
Independent undergraduate study and/or research	___	___	___	___	___
Accelerated degree program (exclude advance placement; include freedom to carry heavier load per term, credit by exam, etc.)	___	___	___	___	___
Study abroad	___	___	___	___	___
Off-campus study in special American subcultures (Indian reservations, Black communities, Appalachian regions, etc.)	___	___	___	___	___
Dual degree with other institutions	___	___	___	___	___
Individualized programs with no specific course requirements (distributional requirements only)	___	___	___	___	___
Individualized programs with no specific course requirements (complete freedom of choice)	___	___	___	___	___
Correspondence and/or other home study	___	___	___	___	___
External degree programs	___	___	___	___	___
Remedial program	___	___	___	___	___
Officially sanctioned leaves of absence	___	___	___	___	___
Internships with local agencies such as newspapers	___	___	___	___	___
Evening courses for adults and other community members	___	___	___	___	___
Seminars for women returning to campus	___	___	___	___	___
Small seminars offered as a concurrent option to lecture courses	___	___	___	___	___

7. Indicate whether your institution has the following kinds of undergraduate facilities or procedures, and the approximate proportions of students currently exposed to them at some time during their undergraduate studies.

Mark One in Each Row

	Do Not Have	Have, Less Than 1/3 Exposed	Have, 1/3-2/3 Exposed	Have, More Than 2/3 Exposed
Computer-assisted instruction	___	___	___	___
Open laboratories (available at student convenience)	___	___	___	___
Closed-circuit television	___	___	___	___
Student-prepared multi-media instruction	___	___	___	___
Independent investigation	___	___	___	___
Modularized teaching materials	___	___	___	___
Audio or video tape-recorded lectures	___	___	___	___
Interdisciplinary projects	___	___	___	___
Interdisciplinary seminars, discussions	___	___	___	___
Women's Center	___	___	___	___
Other (specify)				

_____

_____

_____

_____

8. Indicate which of the following institutional policies or practices are in effect at your institution.

Mark as many as apply

Use of follow-up studies of graduates to provide career information to undergraduates

Impartial channels for addressing student grievances (ombudsmen, etc.)   ___

Involvement of students in making up their own syllabi   ___

Availability of channels for informal, noncourse student-faculty interaction (common lounges, etc.)   ___

Annual award(s) for teaching excellence (monetary or other)   ___

Workshops to improve teaching quality   ___

Systematic research on student characteristics, values, attitudes conducted by your institution   ___

Use of graduate or senior level students to tutor lower-level students   ___

Thank you.

Please return your completed questionnaire in the self-addressed envelope.

202

Institution	Changes	Institutional Status*	Attribution to Project*
Allegheny College	Hire another black recruitment officer	3	3
	Add more minority and older students	2	2
	Establish greater liaison between placement office and departments	3	1
	Have student evaluation of faculty advising influence pay increases	1	1
	Send carbon copy of grades to faculty advisors	1	1
	Require faculty advisor to take students to lunch	3	3
	Establish interaction between advisors and counseling center	2	2
	Increase publicity for placement office	2	1
	Hold job workshops	1	1
	Do follow-up studies of graduates	3	1
	Design brochure of occupations	2	2
	Make available more career information to undergraduates	2	2
	List courses of value in job market	1	1
	Offer more career-oriented programs	1	1
	Offer more evening courses for students	1	1
	Offer more research options for students	2	2
	Have more interdisciplinary offerings	1	1
	Establish internships	1	1
	Establish independent studies programs	1	1
	Collect more student data	2	2
Franklin and Marshall College	None		
Mills College	None		
Northwestern University	Revise statement of character and future	1	1
	Permit earlier student identification with department	1	1
	Have a common room for each department	1	1
	Have a freshman reading-writing program	3	1
	Increase number of small classes for first two years	1	1
	Train graduates to be positive influence on undergraduates	1	1
	Offer more independent work within courses	1	1
	Revitalize honors program	1	1
	Increase support of study abroad and alternatives	2	1
	Foster undergraduate-graduate contact by more overlap of courses and four-year BA-MA programs	3	1

(continued)

Institution	Changes	Institutional Status*	Attribution to Project*
[Northwestern University]	Offer seminar as alternative to lectures	3	1
	Have lectures taught by those good at it	1	1
	Reimburse faculty for undergraduate entertaining	1	1
	Identify faculty adviser corps	1	1
	Have central coordinator for students applying to graduate school	1	1
	Allow students to create own programs	1	1
	Change the quarter system	1	1
	Publicize faculty accomplishments	1	1
	Hold new student week	3	1
	Mail weekly calendar to each student	3	1
	Put out student directory earlier	1	1
	Advertise speakers in all classes	1	1
	Coordinate university lecture series	1	1
	Establish a university speaker policy	1	1
	Provide many living options	2	1
	Encourage each dorm to have an identity	1	1
	Have more student-faculty contact via dorms	1	1
	Put graduates in residence hall Associates Program	1	1
	Hold exchange dinners in residence halls	1	1
	Renovate facilities to facilitate interaction	1	1
	Examine functions of Resident Assistant	1	1
	Examine criteria for funding student organizations	1	1
	Consider alternative student government	1	1
	Increase allocations to Student Activities Funding Board	1	1
	Change standard seating at football games for students	1	1
	Expand recreation facilities— especially weight lifting	2	1
	Strengthen the school newspaper	1	1
	Expand Placement Center service	1	1
Ohio Dominican College	Attain desired balance in population (age, sex, ethnic background, and ability)	1	1
	Examine degree programs: associate and "liberal studies"	1	1
	Expand field experiences	1	1
	Emphasize leisure as well as career values	1	1
	Develop honors program	1	1
	Integrate freshman orientation to college experience	1	1
	Utilize student past experiences	1	1
	Provide housing options	1	1
	Strengthen religious studies, moral attitudes	1	1
	Provide better career orientation and preparation	1	1
	Enhance social life; coordinate social events	1	1

Institution	Changes	Institutional Status[*]	Attribution to Project[*]
	Encourage physical fitness; variety in sports	1	1
	Expand cultural offerings	1	1
	Improve faculty evaluation and rewards system	1	1
	Provide faculty with better pay and sabbatical opportunities	1	1
St. Louis University	Carry out systematic research program on students	1	1
	Organize curriculum around careers	1	1
	Study why few choose "doctor"	1	1
	Establish Women's Center	1	1
St. Norbert College	Create certificate of academic award to students	3	2
	Create $1,000 award for teaching excellence	3	2
	Build library	3	1
	Establish center for student development	2	2
	Hold two-day workshop to improve quality of teaching	3	3
	Do more research on religious attitudes	3	2
	Establish education-by-objectives program	3	1
	Appoint director of research	3	2
SUNY at Oswego	None		
Tulane University	None		
University of Denver	Improve academic climate	1	1
	Improve science and other facilities	1	1
	Offer alternatives for increasing academic orientation	1	1
	Combine living more with learning	1	1
	Offer more interdisciplinary programs	1	1
University of Massachusetts	Utilize a standing group (e.g., office of institutional studies) specifically designed to analyze data and feed it regularly to administrative offices for consideration	1	1
	Give data to already existing interest groups already oriented to change, or to the affirmative action committee established to improve conditions facing minorities and women	1	1
University of Michigan	None		
University of Redlands	Make curriculum more flexible	1	1
	Establish a counselor corps	1	1
	Give students more power	1	1
	Counter bureaucratic officiousness	1	1
	Review library	3	3
	Liberalize graduation requirements	1	1
	Give residence halls more autonomy	1	1
	Raise quality of work	1	1

(continued)

Institution	Changes	Institutional Status*	Attribution to Project*
U.S. Coast Guard Academy	Increase library staffing	1	1
	Offer depth and variety in humanities and social sciences	1	1
	Increase opportunities for under-graduate research	1	1
	Reevaluate core curricula requirements in light of goals	3	1
	Increase flexibility in core requirements	1	1
	Revise curricula for early entry to major field	2	2
	Improve opportunities for social life	1	1
	Offer new outlets for creative activities	3	2
	Offer academic courses in fine arts	1	1
	Make engineering more relevant and meaningful	1	1
	Improve minority recruiting	2	2
	Retention rate to between 62 and 65 percent	1	1
Vanderbilt University	Revise counselor's weekend	1	1
	Revise admissions office brochure	1	1
	Create office of academic research	1	1
	Create "VUCEPT"—student advisee program	1	1
	Create "INTERHALL" residence improvement program	1	1
	Set up action-desk analysis of student questions	1	1
Vassar College	None		
Washington State University	None		
Western Illinois University	Increase non-course personal interaction between faculty and students	3	2
	Review building and funding priorities	3	1
	Identify operational goals	1	1
	Appoint second task force for problem areas	3	3
	Expand graduate education	1	1
	Offer more service to community	1	1
Williams College	None		

*
3 Complete
2 Partial
1 None

Source: Compiled by the author.

ABOUT THE AUTHOR

ALEXANDER W. ASTIN, a professor of higher education at the University of California, Los Angeles and president of the Higher Education Research Institute, is one of the leading scholars in the field of higher education. Professor Astin is founder and director of the Cooperative Institutional Research Program, an ongoing longitudinal study of institutional impact on students. This program, which is jointly conducted by UCLA and the American Council on Education and now involves more than 3 million students and 900 institutions, is the largest ongoing study of the U.S. system of higher education. Dr. Astin has previously been director of research for both the American Council on Education and the National Merit Scholarship Corporation. He has been a recipient of the American Personnel and Guidance Association's award for outstanding research and a fellow at the Center for Advanced Study in the Behavioral Sciences, Stanford, California.

Professor Astin has authored more than 100 articles and 10 books in the field of higher education, including Preventing Students From Dropping Out, Predicting Academic Performance in College, and The College Environment.

CAREER EDUCATION: Contributions to Economic
Growth
August C. Bolino

CRISES IN CAMPUS MANAGEMENT: Case
Studies in the Administration of Colleges and
Universities
George J. Mauer

EVALUATING VOCATIONAL EDUCATION—
POLICIES AND PLANS FOR THE 1970s: With
an Annotated Bibliography
Leonard A. Lecht

EDUCATIONAL POLICY-MAKING AND THE
STATE LEGISLATURE: The New York Experience
Mike M. Milstein and
Robert E. Jennings